PAWHUSKA KID'S STUFF

STEVIE JOE PAYNE

Outskirts Press, Inc.
Denver, Colorado

The opinions expressed in this manuscript are solely the opinions of the author and do not represent the opinions or thoughts of the publisher.

Pawhuska Kids' Stuff
Memories of Pawhuska and Friends
All Rights Reserved
Copyright © 2007 Stevie Joe Payne
V 4.0

All Rights Reserved. Used With Permission.

This book may not be reproduced, transmitted, or stored in whole or in part by any means, including graphic, electronic, or mechanical without the express written consent of the publisher except in the case of brief quotations embodied in critical articles and reviews.

Outskirts Press
http://www.outskirtspress.com

ISBN-10: 1-59800-669-X
ISBN-13: 978-1-59800-669-8

Library of Congress Control Number: 2007923736

Outskirts Press and the "OP" logo are trademarks belonging to Outskirts Press, Inc.

Printed in the United States of America

For the children:

Stephen William Payne, 1967-2003, music maker
Michael Scott Havens, 1970-1988, soul of a poet.
Caroline Goldwood, 1983-2000, brightest of the bright.

ACKNOWLEDGEMENTS

This is my chance to say thank you to a number of people. First, thanks to Marcy Loy Williams, PHS 1963, who showed me how I could connect my essays though they were random and independent of each other. Next, thanks to Jay Lynn Hurt for trusting me with aging and frail newspaper clippings that confirmed there really was a bicycle race and narrowed the time frame when it took place. Thanks to my younger brother, Charles Brave for trusting me with valuable records. Thanks to my cousin, Cathy Smith Alburty (a Revard) of Cleveland, Oklahoma for helping me with the relationship of cousins, aunts and uncles. To my e-mail audience, who let me test some of the concepts and who offered feed back on accuracy and effects go many thanks. Thanks to all of my teachers in Pawhuska, especially those who gave me a love of literature, reading and writing.

Thanks to Lu King for reading the manuscript and offering suggestions. To all those friends from Pawhuska who provided a time and a place for memories to be created go my deepest thanks.

I offer continuing thanks and love to my mother, Bettie Louise Payne, and my grandmother Louisa Victoria Hardy for all that they gave me.

To my author representative at Outskirts Press, Lora

Gallagher, my thanks for encouraging me after my first few questions and for continuing support as I asked for it at each step along the way.

Thanks to my wife, Charlotte, and our two cats Powder and Scooter for allowing me the time, often late into the night, to write, rewrite and edit the essays and thread them together. Charlotte understands; the cats seldom do but they try to help anyway. I only ask that they avoid the delete key.

No book is written and published without the aid of others, and that is true for *Pawhuska Kids' Stuff*. Still, any errors are mine, and I am ultimately responsible for them.

I offer a very special thanks to Ronnie Havens for giving me his book *A Book of My Dreams* and giving me the courage to make a leap of faith.

If I listed everyone to whom I owe thanks, it would be a book in itself. I can not do justice to all those that I owe a debt of thanks. I can only list a few.

And it may be corny in 2007, but I offer my thanks to the God in whom I believe, without whom none of this would have been possible.

Stephen Joe Payne, February 2007

One hundred years of being Oklahoma 1907-2007

FOREWORD

"**H**ome is the place where, when you have to go there, they have to take you in." (Robert Frost)
I have known Stephen Joe Payne longer than I have known most people in my life. I knew him when we were stepping from the security of childhood into the frenetic world of the seventh grade and into what we called junior high school. There was no sophisticated "middle school" transition in those days, you were out of the frying pan into the fire and you had better learn the ropes of pubescent survival quickly or be swallowed up by it. That's why we found each other to cling to so tenaciously that the tie endures half a century or longer.

I was a Franklin kid, and he was a Union kid and we cried,

"Union, Union,
Run for your life,
Here comes Franklin
With a butcher knife"

Union used it too; they just changed the school names around. Now it has faded away—*for good.*

Within weeks those we had been willing to look upon with childish murder in our hearts became our closest friends. There were, of course, Lynn Addition kids and Indian Camp kids but in my life it was Union and Franklin that were the schools of the most immediacy, for we shared an undefined *something* that would eventually bring us together. Booker T. Washington School was, also for the first time, brought to our attention through something called *integration*, the struggle that was setting Little Rock on fire. We anticipated this strange concept with great concern, but that is another story worthy of its own telling elsewhere. The anticipation faded into an anti-climax of emotions and non-events replaced by an acceptance that many of us looked upon with a bit of pride. Though the feelings of prejudice on both sides were, and unfortunately still may be, lurking in the shadows.

In the caldron of the seventh grade, we were all becoming Pawhuskans as the bonds were being forged more firmly through our youthful experiences together. For those of us who stayed the course through puberty and made it to and through the high school experience, it has given us a unique, almost tribal, commonality. We faced the unknown world that bordered on puberty and, beyond that, something of which we had never dared imagined, adulthood. I don't think we really ever regarded ourselves as "children," though we, of course, recognized our place on the ladder of life, but we were merely the smaller models of the persons we would spend the rest of our lives becoming. We were, as Garrison Keillor says, "above average," whatever that means. If we are truly honest with ourselves, we are still in the *becoming* stage, and that's not a bad thing at all.

Steve (he was and is always *Steve* to me) has captured the moments of his life, and of those who have influenced him most lastingly, in ways that those who read his words will be captured and held hostage to another time and another place. *You Can't Go Home Again* is, of course, the book by Thomas Wolfe in which a small town novelist,

George Webber, moves to New York and writes about his hometown.

Though this is not a novel and comes from the metropolis of Bartlesville by way of the United States Navy and a few other places along the way, it is still a book about Steve's hometown. This collection, gleaned from the fertile mind of Steve Payne or Stephen Joe or Stevie Joe, or whatever name you may have attached to him, is a memoir of real events as best they can be pulled from the depths of his memory's soul. It has been a work in progress for as long as I've known him, though he may have been unaware of it in his youth. It has been a creation brought forth through years of deep thought and painstaking research, undertaken to assure him and those who read this work that the facts are as accurate as possible. The research consisted of ideas, thoughts, conversations, probing, inquiries, e-mails, telephone calls, reunions, and attention to every aspect of its creation in his quest for the underlying truth of that *Home* from which we all hail.

This is not a collection of deeply spiritual experiences, unless one regards living life as a spiritual experience; and perhaps in that context *Pawhuska Kids' Stuff* is a spiritual experience. I heard someone once say of life, "We are not human beings having spiritual experiences, and we are spiritual beings having a human experience." If there is any truth in such a statement, and I lean toward it as a reality, then you might find a part of your spiritual being re-experiencing and joining the human journey of one our own natives, a human being, a Pawhuskan (though I rarely use that noun in describing myself or any of you who share that part of our human experience). We will each bring our own perspective to Steve Payne's work, for we see only through our own eyes of experience the emotions that become the joyous words of another. We can almost be inside them for the moment, and there find the understanding of the common ground we human beings have walked. This book, and others like it, will help us to become more like one another, and that is a rather miraculous thing.

In Wolfe's book, the people of home were at first ecstatic when they heard that George Webber was writing a book about their hometown. Things took a darker turn when they actually read the finished work. Their images of themselves were suddenly, and sometimes rudely, stripped of the facades they had built around their own failings and shortcomings. I think you will not find anything of that kind in Steve's literary efforts here. I think you will, as I have, find an honest recollection that is filled with those human experiences we all share, no matter where we call home.

Steve spent seventeen of his sixty-three years in a small Oklahoma town called Pawhuska. I spent nineteen of mine in the same town at the same time. Some who read this little book will find themselves immortalized in print, and it will be of importance in their lives as it will be in mine. Many will not find their names here, but be forgiving of that for there are only so many memories and so few pages to tell any story, and ironically the ones left out are often the ones who have touched us the deepest.

Be assured that you are within the memories of many more than you realize. To be remembered is the sincerest form of flattery and to be remembered kindly is the most touching of human kindnesses. So, dear readers, fellow Pawhuskans, spiritual sojourners to a time and place filled with life's human experience, and for those who may feel they share little of the commonality of those within these pages, fear not and enjoy and become profoundly effected by the experience of growing up among and with the friends of your life. You may remember things slightly differently from the way Steve remembers them, but you must keep in mind that memory is a personal thing. No matter how we may differ in our personality of remembrance or the ways in which we may express those memories, we are truly all much more the same than we are different.

The importance of such a work is that it tends to rekindle the memory of what has formed our lives, both the joys and the sorrows, the humorous and the sad memories, for they are each a part of who we are and have a place in our proper perspective of life. It is in such memories that the spirit's journey has become manifest in who we are. If you read this work in the right light, you will find yourself laughing, crying, rejoicing (and at times wincing) at friendships forged, forgotten, lost, endured and relived within that timeless part of each of us. Nostalgia has its place in life or it would not be such an intriguing part of us.

We long for the good memories, but we should never avoid the tougher ones. No life is lived without embarrassments, sorrows, regrets, hurts and at times the harshness of our fellow beings toward us. Without the full palate of the human experience we could never appreciate the joys.

All in all though, you will find the joyous seasons far outweighing the seasons of sadness in this book. Take the journey with my friend Steve and the reward will be within your own memories as you "...return again to those thrilling days of yesteryear," and discover the treasured moments of your life. So pull up your favorite chair, set your reading lamp to its warmest glow lamp and take the journey with Steve into the timelessness of life. No other creature on earth has the ability to record and relive its history, thoughts, dreams, aspirations, successes and yes, failures, the way we human beings do. It is one of our many gifts. *Home is the place where, when you have to go there, they have to take you in.*

Welcome home Steve. Welcome home to all of us.

Ronnie L. Havens

Pawhuska is a code word for hometown. It is a small town in northeastern Oklahoma. It was an extraordinary place in which to live and grow up. There are probably 10,000 small towns with similar stories. But Pawhuska is the one I know. So, I can vouch for the authenticity of this book. In the 40's, 50's and 60's, Pawhuska was a perfect place to be – or thus it seems to me. It wasn't perfect – my selective memory leaves out some of the nonsense. Stephen Joe Payne has taken the time and expended the effort to collect the memories of his childhood and spread them before us. There are places in his memories that are not common to my experience. I was three years younger than Stephen so I missed out on a few of the adventures he enjoyed.

Childhood was a precious time. We lived large. We went from one adventure to another. Some of them were dangerous. Some of them left scars. Speaking for myself, they all left an indelible imprint on the person I became. The names and places of Pawhuska are signed across my heart and soul. Stephen has invited us to revisit those places and people who were so much a part of his childhood and adolescence. In doing so, you will revisit your own Pawhuska. It is a walk down Memory Lane. There aren't any rose colored glasses or 3-D glasses to distort our vision, but there are memories. And, memories, by definition, are indistinct and frequently inaccurate representations of events that took place long ago. Be assured, the events are real and the descriptions are as accurate as writing from the heart and soul allow. That's where the memories are stored.

Memories have a half life. Over time, the colors fade and the paper becomes very fragile. Just as there is a push to save old movies from extinction, we need writers to keep old memories from disappearing. The best memory may have 10% of the facts but 100% of the truth. Our best writers and poets know a truth. The reader is an interpreter. He or she takes the clues and code words the writer provides and creates his or her own pictures and portraits. We use our mind's eye to see. The best writers and poets create a frame for us. We supply the painting.

There is something achingly familiar in the music Stephen plays for us. The haunting strains of childhood laughter, the one-sided dialogues of parent-child, and the hum and buzz of summer cause us to tilt our head to capture the fading notes. And on the tip of your tongue may be the ending to his next sentence. The sights are fun – like your own home movies of a favorite vacation. Smell the aroma of bakery goodies and smile. Yes, your senses are all involved. Being open to the moment and the momentum will sweep us along, sometimes white water rafting; at other times we'll pole across the mirror surface of still water.

At the end of our day or the end of life, we are left with a collection of reminiscences; some are fresh and sharp. Some of those memories were never quite what we thought they were. In my hometown, there was a drunkard who had the same birthday as I did. I would see him weekly, on Sunday mornings, sitting out on his front porch, whistling and drinking the last of his whiskey. I was on the way to Sunday school, and he lived across the street from the church. I always wished him a cheery good morning, and he would give me a bleary good morning. One day he asked me my name, and I told him Frankie (my Dad was Frank so I was Frankie). The drunkard misunderstood me and thought I said Frenchie. So, every Sunday morning for years I was greeted with, "Good morning, Frenchie!" If you had asked Mr. "D" my name, he would have sworn it was Frenchie. Such is the nature of some memories. But other memories are knife cutting sharp. And bringing them to our consciousness again is a self-inflicted wound. But those kinds of recollections are scrupulous in their honesty and their capacity to begin healing. They are true double-edged swords.

Visit Pawhuska! Prepare to smile and laugh out loud.

It's really good medicine. Stroll the avenues and climb the hills. Let Stephen be your tour guide. Be prepared. Some of the hills are pretty steep. Then, at the end of the day, go back to the places that were special to you and take some time to be still. In the twilight, close your eyes and listen to the echoes - savor the moment. Remember the time...

Frank Hulse

PREFACE

I grew up in Pawhuska, until I was seventeen, which qualifies me to write at least about the period in which I was growing up. A few years ago, I began writing e-mail messages to the salesmen of the company I was working for when I learned that they were not getting any positive or encouraging advice from their manager. I wrote what most of them called motivational material. After some time, I began to expand the list of those for whom I wrote and I eventually began to write about some of the things I knew growing up in Pawhuska.

This was received well, even by people who did not know Pawhuska. One of the audience members was a gentleman from Scotland who finally made it to Pawhuska and used my essays as a guide for things he wanted to see and experience first hand. Essays is an easy word to grab for definition of what I write but more accurately the pieces are personal narrative essays or just personal narratives; it is too long a word to keep repeating so they are essays within that context. I ceased writing to the salesmen when I retired and became a busy student at Tulsa Community College enhancing my knowledge of the Spanish language and culture.

As time permitted, I again began to write for an e-mail audience, many of them from Pawhuska, so I focused more on the time when I was growing up and I did not write motivational pieces although from time to time, my viewpoint slips into my writing.

Over time, I have received notes from other people asking me to add them to my e-mail list and the audience has grown a little but not too much. A few have asked to be removed from the list but not many. And, I have had a number of people who have given me compliments on my pieces and encouraged me to write them. Among those with compliments and praise is Donna Leonard Mazur, from Pawhuska, now of Washington state. Donna, a retired teacher of English, took the time to write a message of high praise and it came at a time when I needed the extra encouragement for there are times when I am discouraged and consider no longer sharing my writing with my e-mail audience. I would keep writing for it is more difficult for me to not write than it is too write; it is a compulsion with me. But sharing and showing what I write is a different option, one I am not compelled to do; it is by choice.

Essays are not my only writing and neither is the subject of Pawhuska. I was writing another book, more serious in nature than this when opportunity changed. I was working on the reunion organization for the Pawhuska All-school reunion which took place in 2006 and some who became aware of my essays and did not have a computer asked about reading them. That has led to this book. The title was simple. I was talking with someone who commented that many of the essays were about kids' stuff so I chose to use that. Because I wanted to make it clear that it was mostly about a few Pawhuska kids, I added Pawhuska to it and it became *Pawhuska Kids' Stuff.*

Stevie Joe Payne
February 2007

A FEW QUICK WORDS OF INTRODUCTION

It was probably in the fall of 1996 when I first met Stephen Joe Payne and it was not long before even I was calling him Stevie Joe; it just seems to follow him.

I was a training contractor presenting a variety of classes to Phillips Petroleum Company employees who were striving for self- improvement. It was during the first day of a three day course I was leading when I met Stephen.

The Seven Habits of Highly Effective People class was not a "quick fix" course, as so many seek, but one with powerful, life changing potential. Stephen always arrived first, I learned, and took the first chair on the right side of the room, on my left. He shared with me that this was his favorite seat, where he felt he learned the best.

As I began the introductions of the thirty people in the class, I asked, "Has anyone read the book *the Seven Habits*"? Only Stephen raised a hand. I later found that he had read it eleven times, in English, once or twice in Spanish.

By the first mid-morning break Stephen had answered a majority of the questions that had been asked. This was so refreshing for me to have a powerful example in the group. As we progressed with the class, I learned of Stephen's appreciation for the book and its concepts, and his mission to share them everywhere he went. I was surprised to learn then, that he had given more than fifty copies—at that time—of the book to other people. He was not a paid instructor so when I say, he had given, I mean he had spent money from his own pocket, bought, and then given them to those he believed the book could help.

Stephen and I became close friends, and as Quick and Payne, we remain close friends more than ten years later. I would prefer that we were Quick and Payne-*less,* of course, but perhaps most people don't grasp the names.

As time went on I was a regular guest in his home where the coffee was hot and his wife and cats shared their company with us.

Stephen had begun writing his essays then, and he added me to the long list of e-mail recipients. His writing was a mixture of memories, thoughts and feelings, and after several years of writing, it began to take on a warm glow for me and Pawhuska became familiar to me, an Oklahoma City boy, with little experience in small towns.

Most of the people who will read *Pawhuska Kids' Stuff* will have a personal recollection of the people, places, and things found within its pages. I had to learn them from his writings.

After a while I started to feel as though *I* knew the Pawhuska kids, Bobby Hughes, Ronnie Havens, and, of course, Hurt and Payne. I even found a short-cut to the swinging bridge; a bridge that now exists in my mind; I saw the window in the ally of the new car dealership garage, where I could sneak a peek before the new cars hit the show room floor. I saw the old reservoir on the ridge, The State Theater and many other unique places.

Stephen has personally escorted me to all of the Pawhuska places, through his written words, and through brief visits to the physical Pawhuska. I feel that I know them, *really* know them.

That is why I am pleased, with a few Quick words, to introduce *Pawhuska Kids' Stuff.*

William Quick

PAWHUSKA POMP AND CIRCUMSTANCES

It was the end of another school year and once again, a Pawhuska High School senior class presented itself in the auditorium where we had come together for so many assemblies, pep rallies, photographs, concerts, awards, plays and more. Yet, this time would be different, for it would be the crowning achievement of a great class, the finale that we called—commencement. They wore caps and gowns as a proud and delighted audience looked on. I wore my black and orange band uniform, minus the hat, with more braid and brass than I would ever wear again, even in the military. My *Leblanc* B flat clarinet rested on my lap; the wooden taste of the reed lingered.

The speaker was tall yet seemed even taller. Silver hair capped off the elegant features of a grandfather and executive and expressed both wisdom and strength seeming to define character. It would not have been an exaggeration to say that he looked Presidential; he did. His persuasive voice, baritone as I remember it, resonated throughout the auditorium. In fact, he was a wealthy and powerful man who represented not only the modern greatness of Oklahoma, as the Kerr name in the Kerr-Mcgee oil company, but also the government of the United States of

America. I wondered; how did *our* little Pawhuska get Robert S. Kerr, United States Senator, for the commencement address?

I do not remember all of his speech, but I did listen to it, the first speech outside of church or school that I had willingly listened to and even embraced for it had meaning to me. I remember that he challenged us, and he frightened some of us for we were not yet ready to face the world. Fortunately, it was not our graduating class though, and we would have a few more years to practice before we would experience all of it. It was the class of 1959, and we were only there to hear his speech because we were The Pride of Pawhuska, the black and orange clad band, and someone had to play *Pomp and Circumstance*.

Scientists have proven that graduating classes can not walk to the stage without the graduation song playing. Donning a cap and gown impedes their ability, and without *Pomp and Circumstance* they either walk too quickly or drag their feet and fall behind. My own theory is that the music hides the sounds of sobbing parents and snickering seniors, seniors who marvel at how they got there. Then again, maybe it's the music that causes parents to sob, not that we played it badly, but it's the nature of the piece, heavy, somber yet sublime. Some of the seniors sob too, mostly girls, although most just sniffle, a polite form of sobbing. It is a time long awaited, yet a time come too soon for it happens just once. Later, some will look back and wish that it could have lasted longer, for the taste, like that of a fine wine, lingers and becomes better with age. And memory, like a fun house mirror, distorts what we see.

"It is called commencement because it is the beginning of your life outside of this institution," he said, clearing up the mystery of why the end is called the beginning.

Something made Pawhuska important enough for the great senator to take time out, travel there-- when it was not easy to do so—and spend his evening with us. Something gave Pawhuska a little brighter star than other Oklahoma towns of similar size. Perhaps something in the rich oilfield history of Pawhuska had created an obligation for him. Perhaps one of the citizens of Pawhuska had special influence with him. Maybe they just paid him but whatever the reason for his being there, I was impressed. For the first time I saw Pawhuska as more than just the small Oklahoma town in which my friends and I were growing up. It was not quite a cosmopolitan center but still, it had importance beyond our lives and, as he had put it, outside of the institution.

The institution--*our* institution--Pawhuska High School, known affectionately as just PHS, the old building where my friends and I attended from 1956 through 1962, was more than just bricks and mortar to us. It was our social system, our opportunities, our challenges and our life. And, yes, it was school, so for some it was boring and tedious, for others it was entertaining and diverse. It was a mixture of both for me. It was the beginning of many beautiful friendships, the beginning of first sweethearts, some that turned into life long marriages, and the beginning of not a few heart aches as well.

Of course, many of us left to seek our fortune and fame elsewhere but, just because you leave Pawhuska, it doesn't mean Pawhuska leaves you. That was many years ago, but as my own case indicates, you can take the boy out of Pawhuska, but it's harder to take Pawhuska out of the boy. I left Pawhuska in 1961 when I was just seventeen.

I have been to Hong Kong, to Tokyo, Japan, to Honolulu, Hawaii, to Singapore, to Manila and Subic Bay of the Philippine Islands, to Jamaica, to Puerto Rico, twice through the Panama Canal, and to too many islands to mention. These were places I only dreamed about visiting as I looked at the photographs in my fifth grade geography book at Union Elementary School. The people in the photographs spoke other languages than the English my language book was desperately trying to teach me, and I envied them. I spoke only an Oklahoma English, and I spoke it with a twang in my voice. The twang was so pronounced that a friend said I had a west Pawhuska accent. I pronounced creek as "crick" because that's the way I heard everyone else say it. I know there must have been other strange pronunciations in my vocabulary. Most of those have been fixed now, rightly or wrongly, and I now speak several languages as well as read world literature in original languages, but for all that, Pawhuska is still a part of me and, I suppose, I am still a part of Pawhuska. I still speak English with a west Pawhuska accent, but I no longer pronounce it "crick."

I have lived in Los Angeles, California; South Heart, North Dakota; White House, Texas; and I have been able to visit and spend time in a great number of our states. I have been from the west coast to the east coast and from the gulf coast on into Canada. Yet the values and lessons that I learned in Pawhuska remain part of me. And most of the friendships that I formed there remain part of me too. What I learned there from my teachers and mentors still helps me to navigate through life.

WHITE HAIR

Pawhuska was named after an Osage chief, Pawhuska, which we are told, translates to English as White Hair. Legend tells us that the young warrior captured a soldier who was wearing a white powdered wig; the wig came off into the hands of the startled warrior. He began to wear the wig himself and while still a young man and long before his own hair became white, he acquired the name that he then gave to the town. Pawhuska was probably not spelled so closely to our current spelling, and it probably had a very different pronunciation, as we observe when Wa-Sha-She can become Osage.

THE TOWN

Too small for a city, too large for a village, Pawhuska lies in northern Oklahoma about twenty miles south of the Kansas border. Ponca City lies about forty miles west along highway 60; Bartlesville lies twenty-six miles east, and Oklahoma's second greatest city, Tulsa lies fifty miles to the south. We always used to say that the population was five thousand people and it has hovered around that most of my life. Sometimes it was a little more and now it is less but the number of five thousand is an easy one to remember so we still use it, perhaps not wanting to admit that it has shrunk below that. Sadly, it seems to be about three thousand six hundred now.

Pawhuska was and is a cowboy town, an Indian town, and an oil town, all at the same time, and lays solid claim to having had the first Boy Scout troop in the United States. Famed as the home of the Osage Indian Nation, Pawhuska also hosts The International Cavalcade and countless rodeos. Oil made Pawhuska great in its time, not once, but several times. Ben Johnson, Jr., who was both an Academy Award winning actor and a champion cowboy, called Pawhuska home. Ben's portrayal of Sam the Lion in *The Last Picture* Show (1971) was real and believable because Ben was real and believable.

But rather than a history of Pawhuska, this is a collection of some of the memories I have of growing up in the 1950's.

PRUDOM AVENUE

I was born in Oklahoma City, not Pawhuska, but my mother and grandmother moved there when I was very young; I had little choice but to join them. I have always thought of myself as a Pawhuskan who was born in Oklahoma City, but a Pawhuskan first. No matter where I have been, no matter where I have lived, when asked, "Where are you from?" I have always responded, "Pawhuska." "Where?" I would hear back, and I would very carefully pronounce it out for them to hear. Of course, they thought I had a speech impediment. Sometimes I had to spell it for them. I worked so hard on pronouncing it for unfamiliar ears that I lost my own ability to pronounce Pawhuska as a native does and as I once did. No matter, as it came back to me, I think, after I was once again in and around Pawhuska. But I think of how much time I could have saved had I only said, "Tulsa," when asked where I was from.

Early on we lived in at least three different neighborhoods but life really began for me when we moved to the big white house at 543 Prudom Avenue. That was about 1950. I had not yet started school, so I did not have that nine months period to help frame my seasons for me. It was hot or cold and I was dressed accordingly. I must have had a sense of seasonal events, such as Christmas and

Easter for they were the seasons that all children celebrated eagerly; I was no exception. The rest of the year was just days and not many of them special, including my own birthday, which I shared with a great and famous American.

The neighborhood was new, and I explored it with curiosity, although I was not allowed to go very far in any direction. I could go up to the alley that lay between Main and Sixth Street, but I was not allowed to cross it, and I was not supposed to cross Sixth Street, the wide and busy street that lay between the house and the park across the street. The large brick building opposite the house was the First Baptist Church, and the double story, long, green house across the street to the north was a boarding house. These limits only allowed me to venture west along Sixth Street in the direction of town but for fear of getting lost, I would turn back at the American Legion building and walk back to the house. Actually, I turned around when fear kicked in and so far, the American Legion had been the marker for that. The neighborhood from which we had moved was, to me, one of daily fights. I was enjoying their absence when a boy about my age appeared on the sidewalk just in front of me as I was heading home. I was thinking that if I ran I might get to the house before he could get to me when he smiled disarmingly and asked, "What's your name?"

I told him my name was Stevie, which was all I used then. My mother used Stevie Joe as did most adults. I'm not sure if I knew I had a last name. He replied that his name was Bobby and asked me if I wanted to play. So began a friendship that would last many years, through many events. It was not always a smooth friendship as we fought each other sometimes and sometimes we stood together against other boys. Still, he was my first friend in the neighborhood. He was wearing a plain shirt and jeans, a Levi jacket and a baseball cap. He had on black with white tennis shoes, and he stood crookedly with his hands in his pockets. We didn't shake hands at that age unless an adult forced us to and then it was fun for it was mimicry of them and a small rite of passage on our way to a vaguely defined something called manhood. But we never shook hands amongst ourselves as small boys; it seems that we started doing that around early high school.

I do not remember where or what we played, but we had a good time. I would learn that he was a legend in the neighborhood, for he had none of my shyness and he would venture around the block, stopping and talking to anyone, child or adult. If he didn't know someone's name, he asked. I had played for hours with boys that I had just met and never learned their names, for I was too shy to ask, and they had not asked mine. And it wasn't important to know someone's name to have fun. The only time I saw shyness in Bobby was later, when it was time to ask girls out, and he stumbled badly with that as did most of us boys.

I don't remember when I was allowed to cross the street, but Bobby probably talked me into doing it before I actually was allowed to; he was good at talking me into things. Once I could cross, though, we often played in the park. It had a tall swing set, a teeter-totter set with three boards and a small merry-go-round.

The merry-go-round was circular and on the floor were metal upside down U frames, where a kid could sit and hold on while someone pushed it round in circles. The flat surface was divided into pie slice shapes of red, blue and yellow colors. A great tree stood in the center of the park, and we could climb it if we could get a boost up to the first branching of the limbs. It was not easy, at six, to get there without help.

There was one more ride in the park, and that was a rotating teeter-totter. It was a metal tube about six feet long with small wooden seats on each end and mounted about eighteen inches from the ground on a vertical pipe. That allowed the teeter-totter to swivel around as well as to go up and down; it was very popular. A metal loop stood on the pipe where the seat narrowed, and we could hold on using this and, as I learned, even put our legs through it to get a super hold. That loop and the speed with which this teeter-totter could be pushed would come back to haunt me later.

I don't know when I learned Bobby's whole name, but it was Robert Gordon Hughes. Bobby was his nickname, but his father, Gordon Hughes, usually called him Butch. This was a time of life that we did not want to hear "Stephen Joe Payne!" from a parent for it meant that we were in deep trouble, especially in Bobby's case for his mother could have won the championship with her "Robert Gordon Hughes!" It even scared me. That is probably how I learned his full name, when, one time she called him just that way. I cleverly left and let them work it out.

When we heard our whole name, there was also a tone of voice with it that measured just how seriously in trouble we were. There is a built-in indicator in children so we know by the words and tone of voice that we might never be allowed to play, if even breathe, again. Of course, most things weren't that serious, and we were soon in a child's world again. The most serious trouble I had been in happened when I set the house on fire before we moved to Prudom.

We were still living at 319 Girard Street on the south side of Pawhuska and one of my older cousins, Barney Hardy, had taken me to a cowboy movie, and I was so caught up in it that I kept reliving it. Indians on horseback shot flaming arrows onto a stagecoach roof which caught fire, and that, combined with thrilling music, brought us to a fever pitch of excitement. I was still excited when I got home. My favorite toy was a yellow, plastic stagecoach with six brown plastic horses, and when we got to the house pure brilliance seized me.

"These matches would make perfect flaming arrows." They did.

A child may not admit it, but we usually know when we are doing something wrong. The proof of that is that we try to hide it. We may take an oath on a stack of Bibles that we did not know that what we were doing was wrong but, inside, down deep, we know it.

I was afraid of the dark but my twin desires of replaying the battle and simultaneously hiding it won over my fear; into the hall closet I went. Underneath the coats and things, I set up my famous Battle of the Yellow Stage Coach at Closet Gulch. As my stagecoach rolled across the linoleum prairie, flaming arrows streaked through the darkened sky, made so by the closed closet door. "Phhtt, phhtt" they sang (actually I made that noise) as my hand guided them onto the roof of the stagecoach, just as they had done in the movie; only...the movie stagecoach had caught fire slowly, and the cowboys had put it out. One of them was struck by arrows and did a masterful dying dive from the stagecoach in the process, while *my* yellow stagecoach had instantly gone up in flames. I would be much older before I understood the flammable characteristics of butyl styrene plastics.

I desperately tried to put out the fire, but it burned faster. Afraid I would be discovered, I moved the burning stagecoach back further behind the coats and things, so that it was safely hidden from view right next to—*the wallpaper*! Old, frail wallpaper can ignite and burn at a frightening rate as my experiment was proving. I began to hear adult cries of, "Smoke! Do you smell smoke?" "Where's Stevie?"

"Steviiiiiiiiiiiiiiiiieeeeeeeeeeeeeeeee!"

"I'm in here!" I cried out, finally, all hope gone for I had hesitated as long as I dared. I'm sure that it was a desperate cry, tinged with fear and tears, for I was afraid, but more than that, I was watching my stagecoach burn to a small blackened hulk of plastic. And I loved that stagecoach. It would soon be gone forever, as the sickening smell was reminding me.

Someone yanked the closet door open and jerked me, by my arm, out into the safety of light and fresh air, and I heard the question that all parents ask when they rescue you, usually from yourself.

"Are you all right?"

"Uh-huh," I sobbed, foolish enough to answer truthfully. That was my second mistake, for once learning that I was uninjured, my mother proceeded to do so with the back of her hand across much of my little body. Worse than the blows though was the constant shaking, because I was trying to explain it away with the time honored, "I was just…" It was so difficult to explain things when my voice was going, "I-i-i-i w-a-a-a-a-a-z-z-z…" If I had known about shaken child syndrome then, I would have argued for her to put me down and save any legal problems for her. But I didn't so I relied on the next best tactic—crying.

Crying had rescued me from the fire but it didn't work here. And it led me to ask the question: Why do parents do that? They fret and worry and ask you if you are all right, and then as soon as they find out you are, they beat you within an inch of your life. But it was a half-inch, a very narrow escape, in this case.

I would be a father later on, and repeat my mother's actions. Yet I would come no closer to understanding why parents do that. Perhaps we only repeat what we have instinctively learned. Perhaps we want to be sure that any damage inflicted was indeed caused by us.

The house was a duplex that we rented from Mrs. Armstrong, and it was saved although the closet was badly damaged and the coats and things in it were ruined. But that isn't why we moved from Girard.

However, it seemed I was able to creatively find trouble before I met Bobby Hughes. So I can't blame him for everything, although he did help me—significantly.

For example, at one time, just a short block south of Main and on Prudom Street was an old yard belonging to an oil company. There were several fun things there, such as an open pit where residual oils were dumped. It formed a small lake, well, a pond, I suppose but we always exaggerated and went for the larger unit, so it was a lake to us. The top was a hard skim much like hot chocolate forms as it cools, and we could walk across it and ride bicycles on it. Then, when it was time to quit and go home, we tracked this marvelous black material right into the house.

There was a collection of discarded tires, and one of the older boys showed us how we could roll them and jump inside and roll quite a ways. Of course, it was more fun if you could get one of the other boys to roll you, once you were positioned inside of the tire. Bobby found a great tire one day, as it was a tractor tire, so he could get inside and get it rolling without having to be so scrunched down. There was only one tractor tire, and we took turns in it. However, since he had found it, he got the lion's share of the time in it. Of course, we weren't supposed to be there in the first place, so we had to wait until the men working there were gone.

One of us, and I think it was Bobby, got the idea of taking some of the tires to the First Baptist Church across from our house. The church had magnificent cement stairways with wide cement banisters that we could walk up, all the way to the top, doing a tight rope balancing act. The banister was about a foot wide so it wasn't really that much of a challenge but pretending was what it was all about anyway.

One of us would take our tire to the top of the steps and one of us would stay down below where we could watch the street. When the boy below yelled, "All clear!" we would scrunch down inside of our tire and start down the steps with us inside, going bouncy-bouncy and end over end as the scene blurred past while we got dizzy from turning over. It was fun.

However, getting inside of the tire took a little time, and we weren't the best judges of a moving car's speed. So, one time after I had received the all clear, got all scrunched down into my tire, and took an unbalanced and awkward start off of the steps down towards the street, I heard Bobby yelling, "Wait! There's a car coming!"

Wait?

We usually just let the tire roll until it ran out of energy and fell over, so we had not figured out a braking system. The smart money would have been on just falling over to one side. I didn't do that. As I was rolling and bouncing down the steps, I had a poor sense of direction and I went wide, out into the intersection, which at least took me away from the approaching car. I did get to look though, and I saw an elderly man with fear on his face, and I heard tires screeching. I was scared to death, but as soon as it was over, we were laughing and telling great stories about how close I had come to being hit. But, shortly after that, a police car came by and picked up all of our tires. Bobby and I weren't the only ones doing it, but we seemed to have been more specifically identified, maybe because I lived just across the street; so we also got into the most trouble over it.

Of course, we had an endless supply of old tires as long as the yard was open; and the police didn't know where we were getting the tires, and they didn't ask us. They just took the ones that we had. We had to lie low for a while, perhaps several weeks. Once enough time had passed, and we felt safe again, we tried some variation of the tire roll. At some point it was over with and I don't know if we just grew out of it or something else happened.

The inside of a tire was as dirty as the outside, and it is likely that our mothers put a stop to it because I'm sure we ruined some of our clothes, shirts in particular. Jeans were made out of steel and could take more punishment and survive. Eventually, the yard was closed, the land sold and something was built in its stead. We had outgrown that phase by then though.

PLAYGROUNDS

Being small boys and having active imaginations created toys out of the natural things of the neighborhood. Trees and anything climbable became playgrounds, and sometimes fortune offered unexpected opportunities.

The telephone company was nearby and the large cardboard boxes for transformers, once emptied, were discarded into the alley between Main and Sixth Streets. These were perfect club house size or they could be a submarine, with the right additions, or an airplane and sometimes a futuristic spacecraft. A vacant lot adjoined our house, and it was sometimes overgrown with tall grass.

Several of us found one of the transformer boxes and we drug it to the vacant lot and set it up as a club house. We had a secret passage through the tall grass and no one knew that the club house was there, except for those of us who had found the box. This box was the nicest I remember, for it was nearly new cardboard and had wood support ribs that made it very sturdy.

Someone knew about making telephones, so we got some tin cans and waxed string and made a complete telephone system. A telephone system is useless without somewhere to call, so we got a second cardboard box, not as nice as this one, but adequate, and ran the telephone system between the two boxes. They were no longer just boxes now as one became headquarters and the other an outpost of some kind. The clubhouse lasted for several days, perhaps a week before it rained and an adult, Mr. Murphy, decided that it had to go. We had put quite a store of things into it. There were water cans, Kool-Aid, peanut butter, an army blanket, and an army helmet, and toy guns; just the sort of things that we brought and then decided that they were safe to leave.

We were playing army, which was natural after all of the army tools that we had accumulated, and it had become our headquarters, when one of the neighborhood toughs came by and destroyed a lot of it. That's when we found out that the grass was not as tall as we had thought; we weren't in secret—at all. And the telephone system didn't work because we didn't keep the strings taut. People who had been walking by on the sidewalk had been listening to our top secret military plans. After the tough tore it up, Mr. Murphy, encouraged by one of the mothers, decided to remove it. We were given a brief notice and were able to rescue most of our stocks.

The Lincoln-Mercury dealer was east and south of us, along Main Street, in a Quonset building next to the Phillips 66 station. In addition to the cars, there were Ford tractors which were left outside. If Bobby and I went in the daytime, we were usually encouraged to stay off of the tractors, but sometimes, we got to play on them. This model, which I think was the Ford Jubilee tractor, was painted gray and red, low to the ground, and easy to climb upon, even for six and seven year old boys. The seat was large and of cold metal, which I pronounced "medal," and there were wonderful knobs, wheels and levers. We knew about submarines and we could make them dive or surface by manipulating the levers. These turned out to be the brakes, clutch, gear, and throttle levers, but I don't think we did any permanent damage since they were never started when we were maneuvering them.

When Bobby and I were in the first grade at Union, and we had not yet learned to tell time, he suggested that we go to the tractor place during our lunch hour and play. I was usually eager to go along, if I thought we would not get in trouble. "Will we get in trouble?" I asked him. "No," he said, "We can hear the first bell from there, and we'll have plenty of time to get back to school before the next bell."

I seemed to operate on a principle of, "It's not my fault; he made me do it," as a belief system of having fun but not getting in trouble for it. It was my version of eating my cake and having it too. But it didn't always work.

We were having a wonderful time playing submarine or spacecraft when a man discovered us and suggested that we should be in school at that time. "No," Bobby told him. "We've got plenty of time, and the first bell hasn't rung yet." The man explained that we were about an hour late, and that the first bell had definitely rung.

It turns out that we couldn't hear it from there.

We arrived, sheepishly, into Mrs. Sauter's class room where, in front of everyone, she asked us where we had been and what we had been doing. That day, Bobby showed the first signs of the master craft diplomacy he would use later to get himself out of trouble, although he sometimes got me into it by shifting the blame. That day, he shared his skill and rescued both of us. He simply and eloquently explained that neither of us could tell time.

How did we happen to be so far from school? Bobby explained that he had been told by his mother to go home at lunch, and he had asked me to come with him, just in case. Just in case of what was never made clear.

How did we get so far from the straight line between his house and Union? Well, it appears that we had gotten lost. Although she was suspicious, he was doing such a good job that she conceded and let us escape punishment. We did not avoid embarrassment in front of our class mates. And, Mrs. Sauter used our adventure to place more emphasis on learning to tell time. I didn't have a watch though, but I supposed any clock would have served us.

I think I understood the numbers and how each larger one followed the smaller number, but I was having difficulty with the day being twenty-four hours long while the clock showed only this many. I do not know when the concept of restarting at twelve finally dawned on me, but I did know how to tell time by the end of the school year. I'm just not sure it was *that* school year. Eventually, I did master it though, and then I was introduced to twenty-four hour time in the navy and had to start all over again.

Sometimes a neighbor would have an old car that no longer ran. It was left at the back of their house, and we sometimes found our way into it to use it for a submarine. Most of the time, someone knew about it, and they just let us play, perhaps thinking we were cute. Once a mother found out though, she would contact the car owner, and we had to hunt for new playgrounds.

There was the park across the street, and Union had a few things on the playground, so we played there too. One of the lumber companies was on Main Street, just off of Rogers, and one of the boys found that it was left unguarded at night and offered plenty of secret passages. I don't remember anything that made good submarines or spacecraft, but there were canyons amidst the stacked lumber so it was a fun place to play.

STARTING SCHOOL

Bobby and I were the same age, born in 1944 with my being about three months older so we would begin school together; but I didn't know that yet, and I didn't know how classes were determined. Now I know that they are determined largely by incident of birth, but I also learned that there are ways in which you can reposition yourself into other classes.

School was a far off concept for me then, for I had heard about it as it had taken my cousins Barney and G. A. Hardy away from me; and I didn't think I wanted to go. I didn't know where it was, but I knew that once my cousins went there, I didn't see as much of them, and there were changes in them. I didn't know that my mother and almost all of the adults had been to school, and they had survived it.

There was a similar yet distant concept for me; Kindergarten. When I heard it pronounced, I thought it was kiddy-garden. I didn't know where it was either. At that time it was not free, and those who wanted to give their child an advantage paid for Kindergarten. For whatever reason my mother did not send me, so I missed whatever learning was offered there. Bobby didn't go either, so I suppose we were dropouts before we had even begun. As it turned out, the school which we would attend was a large building named Union Elementary School, only two blocks away. Actually it was two streets to cross away but really only one block. I never did learn where Kindergarten was then, but in 2006 Jay Hurt told me that he thought it had been held in an area in the basement of Union.

Today I believe that the formal name for our schools had the word elementary in it, but really we just knew them as Union and Franklin Grade Schools; so if I slip and use the words elementary and grade interchangeably, please remember that it's the heart of the schools that counts, not the bricks and mortar and not the technical name of the school.

Elementary may have been too big of a word for us at first. I have just tried to learn to be more accurate as I have accumulated years and experiences and I have learned that errors are repeated and magnified over time. Also, there were other schools in Pawhuska, and it is not my intention to slight them as they were just as important. Most of my friends and I were town kids, and Union and Franklin were the town schools. There were also the Catholic, Indian Camp, and Lynn Addition schools. But, to add perspective, my grandmother told me that if I were bad, they would send me to the Catholic school.

I also thought Lynn Addition was Lynn Edition.

I don't remember when I met my next friend, but I think Bobby knew her and brought us together. It must have been that same year and it couldn't really be called an introduction. We just waved across the street at her, walked over and talked. Introductions weren't really practiced until about the fifth grade, when we were given formal rules about introducing younger to older and man to woman or something like that. The rules have never stuck with me very well.

Her grandmother Jessie lived across the street in the green boarding house, which Jessie owned. Donna visited her often, almost all of the time. For a time, I thought that was where she lived. Like Bobby, Donna would simply walk up and ask your name. I had never done that as I was too shy. "What's your name" was always the first question Bobby and Donna asked new kids.

Over time, we became The Three Musketeers without really knowing what that meant. We were called that one day as one of the residents at Jessie's boarding house said, "Here comes the Three Musketeers." I don't think we yet knew about the world's great literature or even some of its great films, but we accepted that we were The Three Musketeers; it sounded good. And, of course, there was a candy bar named The Three Musketeers, so we felt we were in good company but did not know why.

We were still just six years old at the time. Among the candy bars then were Hershey's plain or with almonds, Mr. Goodbar, Milky Way, Snickers, The Three Musketeers, Milk Duds, Black Cow, Peter Paul Mounds and Almond Joy, Baby Ruth, Butterfinger, Valomilk, Red Hots, Tootsie Rolls, M&M's in the brown paper bag and licorice under several brands; one brand was Nibs which were small black chunks sold in a hard pack then.

Also, there was a small candy square; technically taffy I think, yellow and with a strong banana flavor that you could round out your change with, as they were usually only a penny each. At the movies, they were in their own glass jar and we loved to say the name and even argue over it sometimes. It was labeled Beich, which got some interesting speculations on the pronunciation but in quotation marks after Beich was "Say 'Bike.'" We sometimes pushed the limits of décor in asking the lady for this candy, and we got a frown and instructions to "say bike."

The candies I listed were the candies that I liked, of course, some better than others. My mother had strange tastes in candies; she liked something call Horehound candy, which I would eat only if there were a major crisis.

She liked hard candies and looked forward to that at Christmas time, while I would probably have some of those hard candies today, if my grandmother had not thrown them out. I found them pretty but not edible.

There was also an all time favorite in Cracker Jack, which was molasses flavored popcorn with peanuts; it came in a hard cardboard box with a picture of Cracker Jack on the box cover. We called them Cracker Jacks, but the name was singular and not grammatically possessive. These were a special treat, and it helped that they came with a prize in the box. Most boys ate the popcorn off of the top, then turned the box upside down and finished off the peanuts that were left in the box. The flavored peanuts were the best part. There was a patented process to keep the corn from sticking together, but it didn't prevent our hands from becoming sticky and making us unwelcome in a mother's living room until we had washed our hands. We forgot sometimes though.

I found Cracker Jack in a QuikTrip store and I bought several packages. These were in an improved package, aluminum foil with an easy to tear corner and they were tasty. But I miss the old cardboard box with the flavor it added to the candy. It is said that you can never stand in the same river twice. You can never stand in the same moment twice.

More recently, I found a three pack set of Cracker Jack in the old boxes, and I did research on it. After two boxes accompanied by a Pepsi cola, I have sadly concluded that we lose taste sensation as we get older. This is the conclusion to my research: Eat as many good things as you can while you are very young.

Parke-Davis made a throat lozenge with a licorice flavor. Irby's Drug Store sold it, and we sometimes picked up a box on the way to the movie. It was best shared between two or more of us, and it probably wasn't candy. We treated it as candy though and ate too much of it.

One year a boy came to school with a small bottle of tooth picks soaking in clear liquid. He would suck on one of the tooth picks and make strange faces which got our curiosity up. The bottle contained cinnamon oil, and the tooth picks were soaked in it. Of course, he let us try one, and a few days later, all of us had gone to the G & L Drug and bought a bottle of cinnamon oil. It had a nice taste, but it was also spicy and left us with nearly permanent puckered lips and watery eyes. Fortunately that fad passed quickly.

In summer, we would stop in one of the neighborhood grocery stores, especially during an expedition, and buy a Popsicle. They came in a variety of flavors, grape, strawberry, orange and lemon, and when they were hard frozen they were very good. Sometimes we would not have enough money, and we broke one in half and divided it. They always began to melt before we could finish them, and left our hands sticky with sugar, one more joy for a mother to see us bringing into her house.

FIRST TIME IN UNION

Bobby Hughes had an older sister named Kay, who went to Union, so he had some insights to it that I did not. At least, he had been inside and knew a little about the building. During the summer he led an expedition, which included Donna and me, to the school; at his encouragement we went inside. "Sure it's all right," he said. "I come here all the time," and in we went. We were confronted with the great gray staircase which was both tall and wide. We heard voices somewhere above us, and although it was all right to be there, he had said, he thought we had better stay out of sight. Bobby urged us, two boys and a girl, down the stairs to the right and into a large room with several sinks and strange white porcelain devices rising from the floor.

When I didn't really understand what others boys were doing, I sometimes just went along and did what they did. So, as he stepped to one of the porcelain devices and unzipped the fly on his jeans, I did the same thing only to see Donna standing on my right side with her jeans unzipped. We were six and had a lot to learn. Some of our education began that day as a man discovered us in the strange room and laughingly explained to us that there were separate restrooms, actually I think he said bathrooms, for boys and girls, and she should be in the other one. Of course, he advised us that we were not supposed to be in the school building at all until school began, and he would see us later. He was wearing a uniform of sorts so I think he was the janitor.

UNION SCHOOL

There is a photograph of us, the Union first graders, and it must have been a cold day in late 1950 or early 1951, for we were all dressed in coats and hats and among the smiles appear numb expressions. We were Union's contribution to Pawhuska High School's class of 1962, and the photograph had been taken on the school's back steps. I am in the fifth row up, the only one in a cowboy hat. Our first grade teacher was Mrs. Sauter, a veteran of runny noses, hot chocolates, Christmas pageants and parties, Valentine's Day candies, hearts and disappointments and interminable retellings of the adventures of Dick, Jane and Spot. She seems reasonably happy in the photograph, perhaps realizing she was a year closer to retirement. She was a good teacher, and she tolerated us and even encouraged us, when she could.

I never knew why it was named Union; it wasn't after a famous founding father like Benjamin Franklin for whom our major rival, Franklin, on the hill was named. Perhaps it signified the whole union of the United States of America. We just knew it as Union, and it was our home for six years, longer for a few of us.

Union was located on land that was bordered on the east side by Rogers Avenue, on the west side by Revard Avenue and Seventh Street lay in front of it on the north. It occupied just half of the block, and an alley ran behind the building. The steps where we posed were next to the alley. I don't think Union sat in the center of the land but slightly to the east side, for there seemed to be more land on the west side. On that west side were a dirt and chat basketball court with two goals, rarely with nets in place, a set of swings, a teeter-totter, and what we called a jungle gym. I thought it was Jim because *Jungle Jim* was a movie hero played by Johnny Weissmüller of the *Tarzan* movies.

On the east side and close to the alley was another basketball court. North of that was an outline of a baseball diamond where we played games at recess. We used the sidewalk as the goal line for football. There were no trees, but there were uncountable little grasses that produced stickers that we called goat heads, actually *Tribulus terrestris*; guaranteed to make your bicycle tires flat. They were not very good for your knees either.

Union may have been built around 1910, according to one girl's grandmother, so it had stood for about fifty years when we were the last sixth graders to occupy Union Grade School. The class that followed us began in the new elementary school near the high school on Lynn Avenue. In the fall of 1956, we left for the high school building where we would be, first, seventh graders and, later, eighth and ninth graders but still not considered high school. Not until we reached the tenth grade. Both the Union and Franklin buildings were razed a few years later.

Unlike today's one floor elementary schools, Union had a basement and then three floors above the ground. In the basement were the boys' and girls' bathrooms, as we called them (rest rooms would come later when we were older and apparently tired), which were on opposite sides of each other and next to the stair case. In the back, next to the alley, was the lunch room with its small gray wooden tables and benches. We were served hot chocolate during the winter, often with a thick skim atop it, but it was good, and we sipped it down after a cold recess. I think we had to bring our lunches then, and most of us had a lunch box of our favorite hero or heroine. Some of them were Hopalong Cassidy, Roy Rogers, Red Ryder, Gene Autry, Annie Oakley and Dale Evans. Some of us just had a paper sack in which to carry lunch.

Up a very wide stair case, with wooden hand rails on each side, were the first four class rooms; vertical gray, steel struts about two feet high and about four inches apart supported the hand rails. The first grade class room was the furthest back, towards the alley, on the east side of the building. We spent our entire school year there and began to look longingly across the hall at the second grade class room.

We were already hearing stories about how stern and serious Mrs. Peters of the second grade was, much more serious than Mrs. Sauter; we wondered if we would make it through the second grade. Of course, we still had to get through the *first grade*. Next door to the second grade class room, north of it, was the third grade room, and then back across the hall and next to the first grade room was the fourth grade class.

In the hall, between the second and third grade rooms, was a chilled water fountain, from which you would get cooties if you drank after someone. Since it was the only one, we all drank from it, which probably accounts for our failings as adults. Staircases on each side led up to the next flight where fifth grade room occupied the west side; the sixth grade room the east side. Against the south side of the building and overlooking the alley was the auditorium and music room where Mrs. Harris held forth with the old upright piano, which was moved around as needed. Then there was a slightly raised stage with curtains and a wing back stage. From there came such great theater as *The Christmas Story, Frosty the Snowman* and a version of *The Nutcracker Suite* that exercised some poetic license. I was a

Chinaman in that. I did not know then that Mrs. Harris taught music at both Franklin and Union. Bless her.

All the class rooms were similar with our gray metal lockers against an interior wall near the door. Next to the windows were steam heated radiators with close fitting vertical tubing that gave them an accordion look. The tubing, which was supposed to transfer heat, was adorned with silvery paint which stayed on well enough during the school year, but the radiators probably required *real* maintenance yearly, more than just new paint. In the winter, you wanted to be next to the heaters, and even then, it was sometimes cold enough that we wore our coats inside. We did not have ceiling fans but the ceilings were very high, perhaps fifteen feet. All of the windows could be opened out at the top to let in fresh air and out heat; in the late spring, they also let in wasps, which sometimes caused excitement making heroes or cowards out of us boys. Girls were allowed to be frightened without prejudice to their femininity while boys were supposed to tackle bugs and things.

Our desks were iron frames with wooden seats and tops, and the frames were bolted to the floor so that we couldn't move them. The top had a hole for an ink well, and a hinge that allowed the top to be lifted to store our books and supplies. Some teachers had us change desks during the year, ostensibly to give everyone the same opportunity at being heard, but maybe it was to separate kids who were having too much fun.

In the fifth grade with Mrs. Schirmer, we opened every day with the Pledge of Allegiance with a different boy or girl leading it each time. One of the old jokes was about the boy who asked his mother, "Mommy, who is Richard Stands?" His mother told him that she didn't know and asked why he wanted to know. He explained that each morning they stood and said, "I pledge allegiance to the flag of the United States of America for Richard Stands…"

The seat was bolted to the desk frame and could not be moved, but the desk was wide. For some exercises, we sat two students at a desk to assist each other. Normally, we did not sit with members of the opposite sex, but sometimes that happened too. We did not like to do so. It was apparently one more way to get cooties.

At the very top of the interior of the building and on each side was a small stair case of perhaps ten steps. These led up to the principal's office, Mr. Wagner, at one time. This also housed the secretary, mimeograph machines, paper cutters, the feared wooden paddles and what other office tools we had.

The exterior was made up of large sandstone blocks which gave it the look of a citadel. In front was a sidewalk and along that were metal racks, in which we could store our bicycles, by putting the front tire into a slot.

In sixth grade, we were the seasoned professionals, and we had the honor and responsibility of being crossing guards. We wore white belts with a shoulder band; that signified we were crossing guards. When a group of students came to the corner, we collected them, held up our sign advising drivers to STOP, duly led our charges across the street to safety on the next corner, and returned for another group. Someone had the responsibility for rolling out our helper, which was a metal model of a friendly policeman in a blue uniform with a military cap and a raised, gloved hand; he wore a belt identical to ours, only his was painted on. His base was a metal ring and he could be moved by grabbing onto his upper body and using the base to roll him into the middle of the street, where he was stationed on the two main corners where Seventh intersected Rogers and Revard Avenues.

Union and Franklin school buildings were mirrors of each other. Union was east of Prudom and faced north while Franklin was west of Prudom and faced south. A few friends from Franklin have said that my description of

Union is very close to the way that they remember Franklin, only they remember Franklin as being a better school.

The first year that Pawhuska held Halloween Incorporated, an attempt to keep kids off of the streets and out of mischief at Halloween, Union School was the setting. I remember that the sixth grade room had a cake walk, and I won a cake for my mother. I think I helped her dispose of it.

The classes of 1962 were the last classes at Union and Franklin, and though we desperately wanted to leave and move on into high school, it was sad that Union, and Franklin and the other schools were closed; it was sadder when they were torn down, a part of our lives, and Pawhuska's, like The Raven, gone—forevermore.

AT THE HUGHES HOUSE

The Hughes house often had a lot of boys in it because it had one special thing, besides Bobby, that made us want to go there. The kitchen had a booth-like dining table, sometimes called a nook, modeled after one in a café. The seats and the back were vinyl, just like we saw in the cafes then, and went around the table from one side to the other. On the opposite side of the table where the seating ended, because Mrs. Hughes still had to get around the table somehow, was an open space, and if there were too many boys, she could pull a chair up so that no one was left out of the meal. It was great fun to eat there, for we could pretend that we were in a restaurant, although we weren't really restaurant broken yet. Unlike a dining table that could be moved around and the chairs moved up against it, all of this was fixed in place, and we had to move around on the vinyl bench seat. The only thing better would have been swivel stools.

I think Mrs. Hughes, Evelyn, even accommodated us some by letting us place orders, although she then gave us what she chose and not always what we wanted. But she did serve it just like we were in a restaurant except that she never asked for a tip; it was great fun for us. She had one specialty though that was wonderful, and that was seared wieners that we put on hot dog buns and covered with mustard. My grandmother boiled wieners; seared wieners were better. Technically, there were two major parts to a hot dog; the wiener and the bun. Once put together they became a hot dog but the meat was called a wiener. The buns were labeled hot dog buns, so there was an inconsistency. Sometimes the wieners were split in half and served on plain white bread, but it was the blackened streaks across the wiener that made them special. The secondary parts of a hot dog were onions, pickle relish, mustard and catsup. Everyone I have known has pronounced it ketchup, and some labels were spelled that way; usually though, it was catsup. I would have thought it completely affected had someone actually said, "Cat soup, please." That was one more inconsistency, and I was beginning to develop mistrust in adults for these inconsistencies. At that age I could not read anyway, but I certainly could recognize a lot of things and I could tell ketchup from mustard in a flash.

NOT TOO FAR AWAY AFTER ALL

I loved the new neighborhood, but before we moved to Prudom my cousins Barney and G. A. Hardy would take me to the movies at the State Theater. Secretly I was afraid that this would end because we were moving away, and I didn't understand that away was not that far. There was no television then, so it was movies or not much else. I did have a book for children called *Mr. Bear Squash You All Flat*, but the story never changed when it was read to me. I became able to predict the ending.

The State was only about two blocks from us on Girard Street, so we could walk there and back, but I did not know the way so someone still had to take me. Barney was older and fun, but he must have had that older child's resentment at having to take me, for he sometimes played tricks on me. Since I couldn't read, one of his tricks was to tell me that a monster in the movie was real. He would tell me that it said so on the writing at the end of the movie.

I was mostly interested in the cowboy movies but sometimes we saw something that left me frightened, and one day Barney brought me home from something that had me so scared that I hid under the bed. No one could find me and the usual hunting and calling began, but I wasn't coming out until it was safe, so I stayed absolutely still beneath the bed. Someone eventually looked under the bed, and once they had pulled me out, there was the dreaded question, "Are you all right?"

I never learned to say, "No, I'm not all right," so I got the usual treatment of being shaken by the arm and threatened with, "Don't you ever hide under that bed again or...," until I was not all right. I have never found out what the "or" was, but it must have been horrible for no one ever actually said what it was. Even in the navy I was sometimes told "Don't ever do that again or..." The only thing more threatening was, "...or else..." So, to me, the "or" and "or else" remain mysterious monsters hiding in the shadows, and I am afraid to find out what they are. In the navy I learned to ask, "Or else what?" but immediately learned it was not always the wisest thing to ask. Sometimes they told you what.

So, the only thing I did not like about the move to Prudom Avenue was that I would not be able to go to movies, at least I thought that. Our move was actually only about four blocks, but it was life changing for me. Years later I would show my son where Girard Street was and the short distance to Prudom, and that was when it dawned on me how much it had changed our lives, especially mine.

The State Theater was now farther from me, but it was still within reach so I still got to see movies. I just did not know how to get there alone. Most of the movies that I saw were on Saturday during the matinee, and these were usually a western movie plus a cartoon and a serial. A funny thing was that I did not know what matinee meant, so if I were asked if I wanted to go to the matinee, I always said no. If I were asked if I wanted to go to the movies, I said yes. Barney still took me, and he still fed me his own interpretation of the movie. My grandmother might have been paying Barney to take me.

One thing that he told me was that the cowboys we saw

were actually killed, and I felt very sad about some of them, the good cowboys. I cheered, right along with the rest of the kids, when the bad cowboys got it though. The rules were that the good cowboys never killed anyone unless it was unavoidable. There were fist fights, of course, and the bad cowboys always fought dirty. They also always wore an outfit that made it obvious that they were bad. I could not put my finger on it to explain it, but I knew by the way they looked that they were bad. The word villain comes to mind, but villain seemed to be a caricature word, something that reflected the old mustachioed, top hat attired vile man who would take away the widow's home as he gleefully said, in an aside to the audience, "It's all mine" or he muttered under his breath as he was spurned by the widow, "Curses, foiled again," These were outlaws rather than villains.

An outlaw was tougher than a villain, more physical, more obvious, although often the outlaws were just hired thugs who worked for a villain who was hiding back in the town saloon. The outlaws often had a moustache or several days' unshaved whiskers, and they always had a mean way of talking, often out of one side of the mouth. Some of the bad men were played by actors Glen Strange and Sam Bass, and later, I would understand they were both kind men who were only playing bad men. Back then, I really didn't like them.

Roy Rogers and the other good cowboys wore outfits that let us know that they were good and, as trite as it may be, they usually wore white hats. Also, if someone asked Roy or Gene a question, instead of just answering they would break out a guitar and sing it, especially it there was a girl present. In my first grade class photograph I am wearing a black cowboy hat but, it might have been red since the photograph is in black and white. I do think it is black although I don't think I was one of the bad guys, just misunderstood. In the first grade I was certainly misunderstood at times.

Two incidents stand out for me from the second grade, both involving Roy Mitchell. One recess, Roy was running around a corner of the building at top speed, and a girl was running in the opposite direction, laughing with her mouth wide open. As they met, her teeth came down over his lip and cut it badly. The lip was hanging on by only a thin strand of flesh and Roy was taken to a doctor. Both of them were hurt and cried a long time. Roy had stitches, perhaps seven, and immediately rose to the top of our list as a hero. All the years that I knew Roy, I would see the scar from his crash with her and remember it. Sometimes I reminded Roy of it, and I don't think he liked that.

Mrs. Peters was a stern teacher, and years later, one of my life long heroes told me that he was scared of her the entire year. I was too, at some level. One day, Roy, who sat behind me several seats, began to sing.

There's a place in France
Where the women do a dance
And the dance they do
Was written by a Jew
And the Jew wore pants
And the pants he wore
Cost a dollar ninety-four
(Plus tax).

The ditty was sung to a definitely Arabic sounding song. Mrs. Peters started towards Roy as he began to sing and as he began each verse, she was closer and closer. She was standing before him as he sang, "Cost a dollar ninety-four" and frowning. We thought she was going to hit him.

As he added, "plus tax," she smiled, and said, "Are you finished Mr. Mitchell?" "Yes, ma'am," he said, and she smiled, broadly, shook her head and returned to her desk. Only Roy could have got away with that.

IT'S JUST A STEP TO THE LEFT

Downtown was not very far from us; it was easy to find, just out the back door and a step to the left, you might say. Prudom ran north and south in front of the old white house, and Sixth Street lay on the north side where the back door was. We called it the back door, but it was on the side of the house. Downtown began just two blocks away along Sixth Street, and I always believed that downtown began at the bakery. The businesses along the way up to that point were serious businesses, for adults. On my side of the street were the American Legion building, an insurance company, the Monk Apartments, Fruehauf, Webber's Wholesale and the bus station and then...the bakery. This was Llewellyn's Bakery, on the corner of Sixth Street and an alley. The alley was between Leahy and Ki-He-Kah streets, and the back doors of stores such as JC Penney, Oklahoma Tire and Supply Company and Firestone opened onto it. I had always thought it was a street until I tried to find a name for it, and then I concluded that it was only an alley.

You could smell the bakery a mile away and what a smell it was. When I would see one of the cartoon characters, usually Goofy, with a wispy finger of smoke pulling him by the nose into a bakery against his will, I knew how he felt. It was difficult to walk past without stopping and once inside, it was impossible to leave, if I had money, without eating something. My favorite was brownies with a close second being anything else. There were rare times when I could not eat two brownies, luscious chocolate and nutty cake topped with even richer chocolate icing. And then I would go into one of the stores and with sticky hands, examine toys and things.

On the other side of the street along Sixth was the big green boarding house, the funeral home, a building which would become the Safeway store, the post office and the Ford dealer, a few small businesses and then, finally, Lennon's G & L Rexall Drug store. This was another treasure house as they had comic books, several racks of them, and there were booths where you could sit down and enjoy what you might have just purchased: a milk shake, a malt, a coke or other drink and sometimes ice cream in some form. When we said "Coke," it was meant as a generic term for soft drink, often called a soda. No matter your drink preference nobody said, "Let's go get a Pepsi or a 7UP;" it was always, "Let's go get a coke," much as one might say "coffee."

Lennon's served milk shakes in white cardboard pint and quart containers and the container gave a unique taste to the milkshake. Plastic laminate would later be added, and the container was more secure with fewer leaks and it lasted longer, but I missed that unique taste that the old cardboard jars had given the milkshakes. I could never tell a milkshake from malt, but I favored milkshakes. I settled on that and stopped ordering malts.

I also struggled between chocolate and strawberry but I usually leaned towards chocolate. I never really liked vanilla; perhaps because it was too vanilla.

Beyond the bakery was another serious business, the bank. It was a marvelous building though, in spite of being an adult building, and I liked to climb up on the side where there was a ledge on which I could walk as I tried to go from the back of the building to the front, without having to touch down on the sidewalk again. I never made it.

Inside of the building was an elevator and a man operated it with a device that was round, looking very much like a polished dome with a handle sticking out of it. He would ask, "Floor?" and when you told him, he moved the handle first one direction and then back again and the elevator took off. When we reached the floor he moved the mysterious device again, and we came to a slow stop, sometimes just above or below the floor. He made minute adjustments to get the car just right and then opened the doors.

At one point in my life I had decided that this was what I wanted to be when I grew up, an elevator man. Boyhood was fraught with that question: "What do you want to be when you grow up?"

The first time that I rode an elevator in which I could select the floor myself by just the push of a button, I was very excited. But then when I thought about how much fun it had been to ride with the elevator man, I missed him and the fun we had had together. He was a short, heavy set black man with a wonderful personality and attitude and the most brilliant smile I ever knew; he always seemed happy.

At the front of the bank was Ki-He-Kah Avenue, and it was here that I thought the heart of Pawhuska lay. Turning left and southward I learned where the toy stores began. First, there was F. W. Woolworth, which was the toy capital of Pawhuska, for it had toy soldiers, space men, trucks, tanks, boats and airplanes, as well as games and other things. At the age I was when we first moved to Prudom, that was probably the store of stores for me, but that would change as I got older. Further in that direction was the Oklahoma Tire and Supply store, which had some toys among its wares. The toys were not as abundant as in the Woolworth store, but OTASCO, as it was abbreviated, had bicycles, scooters, wagons, fishing gear, and other things that were interesting. And then there were the stores that I called boring, because all they had was clothing. These were the JC Penney and C. R. Anthony stores. It was easy to tell clothing stores as they had two initials before the name.

If I turned right and northward from Lennon's Drug store, I came to Longstreet's Variety Store, which I thought of as Longstreet's Toy store, for it also had the same toys as Woolworth. Next door to it was Manley's Army Surplus store, where we could examine army helmets and other things that we could use in make-believe battles. When I had lived on Girard a close friend was Jackie Manley, who was a year younger than I was. His father ran the store, and Jackie had many of the toys from the store. Of course soldiers' helmets, web belts, camp spades and bayonets and such weren't toys, but we saw them as toys. Almost anything can become a toy for six year old boys.

I mentioned Llewellyn's bakery because it was the closest to us and the first one we came to, but actually my favorite bakery was Crockett's Bakery on Leahy Avenue and Ninth Street. I suppose it served the same fare as Llewellyn's, called Lew's when you couldn't pronounce it, but the man and woman that I think ran Crockett's were very nice people. Lew was a bit of a grouch, and perhaps it was justified because he was much older and people had played tricks on him before. And I was six or seven and it's easier to see grouches at that age. Truthfully, I was very saddened when Crockett's Bakery closed.

CORNUCOPIA

We were fortunate in the Pawhuska of that time, for it was a small town yet had many of the advantages of a larger town. Then as now, there were towns nearby and some were close in size to it, yet Pawhuska *seemed* to be larger than the other towns; it seemed to offer more. Perhaps that was because it was the county seat for Osage County; perhaps it was because it was the home of the Osage Nation. Perhaps it was because of the oil production in the Burbank fields. Perhaps it was just an illusion, but if so it was a shared illusion.

Pawhuskans traveled to Tulsa, Ponca City and Bartlesville to buy things for there were more stores in those places and more things to buy and more things to do, but Pawhuska had many stores: Oklahoma Tire and Supply Company (OTASCO), Firestone Tires, B. F. Goodrich, and Western Auto Supply, for tires and parts. For clothing stores, Pawhuska had the national brands of JC Penney's and C. R. Anthony's. I don't remember Hominy and Cleveland having such stores. For men, there was the Hub Clothier store, which sold cowboy boots and hats, suits, shirts, pants and belts, all of good quality. Women's clothing stores were abundant, and my grandmother supported several of them.

The commercial heart of Pawhuska was the area around

the Triangle Building, on both sides of Ki-He-Kah Avenue as well as on Main Street. The JC Penney's store was on the east side of Ki-He-Kah opposite of the Triangle Building and just north of Main Street. But, at the entrance in a now empty space further north along Ki-He-Kah and between Whiting Hall and Sally's are embedded tile letters reading JC Penney's so the store must have been there once. Sally told me that she thought it had outgrown its space and moved to the newer building.

I don't remember seeing Mr. Penney, but he was still living then, although elderly, and I think that he did visit the Pawhuska store as he was famous for visiting the Penney's stores in person.

Triangle Building

What fascinated me most in Penney's was the system for moving payments, tickets and receipts. There were at least two floors in the store and the merchandise was downstairs while the administration was upstairs. We took our merchandise to the counter where it was recorded, and then after we paid our bill, a small wooden container on lines of rope was sent down to the counter and money was placed inside of it. Then it was retrieved, rapidly, back up to the next level, and your receipt returned via the same method. It was the most fascinating thing I had ever seen, and I liked to buy something there, just to watch the system at work.

HOW MUCH IS THIS ENOUGH FOR?

I find myself writing, "If I had any money…" and it needs explanation. Starting from those first moments when I was allowed to have money, it was usually just pocket change and very little of it. But it might be enough to get a Coke and a candy bar. At first, and before I started at Union, I really couldn't count. This was true of most of my friends of that age. So we had a system in which we basically said what we wanted and showed the man or woman behind the counter our entire fortune and asked, "Is this enough?" Sometimes they would advise us on how much we had and just what it would buy. I think it was both cute and frustrating for them, for it was a bit time consuming. It worked better on a woman for me. Sometimes, just because we were in that cute stage, one of them might make up a deficit of a nickel or a dime. I know it is difficult to look at a group of men and women who have passed their sixtieth birthdays and believe that they were ever cute, beyond an ogre sort of way, but trust me; we did pass through cute on our way to here.

If the clerk did not or would not make up a deficit in pocket change, sometimes your friend with you might have that extra nickel and loaned it to you. Loan was a euphemistic word for "gimme" as very few of those nickels and dimes were ever repaid; they were just loaned in the opposite direction later on.

Even as we got a little older and could count, larger numbers such as $.75 or something over several dollars, had small children standing at the glass counter that guarded the candy at the movies and asking, "How much is this enough for?" as they held out their entire fortune for the lady to see. I can imagine the frustration of the people behind the counter and the beautiful blonde woman that was cranky, sometimes became really cranky. I was so intimidated once that I pushed everything back to her except for my basic Coke and popcorn, which I suspect had become a Pavlov response for me: See movie, must have Coke and popcorn. It must have been an addiction for it stayed with me well into the year 2000 and I even considered founding a group for Coke and popcorn eaters anonymous.

GIRARD AND PRUDOM

The duplex on Girard had an icebox, not an electric refrigerator, but a real ice box in which we put ice. The exterior was made of wood, probably oak, and the inside was galvanized metal with small shelves. A block of ice was placed in a shelf at the top and cold air drifted downward to cool food. The ice slowly melted into water which ran down a tube and collected in a drip pan underneath the ice box. The pan had to be watched and emptied to keep the floors safe. I missed the icebox once it was behind us, not per se, but the delivery and the ritual of the iceman. Service people, who were invariably men then, were nice and they were always nice to me, a kind of larger play mate and they often had something to give me: candy, gum, a penny. Of course, I didn't have to clean the icebox or find money to pay for the delivery.

The house on Prudom had a refrigerator which only required plugging in and then periodic defrosting. Defrosting anywhere in the neighborhood was a delightful experience, for if we kids were around, we got to eat some of the treats that might otherwise go to waste. There were no published schedules; you just had to be lucky and be there to get in on it. Most of the things that might go to waste happened to be ice cream and popsicles.

This was akin to being there when someone's mother

made a cake, especially one with chocolate frosting, which we also called icing. Before the easier cake mixes, frosting was made by hand and there was inevitably a surplus which no one wanted to see go to waste, so Bobby and I volunteered at times. Besides, it was probably difficult to clean up so we were doing her a favor. If you had two or three boys standing by, you passed out spoons and then the bowl, egg beaters and utensils were almost self-cleaning; the innocent bystanders of furniture and walls were not.

The house on Prudom was furnished, and we owned very little. I don't know why we had so little at the time, but we had no furniture, no car, no washer nor dryer so our lives were simple in 1949. We had a record player that played records of 16 rpm, 33 1/3 rpm, 78 rpm and 45 rpm; I have still never seen a 16 rpm record. My favorite record at age five was *Froggy Went A'Huntin* or at least I knew it by that title, and I had them play it for me until it was worn out. It might have actually been called *Froggy Went A'Courtin* though. They would not let me play records on my own due to the expense of needles and my combined eagerness and clumsiness. We had a radio which I think was a Philco brand. My grandmother, Louise, listened to Johnny Lee Wills daily with the musical introduction, "Here's Johnny Lee and all the boys, here to play for you." The sponsor was Shawnee Mills, and it became so burned into me because of that association that I still favor Shawnee Mills brands.

We did not have a television then, and I think that there were few in Pawhuska. In fact, I'm not sure if I knew what a television was yet because I remember my first television experiences came later.

My mother, Bettie Payne, worked as a telephone operator, and the office was a short walk from our Prudom house. Her walk from Girard had been more difficult so she was happier on Prudom. The telephone building, which housed the business office, telephone operators and switching equipment, faced Main Street from the middle of the block. The block was bordered by Prudom to the east, Leahy to the west, and Sixth Street on the opposite side north. The Servall Grocery was directly across the street. Main Street was wide but parking along this section was diagonal, which reduced it to two lanes in the center.

The operators worked upstairs one flight while the business office personnel were downstairs as one entered the building. The operators were all women then, mostly young women, and it was a good job but the hours were often difficult, especially for young mothers. The operators had to bid on shifts which were awarded, in part, on seniority so young operators often got the worse shifts or shafts as some said. This could mean working at night, all night, or in the evening. The worst shift for my mother was called the split shift. She would work about four hours, have two or four hours off and then return to finish her day with the second part of her shift. The issue of split shifts and how frequently she had to work them was probably why the short walk made her happier.

THE RED AVENGER

I was intrigued with heroes and superheroes from an early age on. They were in the movies mostly, but one day, I was fortunate to meet one in person. I do not remember what he called himself, but it was something like The Red Avenger so I am using that.

I met him in the park on the corner of Seventh Street and Prudom, and he was older than I was and a nice, friendly boy. We played together some, and as I got to know him he decided to trust me with this secret; he told me that he was the Red Avenger. I was skeptical because he did not seem to be more than another boy but he showed me the secret place where he hid his red cape, hat and mask. At the age I was then, I was convinced, and I was very impressed. Of course, I couldn't tell anyone. It was a secret, and I had a clear vision of what a secret was then. Later, I would learn that a secret is something you tell one person at a time. I was burning to tell someone.

Above all, he told me not to tell Bobby Hughes. Darn!

One day the boy and I were in the park and some girls came in, walked a bit and were just talking when two tough boys came from a movie. There were some words exchanged, and the boys impugned the honor of the girls, and it was getting close to a fight or something. I didn't believe in fighting girls, and I didn't think that girls fought.

Suddenly, my older friend told me that this was a job for the Red Avenger, and he took off running towards his house, I thought. I assumed he was going to get help, so I waited. It was getting worse, the boys were becoming ruder and more sarcastic, and I had said something. They told me to shut up or get beat up. I shut up.

Suddenly, from the hedge that ran around the park came a cry of something like, "Leave those girls alone!" The two tough boys looked at him, startled, and then began to laugh.

The Red Avenger walked into the park, his red hat on, a red mask, much like the one that the Lone Ranger wore in black, a short, flowing red cape and he might have had a wooden sword. All of his red costume looked suspiciously like women's clothing. The undisguised voice was clearly his, and everyone recognized him. I stood by, impressed with the courage he was showing, and waited for something to kick in, something like Popeye's spinach that would make him tougher than them. One of them called him by name and told him to go home. He stood his ground. The boys would not stop pestering the two girls, The Red Avenger would not retreat, and in short order, they had beaten him to a crying baby. But he didn't quit. Then the girls got upset with the boys and even started hitting them, telling them to leave him alone.

The boys were being shamed and knew it so they gave up, apologized to everyone and left the Red Avenger crying in the park, still in costume but beaten. I waited for him and after a while he quit crying, wiped his eyes and stood tall. Then he said, "Once again, the Red Avenger has brought justice to those in need." He either never grasped or never understood that he had been completely defeated. But he didn't give up. The girls stayed and talked a while, humoring him a bit, and when they left he put his costume back in the hedge in its secret place to await another episode of injustice, another need for The Red Avenger.

The place was in the hedge next to a tree and anyone

walking by could see the costume. No one ever bothered it as they seemed to know to whom it belonged. Like me, he had seen too many movies and had a fanciful imagination, and he wanted to be more, to contribute to the values of America, as he understood them. Even though he had been soundly defeated, he was my hero, perhaps just because he tried, because he showed so much courage in the face of insurmountable odds.

As he got a little older he passed the point where boys my age were too young for him, and we were not as close as we had been. I always liked him, even through high school and I always spoke to him. We just weren't as close. He was very intelligent, smart as we said, and that was another thing to admire. Even though other things happened in his life—and mine—when I think about him today my fondest memory is of the fearless, but hapless, Red Avenger.

THREE BOBBIES

I was giving a seminar on drilling fluids at Texas A&M University in 1985, and I liked to have a student help me with one or two tests, to show that they were unbiased and anyone could achieve the same results. When I reached the critical point, I looked out into the audience and asked, "John, could you come up here and give a hand?" It was something I had learned from watching *Mr. Wizard* when I was a kid. A handsome young man, startled at first, pointed at himself and asked, "Me sir?" "Yes, John," I said, "Come on up and stir the thinner mix for me." Afterwards, the professor asked me, "Stephen, did you know John." "No sir," I said. "I used an assumption, that certain names will always be used and there is a likelihood of one of them being in a group of young men." And John was there.

When I was a kid, John was common then too, but my world was full of Bobbies. By the third grade, we had Bobby Hughes, Bobby Cole and Bobby Green. There were a few things common to all of them as they were all funny, usually smiling and a tad ornery. I always thought Bobby Hughes was the funniest of them for he seemed original most of the time. Bobby Green was a great imitator, and his father had a collection of comedy records. Andy Griffith had begun to make his mark on the comedy world as Deacon Andy Griffith and his major routine was a story called *What it was, was football*, in which he told the story of how he was going to a tent meeting and saw a sign for food which led him into a little cow pasture and so on. It became a comedy classic. We didn't need the record for Bobby Green performed it everyday with accents, gesticulations and theater to the point that we were there. I did acquire a CD of Deacon Andy in the year 2001, and I have most of his comedy routines.

Bobby's dad had other comedy records too which Bobby could do just as well only, some of them were not intended for general audiences. We went home with interesting questions related to Bobby's stories. For all of his humor, Bobby went on to have a career with the Oklahoma Highway Patrol where his courage counted more than his funny bone.

Bobby Cole was funny as well, and I spent a lot of my time laughing at him. Bobby was funny for the way that he told a story, even if the story wasn't funny. My memories of him are of a boy always smiling, right down to his eyes, and laughing loudly. Both Bobby Cole and Bobby Green played catcher when we played baseball, and catcher is a position that requires courage as well as skill. I always admired them for playing catcher but also, both of them *wanted* to play catcher. I usually played left or right field as Jay theorized I could do the least amount of damage there.

We did have Jon Horn in my classes, and Jon was with us at Union and also in band. But I remember having more Bobbies than any other name. I was the only Steve, Stevie or Stephen in my class, even when we combined Franklin and the other schools. There was Steve Horn, class of 1961 and Steve Carroll, class of 1961. We were a rare name then, but after Steve Reeves became the Arnold Schwarzenegger of our day, except that I think he could speak English, many women named babies Steve.

My spelling is Stephen because the name came from the Greek, Stefanos, who became Stephen the martyr of early Christian history; the f from the Greek is transliterated to the ph of English. Only, my name was given to me for my aunt Mae Dean Payne whose maiden name was Stephens. I'm glad that the s was omitted. When I lived in North Dakota, the residents pronounced my name as Step-Hen which I am glad has been lost to history.

THE BOY WITH GREEN HAIR

The *Boy with Green Hair* was an important movie for me. Not because it was Academy Award material but because it taught me a survival tactic that saved me one day; it also taught me a lesson. Although the movie was released in 1948, I only saw it when I was in the third grade, about 1952.

I was having a problem with a boy that was picking on me and not for any reason; just because he could. Although he was about my height and weight, he was more aggressive than I was, and he had his bluff in on me. Also, he always started something with me for no reason, and I was frustrated with him. I only remember two things from the movie. The boy had green hair, and in one scene a bully was chasing him. At the last possible moment in the chase, he dropped to the ground on his hands and knees, covered like a rock, and the boy went over him, crashing into the ground.

Meanwhile, back at Union, the boy started pushing and shoving me, taunting me, and then he hit me. I turned and ran, just as I had seen the boy in the movie do, and—he took the bait! Step for step we ran across the west side of Union, heading for the back door when suddenly, I folded up and dropped right in front of him. I landed on my knees right in the goat heads, and the tiny but stubborn thorns hurt like the dickens.

The boy went over me, just like in the movie and crashed on his face. I thought *I* was in trouble, but he landed face first, ahead of me and in the middle of the largest patch of goat heads on the school yard.

Had I won?

No. I was hurting but I felt so sorry for him, and I was worried that I had really hurt him, even though I had not touched him. I liked the boy and wanted to be friends with him, but he had to pick on me. All I really wanted to do was to get him to stop.

I went over to him, helped him up, and he was bleeding and crying and I was scared to death. I felt so bad about hurting him. And I asked him, "Are you all right?" It was already starting; I, too, was picking up the habit of asking someone with major injuries if he was all right.

He said something like, "Ifellinapatchofgoatheadsandithurtsrealbad-waahhhhhhhhhhhh." I didn't really understand it but that was as close as I could get to it.

A teacher was coming, and we looked at each other as two men condemned to be hanged might look at each other.

"What happened?"

"I fell down," he said, as calmly as though nothing had happened.

Eyeing us suspiciously, she mumbled something about, "Be more careful when you play boys." She did not believe us, and she did not trust us.

Neither of us told. We helped each other get the goat heads out, and we never had another fight. We became pretty good friends and remained so for as long as I had any association with him.

My lesson: I hurt when I hurt someone else, and it's just not worth it to me. It's my own personal lesson, and it's not for everyone. Some people have to be tough in this world, and I'm just not one of them. It hurts me too much to hurt others.

That being said, I hope I never hurt another human being as long as I live.

WHAT THE DICKENS?

For much of my life I have said something similar to, "That hurts like the dickens." There are many variations of it: stings like the dickens, burns like the dickens, feels like the dickens. Most of them seem to be negative and I have never heard one used in a positive sense. What is the Dickens?

As humans, we seem to have a need to express ourselves about negative things. As children, we begin to pick up whatever phrases are lying around, left by an uncle or an aunt, a cousin or a well meaning friend. Most parents would remain ecstatic if The Dickens was the only phrase that their children chose to use. I won't list them because there are too many resources where they can be found, and on the job training is provided in pool halls, the navy, the oil patch and at most truck stops.

Like the Dickens seems to have no real meaning beyond an expression of saying, "Ouch!" in a way that our friends will understand. The closest meaning that I could find was that Dickens was another name for the Devil from early times, back when we were first learning English. "That hurts like the Devil," still means, "Ouch!" It goes to our need to use superlatives and hyperbole to express ourselves and somehow, get the most attention. It is obviously one more holdover from our experiences as children, when we first felt the need to be competitive and gain the attention of someone important to us.

I have explained the Dickens out of that.

THE NEW KID IN SCHOOL

Jay Lynn Hurt is not in our first grade photograph because he wasn't in our school then. Jay is always the first member of our class to have a birthday, unless it was one of the kids who were invited to stay another year in some grade.

But Jay Lynn was born in a twilight area that meant he was one day too young to start with the class of 1961, so he was with us, the class of 1962. His birthday is November 3rd so he always reaches that next birthday before I do, and I always do something to help him remember his birthday. For his 50th birthday, of which I was rather proud of his reaching, and felt it should be celebrated magnificently, I bought a **GIANT** birthday card. I signed it with my famous signature, of course, and then I got everyone I knew in the class of 1962 to sign it.

Because it was so large, it didn't look filled to me, and I wanted it to be filled so I took it to work to have everyone sign it for him. Did they know him? Of course not but it didn't matter since I wanted lots of names on the card. I carried the card everywhere with me for weeks, and I asked everyone that I saw, at the post office, the mall, grocery stores, my doctor and my barber—everyone, to sign it. I had to meet my cousin Pan at the Tulsa Airport so I took the card and Pan signed it as well as several hundred people waiting for others there. I had some Korean people sign it and a Russian or two and then, Friday night, I took the card to the Dewey, Oklahoma (where the traitor was coaching) football stadium and passed it among the spectators. When the evening was done, we may have had five or seven hundred names on it, and I think he was impressed since he actually only knows six people. Jay Lynn has asked me not to remember his birthday so well and often, and that has only encouraged me.

Jay Lynn Hurt

At Jay Lynn's fiftieth birthday party Gary Abbott offered a toast in which he said, "Jay, there are only two kinds of football coaches; those that have been fired and those that will be fired." Gary knows this because there are only two kinds of performers.

Jay Lynn was one of those people that, for some reason, we rarely spoke of just Jay and used Jay Lynn most of the time, even when we were talking to him. I suppose it is that version of –ying or-ieing a boy's name; such as John becoming Johnny, Bob Bobby, Steve Stevie and so on. You can't do a good –y or –ie on a name like Jay; no Jayy or Jayie, certainly not on a boy. So I guess he got Jay Lynn to fulfill our southern or country need to add syllables to a name. But in rapid pronunciation the Jay Lynn became a sort of JayLen or JayLun, depending upon whether you were from east or west Pawhuska; the emphasis is on the first syllable. He was JayLun before Jennifer Lopez was J-Lo.

Jay Lynn had started school in Barnsdall and transferred to Pawhuska, starting with us in the second grade. I'm sure there is mystery surrounding the circumstances of why he had to transfer from Barnsdall, but since he was a juvenile, the records may be sealed. No matter; he transferred and came to Union. I don't remember that he was introduced to the class, but there were rumors of a new boy being in school and actually in our class. I remember someone pointing him out, and I soon learned that he was a tremendous athlete. We boys were competitive, even at that age, and there were soon challenges to young Jay Lynn who, being new, had to prove himself as all new students do. We were playing a loose game of football on the west side of school, and he threw a beautiful pass, an actual spiral, which was the first one I had ever seen.

It is easy to forget or to misunderstand how difficult the football is to handle. I think it is only called a ball because that is the closest word in English for it. It isn't round and is too large for most things so it isn't conducive to being hit with a bat, racket, club or much else, and it doesn't bounce, with control that is. Fumble one and it will bounce, but seldom in the direction that you wish. Few people go round dribbling footballs and those that can, I don't think I want to meet. Maybe we should have just called it a foot- and stopped there, leaving off the word ball; maybe a foot-thing then or even have created a new word for it, perhaps Kabeezle.

I always had trouble handling a football, and especially if I were taking a snap from center and trying to throw the ball. You have to take the snap, back up quickly and get the football into your hands with the seams in the right place so that you can put spin on the football and make it spiral. I could do that, once in a while, if I had a lot of time to hold the football and look at the seams. Taking the snap from center with the defense rushing at you when you are the quarterback did not allow the time that I needed. So, basically, I threw bad passes.

In grade school football, almost all of us got to play quarterback at some time, especially if you were the boy who owned the football. But Jay Lynn was authoritative as the quarterback, and we let him play that position; to humor him. Jay Lynn was good at football, baseball, basketball and track and, truthfully, speaking from today, he was the best all round athlete that I have ever known. Of course, I knew that back then. I admired him for those skills. I was also a little jealous, which is to be expected. I was never meant to be a lineman, but that's where I usually played, right next to the center. I wasn't big enough, but it required less special skill; and you didn't have to handle the ball.

There was a bully in our school, actually there were several, but one in particular who had been held back a year. The story is that the bully went to find Jay Lynn and told him, "I'm the toughest kid in Union school." Who threw the first punch or how it started is insignificant, but when it was over, Jay Lynn said, "Now you're the second toughest." So he established himself right away. I liked Jay Lynn right away, once I found out that he was a pretty nice kid. Like anyone, you had to get to know him, and I was always shy, but Jay Lynn made friends with me first, which was wonderful. I was not an athlete. The actor Audie Murphy once told a critic that his performance was not his fault because he was working with a handicap. "What is it?" asked the critic. "No talent," Murphy deadpanned. Athletically, I had the same handicap.

Jay Lynn took me under his wing early on and taught me things about baseball, basketball, football, and girls; he never told me that I was not good, which some people did. He encouraged me and spent a lot of time in practice with me. One of our favorite games was called burn-out. Basically it is the metaphor for the shoot out at high noon seen in the western movies but without music. Two boys stand facing each other and throw the baseball as hard as they possibly can, and you catch it until your hand no longer works or is burned out, hence the name of the game.

Jay Lynn and I played a lot of burn-out, at his house, and in the park across the street; I learned a lot about catching the ball. My first lesson was—do not let the ball hit you in the mouth.

I played hard, and I really improved with his helping me and teaching me so much, but he always won our burn-out contests, not only with me but with just about everyone else. I guess you could say that he had a strong right arm, for it was in the games where he was the shooter that he excelled most; quarterback in football, pitcher in baseball and he was a pretty fair shooter from the basketball court. He wasn't as good as the Marble King though, when it came to shooting marbles.

A COUNTRY LAD

And thinking about the park that was directly across from Jay Hurt's house and kitty corner from Bobby Hughes's house reminds me of someone I met there.

The park was small with a large tree, and there was a cellar, which we called a fraidy hole, in it. It was into this cellar that we went when there was a storm alert, and in the Oklahoma spring there were always storm alerts. Pawhuska had experienced a tornado in the early 1940's that resulted in a loss of life, and many people remembered it. My grandmother was one of them, and she headed us towards the cellar at the first sign of any severe weather. I hated the cellar. It was dark and dank and someone who was drunk always showed up, so we had to smell the dampness and a drunk at the same time. There was always water standing on the floor and at least seven varieties of insects lived in it, all of them deadly to my way of thinking. I always felt that given a choice, I would easily have chosen the tornado over the cellar. Other boys with whom I have spoken in the last few years felt the same. The tornado *might* get you, but certain death lurked in the cellar. Of course, we all survived it and have those joyful memories to share with each other.

The park had a neatly trimmed hedge that ran around its edges, and it was in this hedge along Prudom that the Red Avenger hid his costume. We played baseball in the park and sometimes two or more of us would get together and just play catch with our gloves, sometimes burn-out.

To this point we were all just boys with little differences between us, statistically speaking, less than two standard deviations. But I was about to meet my first true character, outside of my own family, of course. Sometimes you never forget the first time you meet someone, and I have never forgotten my first meeting with Henry.

Jay and I and some others were playing a modified version of baseball, because we did not have enough boys to form two full teams. So we were playing something in which we covered a base and a half instead of each base. The park was small, and the outfielders played in close.

As we were playing, a boy and a man were walking towards us. When they got close, the man let out a man's version of Minnie Pearl's "Howwwwwwddddddddddddeeeeeeeee!" and came over to us. The sight of the man struck me right away, for he was smiling and laughing in spite of having his broken arm in a cast and a sling. He came right up to us and the game came to a complete halt, as one of our players knew him and walked over and began to talk to him excitedly.

"What happened, Henry?" he asked.

"Well, I bruck my arm," Henry said as he lifted the arm in the sling to show us.

I had never seen a broken arm for real and up close, and I was impressed with how tough he seemed. I had seen Roy Rogers winged a few times in the movies, but he only wore a sling, not a cast.

About that time one of the boys told us that this was Henry Jones, and I wondered how a man knew so many kids so well and how they knew him. It turned out that Henry was really only a boy a few years older than we were, and he apparently went to school at Lynn Addition. But he seemed to be an adult, at least until you got to know him.

"How did you come to break it, Henry?" the boy asked.

"Well," Henry began, still smiling, "I had just come from seeing the Tarzan movie, and we got to this tree," he said, pointing to the big tree in the park, "and I clumb it, got way up there, took my shirt off, beat my chest and went augh-augh-augh-augh," giving us his best, and a formidable, Tarzan yell, "and I grabbed onto a vine like he did, to swing over to another branch." He paused, laughing hard at his own story, "and I went straight down like a rock. Bruck my arm right away. I knew it was bruck as soon as I stood up."

Henry was tall, muscular in a farm hand way, and strong. He had an unforgettable face, more square than round, and a shock of jet black hair that might be combed but had its own life to live, and it was always over his forehead. He had a laughing, booming voice and was never shy about using it. If I had a twang in my voice, Henry had a hillbilly band in his. I don't know where his accent came from, but it was the first time I heard a true hillbilly voice. And I loved it. Henry could entertain just by telling you he had just come from town. I had thought he was a man instead of another boy because he acted like one, at least at first impression. He was older than we were and further along in school but by the time we arrived at PHS together, he was in classes with us; so he must have been enjoying school but not studying too much.

I had an English class with him in either seventh or eighth grade, and he and I were picked, by our female teacher, to give descriptions of each other, out loud. I had tried to describe him accurately but kindly and yet for all of my efforts, I caused some laughter; no one could describe Henry without getting some laughs.

Then it was Henry's turn. Henry did not say "well;" He said "wayail." And that is how he began to describe me, "Wayail, he's got sort of brown hair, kind of like a dog I had, and it ain't long but it ain't real short like ol' Butch

(Hughes) is neither. But I always get a kick out of his ears. His ears are real big for a little guy, so I always look for his ears if I see him in the hall..." and he went on, gaining laughter from the class, especially the girls, as he went along. I was red faced but not angry. You couldn't get angry at Henry. And I might have been that funny.

When he started football, the coach told him that he would have to get an athletic supporter and Greer's Sporting Goods was the store that a boy went to for that. Henry grew up around farm animals, and things that we did not talk about or admit to know about were commonplace for Henry; and he saw nothing wrong in speaking plainly about them. We had to be cautionary with him as he explained how he knew that they were going to have a calf soon, or how the calf got there in the first place for his language was plain and straight and sometimes a bit ornery as he liked to make the girls blush, even if he eventually made himself blush more.

Henry went to Greer's, up to the appropriate counter and found a young lady working there, one he knew from school.

"May I help you?" she asked.

"Yup. Coach says I need to get a jock strap," he said, going for the common term versus the polite one.

She blushed and after a moment of realizing that this was her job, what she had to do for the male customers, she gathered herself and said, "And what size?" meaning waist band.

Henry, smiling and with his hands offering measurements, said, "Oh, bout this big."

At this the girl, embarrassed, gave up and went to get a male clerk to deal with Henry.

Off and on I had some contact with Henry and I was always glad to see him, to be around him. It was always casual contact though, maybe at the Dairy Queen or at the football stadium. Henry loved people and I never met anyone who didn't like Henry Jones.

Henry joined the Marine Corps, and I saw him one day in Pawhuska. "Are you on leave," I asked him. He was standing with some other boys and in just his civilian clothes.

"Nope," he said. "I ain't in no more."

"How come," I asked.

"Well," he began, with his special multiple syllable pronunciation of the word. "I was in the barracks and our Sergeant come up to me and said, "Do you like the Marine Corps, son?" ""Yes sir,' I told him.""

"Then he hauled off and hit me in the stomach real hard."

""Do you like it now?" He asked me"''

"'No sir' I said, and here I am.""

That was the last time I ever saw Henry. He was later killed in an industrial accident. Henry had married and been divorced and I heard many people talk about how much Henry loved his child. My class sorely missed Henry Jones, a Pawhuska original. As someone said, "When God made Henry Jones, he broke the mold on that one."

THE MARK OF COURAGE

When we lived on Girard, some rail road tracks and a station house, long since closed, were just north of us. We children, both girls and boys, liked to find something and put it on the track for the trains to run over. To help us out, someone had discarded a lot of ceramic pipe, and we found that putting a half piece of it, shaped as a semi-circle, over a track was a lot of fun; when the train hit it, the pipe was broken and sent flying, usually in our direction. Because we were hidden, it missed us. Of course, it could have hit one of us and left us maimed, stupid or dead.

There was a small tree there and I climbed it often, and as proof of that, my current X-ray images show fracture indications in three separate places on my collar bones. I broke one in a fall from the tree, and I had to wear a miserable white canvas brace while I healed, six weeks, I think. I had just recovered well when I made a second climb followed by a second fall, in which I broke the other collar bone, and then, when I had healed well enough, I broke the first one a second time. In my final fall I did not break my collar bones because I hit on my nose. I don't know if I actually broke my nose, but it was the most blood that I had ever seen. My grandmother indicated that it was the most blood she had ever seen as well.

But none of my Union friends knew about those bone fractures and my nose, and they did not seem as important to them as a broken arm or leg did. I would tell them that I had broken my collar bone, and it didn't seem to get the respect that I thought it deserved. I think it was because a broken arm was so visible. Usually it was also supported by a sling, until the arm was far enough along to stop using the sling and wreck havoc by using the cast as a club.

Henry Jones's was the first broken arm that I had seen until later when Jay Lynn introduced me to his neighbor, Earl Brunger. Earl was a little older than we were, and he went to Indian Camp School. I was in awe of Earl when I met him for he was a lot more experienced in about everything, and he had a broken arm. I think he was out of the sling but still wearing a cast, and it had been signed by a lot of people. Also, Earl was a character.

"How did you break it," I asked.

"Playing football," he replied. "In fact," he continued, "I didn't know it was broken and kept on playing for a while until Mrs. [and he named the teacher] came and got me and said, 'Earl, I think your arm is broken.'"

I was very impressed then. Usually, we called Earl "Chunker." I don't know who gave him the nickname, but it was about all we ever called him. Many of us had nicknames, and a lot of them were the type that we would like to forget and hope that others have. One of the boys I knew got nicknamed "Stinky" during a band trip. Most people don't want to be known as Stinky when they are adults.

I was still called Stevie Joe through much of that time, but I was beginning to *try* to grow out of it.

As an adult I have heard many stories from people about a nick name and how they despised it; most of them have tried to change from being called by a nickname to using their given name. And I have tried to be considerate of others and stop using those nicknames, for the most part.

Some people keep a nickname all of their lives and even benefit from it. Somewhere along the way I learned that Blackie Ricketts name was William B. Ricketts, but I never heard him called anything but Blackie. He liked it, and everyone else seemed to like it; he seemed to benefit from his nickname. Maybe the B. was really for Blackie.

One boy of the 1962 class was Robert McQuay, but Robert got stuck with the nickname of "Goober." Almost everyone called him that. Robert was in a biology class with me in the 10th grade, and our teacher called him Goober. It was a nickname that stuck hard to him.

A few years ago, at an all school reunion, I apologized to him when I accidentally called him Goober. I corrected myself and said, "Robert." "Please. Just call me Goober," he said. It was a nice touch on his part.

I asked Earl Brunger if we still called him Chunker, meaning, is it all right to call him Chunker. He told me that we could call him anything as long as we called him for dinner and payday. I explained that I wanted to use Chunker for this book, as it better fits the times I am writing about. I am grateful that I can call him Chunker for this. I suspect that Earl will never outgrow being called Chunker, at least by some of us.

There were the two boys so far, Henry Jones and Chunker Brunger, who had worn the mark of courage, the broken arm in a cast for all to see. The rest of us talked about it a lot, wondering if we would be able to stand the pain, and have the courage that it implied. I was frankly scared but also envious of Chunker. We looked up to the boys who had broken arms. It showed more courage if you had a broken leg, but of course it was harder to do and riskier. A broken leg was more obvious; you had a bigger cast and had to use crutches for a while. You had to have a pair of jeans either cut or torn to fit over the cast and you got a lot of sympathy and help; also a lot more admiration. Of course, there had to be a good, courageous reason for the break in the first place. Few would give you sympathy or admiration for breaking it falling out of a chair while watching cartoons.

Not that any of us tried to break an arm; we didn't. But if you came by one naturally, doing something courageous like playing football or baseball, then it was all right in some sort of way, and I suppose falling out of a tree carried the same mysterious connotation. It is sort of like that moment when you see a football player carried off of the field, and the whole stadium stands and cheers for him. It also helps if your team wins.

Most of us had a lot of skins and bruises, from playing football, baseball and basketball. And there were many skins and bruises from bicycle accidents, for the bicycle was more than mere transportation. It was a device to show your cleverness, your ingenuity, and your daredevil side. Most boys' favorite trick was to ride with your hands off of the handlebars and, as usual, in this I followed someone else who had done it. I was successful too, until I hit a curb and went over on my nose.

One of the boys gave us this refrain of a boy who was riding his bicycle and showing off. At each pass by, he would utter one line, then the next a new line and so on, like this:

Look ma, no hands,
Look ma, no feet,
Look ma, no hands, no feet,
Look ma, no teeth.

We spent a lot of time with the bicycles. Some were Schwinn bicycles, which was probably the best American brand of the time. I had a Monarch bicycle that my grandmother had bought me at OTASCO. Mine was still standard and had all of its parts; a front and rear fender and a metal piece that filled in the gap between the two crossbars. Some of the boys stripped them down to make them faster, so the front and rear fenders had been removed. Everything we did with bicycles was in a small way trying to imitate what we saw with motorcycles. One of the boys took a deck of playing cards and fitted them to the spokes in such a way that they struck the frame of the bicycle and made an engine-like sound. If one boy did something successfully, we all imitated it so a few days later, there were parents' playing cards with shortened decks. Only a few of us had our own real deck of cards so, we borrowed what we needed from our parents. You couldn't tell them what you wanted the cards for so you didn't ask. And, besides, you were *going to* put them back in a few days anyway; talk about marked cards. My grandmother played Canasta with several of her friends on a periodic basis and kept several decks of cards at the house, so I borrowed one and shared it with the other boys.

Not every boy had a bicycle, and there were times that your bicycle was in the shop or had a flat tire so you had to ride with another boy. Riding double had variations and the best case was one in which the bicycle had a rack on the back; a second person could sit there safely, sort of. Riding double on a bicycle was never completely safe. A more common option was that the passenger sat on the cross bar, boys' bicycles only, in front of the driver. Sometimes the passenger sat on the seat, and the driver stood and pedaled wherever they went. The most dangerous though, which I did a few times, was to have the passenger sit up on the handlebars. The bicycle could be ridden and even controlled that way, but it took a strong boy to handle the bicycle. Butch Daniels was probably the best at that, and I trusted him. If you had to stop with someone on the handlebars, you usually just dropped the passenger and crashed. Fate was random about which one of you got the worst of it.

Most of our bicycles had the brake as a mechanism

inside of the rear hub so it was operated by pressing the pedal backwards. It was good most of the time, and one stunt was to ride as fast as you could and then slam the brake on leaving a good length of rubber on the pavement and making a good noise. But, if your chain came off, broke, or something else happened to it, the brakes did not work. All of my accidents that way were minor, but one boy said that he had been going down Grandview hill, going as fast as he could and as he passed the courthouse, his chain came off. He said that he went flying down the hill screaming, "No brakes! No brakes!" and dashed across the street, narrowly missing traffic and pedestrians and navigated his way past the police station and around the old firehouse. Maybe it happened that way. We all had a tendency to exaggerate our stories.

Chunker had a large tree at the back of the yard, just to the side of the chicken coop, and he talked Mr. Brunger into letting us build a tree house there. It started with a single layer of several boards and a simple ladder made of small boards nailed into the tree to climb up and down. Chunker was generous and let all of us climb up into the tree house. Soon other boys were getting architectural ideas, and the tree house slowly gained walls so that it was enclosed. Then there was a second floor and the beginning of a third. You might say it was a split level structure. One of the boys suggested that we needed a fire pole for emergency escape in case of a fire. Almost all of us pronounced escape as "excape."

One of the boys got a pipe about twenty feet long, an inch and a half or so in diameter and set it up as our emergency escape. It was a little rusty and not smooth like the fire poles in the fire department house; but it was usable, and we practiced using it. I was eager to try it and was probably one of the last ones, as the others kept going down it, taking my turn. Of course, once you went down, you had to climb all the way back up. The ladder had been improved though, and it might have even been a real ladder by then, at least for part of the journey back up to the tree house.

There were rules, of course, and the first one was: NO GIRLS ALLOWED.

That was our rule, by the way, not one imposed on us by a parent, but one of them probably would have done so had they seen a girl climbing the tree.

There were starting to be too many boys for the tree house in spite of its multiple layers of growth, and someone recognized the need for a second tree house in a different tree. I don't think we had a falling out as someone has suggested. We just needed more space. Some of us moved over to the tree in Jay Lynn Hurt's yard and started the new tree house with plans for a bigger and better one.

We were doing fine building it, and Chunker was even giving us lumber—well, leftover boards that is, to build the new unit. Economic growth and expansion you might say.

We had a tall stepladder positioned against the tree, and I had made several trips up and down the tree. I was laughing and joking, and I had started down the step ladder, facing outwards as I stepped down, carrying something when I suddenly realized that I was moving forward and downward at a high rate of speed. Fortunately my fall was broken by hitting the ground, so I only dropped about the height of the stepladder, whatever that was. It seemed much further though, than when I had been climbing it; five or six feet going up and now some fifty feet or so going down. In every accident, there is a moment when time seems to absolutely stand still and in that framework, you feel like you have time to go around and say bye to all of your friends, get something to eat, read a book or a few magazines, lots of time to do anything you want, and then—suddenly, all of that suspended in perpetual slow motion moment is over and the hard reality—especially if it *is* something hard, like the earth, is back and quite real, coming at you much faster, inescapable.

I hit the ground, face down and then, after a while, I stood. I was very frightened then for I had fallen onto discarded nails and a number of them were sticking out of my skin in various places, mostly on my forehead. None had actually penetrated but were only superficially stuck onto me. I didn't know that right away though, and I let out one of those blood curdling, ear piercing shrieks that only an eleven year old boy can make. I thought I was dead.

I was in a great deal of pain where the nails were, but after a while most of the pain had shifted to my left arm. Jay Lynn and someone walked me the long block home as I cried and tried to talk at the same time, which resulted in "I-I-I-I didnnnnnn meeeen toooo..." Unintelligible babble at best. I was embarrassed for one thing. And, of course, my mother asked how I had done it. "I was just..." I replied, not finishing it. I wasn't really sure what I was just doing. Building a tree house, of course, but I felt I needed more explanation than that. Why was I the only one to have fallen out of the tree?

That's a good question which I can answer fifty years later: I was clumsy. I didn't want to admit it then, but substantial evidence from having lived long enough suggests this as an unimpeachable and well qualified answer.

My mother took me to see Doctor Loy in his office in the bank building. All I wanted was one of the miracle drugs I had heard about in war movies, morphine or anything like that to stop the pain and it seemed to be taking forever to get my examination, which included X-Rays, completed. I don't remember if it was Dr. Dick or Dr. Bill, but I think it was Dr. Dick, as it seemed my care had been turned over to him. Maybe he was just the Loy on call. He came in, showed us the X-Ray, and told me that I had a broken arm but it was not separated, just a green fracture and he explained a green fracture by analogy to a green twig from a tree.

But it would require the same care as a separated fracture, so I got a new cast and sling to help me through the six weeks of healing that awaited me. I went to school the next day, wearing my sling and cast and feeling a little proud, between the pangs of pain, for I had joined that special boys club of Henry Jones and Chunker Brunger, boys with broken arms. I had earned the right to wear the mark of courage.

I don't remember Jay Lynn ever breaking an arm, but one day he started down the steps at Union, missed one and fell down the rest. He had a concussion which moved him to the top of the list, for he was the only one we knew who with a bona fide concussion. The Hurts had moved to the green house on west Main Street just next to the Bird Creek Bridge, and we would ride over on bicycles and visit him. It was odd that he received so much attention since he didn't have bandage; just a strange look in his eyes.

I WAJ JUST...

I have mentioned the time honored defense of "I was just..." but it is so good and universal that it deserves more than just mention. Maybe it is instinctive, for I don't know where we learn it. There is no formal course; it isn't taught at the university and there is no major for it. Yet, we learn early on that it is one of the world's great refuges against accusation. We use it quite naturally for the first time as children, when we are caught in an act.

We are startled, nearly to death, when we hear, "What are you doing?" As our hand jolts out of the cookie jar we reply, "I was just..." and we are not sure what it was we were just doing. The truth is we *did* have our hand in the cookie jar, we *were* playing with matches, we *were* teasing the dog, we *were* finger painting the wall in the hall, we were...guilty as charged.

We almost never finish the sentence because it would admit our guilt. "I was just getting a cookie." We were probably getting two or eight to go with the glass of milk but in for a penny, in for dollar. Once we are apprehended, it doesn't matter. We are caught, cookie dough handed, often chocolate chipped, in fact, as that is one of the great all time tempters.

I learned I was addicted to chocolate chip cookies. I could not eat just one and stop. Whatever was there, I ate, unless I became sick before I could finish all of them, and I was burdened with being an only child, so I had to eat all of them myself. Yes, it was a tough assignment but someone had to do it. In retrospect, it's fortunate that it fell to me as I seemed to have special fortitude for it, no matter its difficulty. In fairness, sometimes Bobby Hughes came over and helped me. He could smell chocolate chip cookies a mile away. He could smell Llewellyn's Bakery from his house with the doors shut. Ah, I miss his nose for food.

Before I knew I was addicted though, and had something beyond my control to blame, I tried to quit, and sometimes I resisted eating them before dinner. I was told that they would spoil my dinner. How could they when they *were* my dinner? And as to blame, I have mastered the passive voice: Cookies were eaten. That would have combined nicely with, "I was just..." to form: "Cookies *were* eaten but I was just...inspecting the cookie jar?"

If I heard, "What are you doing?" I had to wonder about my mother. Did she not see well? Did she not understand something so basic, when it was obvious that I was sneaking into the kitchen, working hard to find hidden cookies and rescue them from their tiny, darkened prison, to give them a brief moment in the world of light and air before..."What are you doing?" rang louder in my head and I responded, as God must have given me the answer, "I was just..." "Just what, young man?" she asked. "I was just getting a few [more] cookies before dinner...uh, so that I...didn't eat too much of something and...spoil my dinner!"

If she had to ask, maybe she really didn't know, and I had found the answer. Parents liked that about not spoiling your dinner. However, I'm sure that I was not the first child to tell his grandmother to send the food that she had so worried about on to the Europeans, who were starving. She worried a lot about those European children.

And there was the title, Young Man, which was just a

degree below Stephen Joe Payne! If they stayed at Young Man, I was not in serious trouble. If they went on to Stephen Joe Payne, something was going to happen, and it wasn't going to be good.

Stephen Joe Payne was never spoken either; it was barked, and so brusquely that an outsider might have thought she was speaking a foreign language. In fact, it was more STEVNjopane, one word of multiple syllables with vocal stress on the first part rather than my three names put together politely.

"I was just..." worked so well for me that I carried it on into grade school, refining it with more complete sets of nouns and adjectives. A teacher caught me talking to a girl in seventh grade class: "What are you doing?" "I was just..." "Go on," she said. "Talking to..." "Yes and what about?" I was trying to get a date with her. "We were discussing last night's homework." "I see," Miss Updegraff said, without conviction. "Let's discuss it after school then."

Did that mean that Miss Updegraff and I would discuss it after school? "Yes ma'am," I replied not volunteering to actually come back after school, knowing that I had escaped the board one more time. The board was The Board of Education; it was not a committee. It was a board about one-half inch thick, four inches wide with a narrow handle to fit a teacher's hand, and it was ten feet long (perception is in the eye of the beholder). I had not always escaped it, having been twice elected at Union. But this was my first escape in the big building,

It worked in the navy too where I seldom had to complete it. Hakenjos, my First Class and my boss would ask, "What are you doing Payne?" "I was just..." "Yeah...," he would interrupt with a laugh, and I was caught, rescued and forgiven all in one brief exchange, provided I stopped and started what I was supposed to be doing.

It served me well for thirty-three years at Phillips Petroleum too. My boss would say, "Did you finish the Newpark proposal." "I was just….getting to it," I would say as I shuffled the papers of my in-basket hoping there was something in there that hinted it was the Newpark proposal. What *is* it I wondered? My in-basket was really an in-tray but years of calling them in-baskets made us say that regardless of their form.

I have found it useful while writing as well. If I have an assignment that I am late on or have forgotten, I can always explain my failure by saying, "Well, I was just working on my book…"

MY FAVORITE YEAR

I think everyone must have a favorite year, one period of time that seems to stand out more than all the rest of them, and I am no exception. Also, if you have reached a mature age, you have more years to choose from.

We talk about decades as the fifties and the sixties. I noticed that, since I was born in 1944, my first awareness of decades came in 1954 when I was ten years old. I like the music of the fifties and sixties, but it's broken down like this: I like the music from 1955 through 1965 so it is really the decade from being ten to twenty more than the whole decade of the fifties or sixties.

My favorite year on the calendar was 1956, but it was really parts of 1955 combined with parts of 1956 and probably twelve to sixteen months in duration.

Maybe that was my favorite because I was just getting to the age to notice cars more, and the 1956 models intrigued me. It was probably the first time that I had the skills to clearly distinguish one model year from another also. My grandmother bought a 1956 Oldsmobile and Jessie Garcia, across the street, a 1956 Pontiac. My uncle Bud Lessert bought a 1956 Cadillac. Earl Brunger's father bought a 1956 Ford station wagon, and I remember the words "Thunderbird" on the fender to indicate that it had a Thunderbird engine. Ernest Daughtry's father had a 1956 green Dodge, so a lot of people that we knew had 1956 models, and I noticed them more.

I loved the 1956 Ford Thunderbird and the Chevrolet Corvette as well; it would have been a difficult decision for me to have to pick just one. Of the three model years for the first class of Thunderbirds, which were small, two seat vehicles, low to the ground and with lots of power, I liked the 1956 best. It improved on the 1955 model yet it still did not have the slight fins that the 1957 model had.

Slight nubs of fins had emerged in 1955 and enlarged in 1956. The 1957 models got larger, and it took a near automobile revolution to get fins off of cars. Also, design engineers were playing a clever game of hiding the gasoline tank cap. In the 1956 Chevrolet and Cadillac models, the gas cap was hidden in the tail light assembly.

Not every Thunderbird had them, but one model had small windows, in the sides and to the rear of detachable hard top, that we called Queen Mary Portholes. Whether that was the official name or not, it was what we called them. The gear shift lever was on the floorboard and the speedometer indicated 150 mph, and I believed that it could really go that fast; I didn't believe Mr. Brunger's station wagon could though.

It didn't occur to me that there were only a few Oklahoma roads on which a car could reach that speed. But I was very fanciful, and I had a wild and reckless imagination that didn't let reality disturb it unless they, imagination and reality, actually collided with each other. I had never driven either, so I had no serious idea of how fast a car could really go through a curve.

Pawhuska had an interesting communication system for news. One night my mother was driving through town, and we stopped near the Packing House Market because there was an unusual automobile parked on the street. It was a 1956 Lincoln Continental Mark II, and the only one I ever saw on the streets. Research indicates that only 3,000 were built for the years 1956 and 1957 together; it sold for $9,695.00. A Chevrolet sold for about $2,000.00.

We stopped and looked at the marvelous car, a giant version of the Thunderbird. Soon, there were thirty of forty people gathered and looking. The owner never did appear, but I always marveled at the system that quickly let people know that something was happening downtown and how it attracted so many spectators so quickly. I have seen several Continentals at automobile shows and auctions, but that was the only live one.

This happened other times also; one day, in front of the Crystal Coffee Shop, a Mercedes-Benz Gull Wing parked and within a few minutes, a large group of Pawhuskans were gathered there, looking, admiring and talking about it. It was the rarest of cars to see on the street and especially in a small town like Pawhuska. That was the only Gull Wing I ever saw on the road.

The method of announcing that a new or unusual car had just appeared in town must have been part just driving by and part driving through the drives at the Pig Stand or Dairy Queen and telling someone. I doubt that most people ran home, and called someone just to tell them that there was a strange car in town; and the rapid communication via cellular telephones existed only in Dick Tracy's communication watch. Whatever it was, it worked and there were soon large crowds examining the strange beast. These were not large crowds by New York standards but certainly by Pawhuska standards.

What really made that my favorite time though was that I had just wonderful friends. I was close friends with Butch Daniels, Jay Lynn Hurt, Bobby Hughes, Earl Brunger, Mike Avery, Chuck Carnagey, Hughie Hollowell and a few others. I had a wonderful teacher in Mrs. Schirmer, and I was enjoying being in school more than at any other time. We had a weekly school news magazine to which we had to subscribe, and we studied from it; so we knew a lot about current affairs, for fifth graders.

The music was magnificent for we had Elvis Presley, Sam Cook, Pat Boone, Frankie Lymon and the Teenagers. We also had Frankie Laine, Rosemary Clooney, Tony Bennett, Perry Como, Gale Storm and some others, but when we discovered Rock n' Roll, most of us left them behind to follow the new music. But, truth is, Frankie Laine and the others were pretty good. Everything seemed to combine with a wonderful magic that made them seem special to us.

It wasn't a perfect year for I broke my left arm in 1955 and Butch Daniels broke an arm, his left also, I think, in 1956. For both years, Butch and I gave a demonstration on gun safety for the 4-H Club, of which we were members, and one of us had to do the gun demonstration while the other did the speech that went with it. Butch didn't like to speak in public and I did, after a fashion; so I did the speech both years. Butch was supposed to do the gun demonstration, but the year he was in a cast and sling, I had to help him a lot with the demonstration. We, the demonstration givers, had to memorize our speeches and I had given it for Butch and me many times. We had been able to practice in front of the class at school, so we were totally prepared. Right. All of the practice helps, but when you are eleven and find yourself before a panel of adult judges and see them suddenly making notes about your performance, your legs go to jelly anyway.

From today's standpoint, you have to think about that for just a minute. There we were, two eleven year old boys that first year and twelve years old the following year, going to our class and carrying a 22-caliber, single shot, bolt action Stevens rifle to school, into the class room and demonstrating how to handle the weapon before a class and our teacher.

Could a child walk to school in 2007 carrying a rifle? Could a child take the rifle into class in 2007 and show the other kids his talent with it? We were not allowed to fire it, but I think we had a box of ammunition with us just to hold up and show what bullets looked like. We may have had to remove the firing pin for the demonstration, but I'm not sure one could even take a realistic looking toy rifle to class today.

We were quite a pair with our broken armed acts those two years, but we won a white certificate one year and a blue certificate the following year in spite of jelly legs. The only problem is, today, I don't know which of the colors was first, second and third.

Also, in 1955, I was taking ball room dancing lessons from Evelyn Whitsitt at her studio down town, and that made the music more special; for I had something to do besides just listen to the music. Tennessee Ernie Ford had a hit record with *Sixteen Tons*, and Earl Brunger was teaching us to dance to it, dancing what we called simply: The Bop. The way that Earl taught us was to move one foot sideways, heel and toe alternating so it moved us across the floor. Then the other leg was moved back and forth, crossing alternatively right and left over the foot that was moving the body, sort of a modified Charleston. The rhythm of *Sixteen Tons* was perfect for it. Some mothers did not approve of the bop because someone had said that it was dirty dancing. It's good that they have not seen dancing today.

Television was still young and imperfect, and there were only three channels to watch. There was Public Broadcasting, but I think it was called Educational Television then and the word Educational usually turned young students away. The channels, out of Tulsa, were 2-NBC, 6-CBS, 8-ABC and PBS was channel 11. When I got home from school I watched Superman, actually I think it was *The Adventures of Superman*. It was a half hour series in black and white, always on our television, but we had only black and white anyway. "Hey kids! What time is it?"

opened the Howdy Doody show, and I didn't like it because I thought I was too old for it, too sophisticated, but I watched it sometimes because it might be the only thing on. And at one time, I even had two or three Marionette puppets myself, such as were featured on the Howdy Doody show. I struggled with them for some time, but I never developed the patience or skill to be good with them. Murphy's Law was made for small boys with Marionette puppets: If something can go wrong, it will go wrong. However, I fooled some people and put on small shows in the neighborhood.

Some of the boys were talking about the Mickey Mouse Club show, which I thought was too immature for us until I discovered that they were watching it to see Annette. If you are a certain age, then Annette is all that needs to be said, I suppose like saying Brittany today; everyone knows whom you are talking about. Annette Funicello was a brunette, who was a regular on the program, and she was probably the first girl on television that most of us boys fell in love with. Also, her career paralleled our growing up as she moved into movies, mostly with Frankie Avalon. She and he made a lot of movies that will not stand the test of time to become classics, but a lot of us went to see them. They will not stand the test of time because they were dumb.

They are basically a simple story of boy meets girl, boy loses girl to his rival, boy gets girl back and they live happily ever after to the tune of badly written Rock n' Roll songs used to make the dances make sense. The titles were *Beach Party, Muscle Beach Party, Bikini Beach, Beach Blanket Bingo, Dr. Goldfoot and the Bikini Machine* and a few others. Yes, I saw them; yes, I'm embarrassed. But that was later.

In 1956 there was a local television show on KOTV's channel six called *Zeta on Satellite Six*. It appeared in the afternoon between the end of school and before the early news came on. An actor named Jim Ruddle played Zeta, and he had a device called a Zetascope into which he would gaze and voila! We were watching a *Little Rascals* film. I think he wore goggles and a hat with a uniform. Zeta allowed parties of kids to come watch his show live, and Earl Brunger went for his birthday one year. He was one of the few among us that went to a live television show; and he was the only one till then. One day the camera swung to Zeta and caught him smoking a cigarette. He tossed the cigarette into the air, began to fan the lingering smoke and shouted, "Gas! Poison gas! Get away! Get away!" and the camera swung away from him and to a rattled announcer that stammered out, "Well kids, Zeta will take care of that, uh, poison gas situation, and we'll be right back for more Little Rascals and other things." [Cut to commercial].

That is a true story, but after writing it and letting it simmer for a few days, I realized something important. It was not my story. After Earl Brunger had been to see Zeta, we were talking about it one day, and one of the boys said, "Did you see Zeta yesterday?" "No, why? What happened?" And he told that story. I have repeated it for years and became convinced that I actually saw it, but the truth is that I am only repeating it. I chose to leave it in with that stipulation because, if it were true, it is too good to omit.

And, for awhile, the real George "Spanky" McFarland of *The Little Rascals* hosted a television show on KOTV, in which he introduced *The Little Rascals* films and commented about them. I don't remember anything that he said but I do remember his hosting the show; I was fascinated with him. Of all the Little Rascals, I liked Spanky best, but I also liked Alfalfa, who was played by Carl Switzer. Spanky was the boss but not the brightest in leading them as he was, like us, a ten or so year old boy. Alfalfa was probably the intellectual of the gang but he too suffered from misinformation.

Few of us got nicknamed Spanky, but several of us got

the Alfalfa name, including me, because Alfalfa had a strand of hair at the back of his head that stood straight up and refused to be combed. I did too. Many of us were struggling with our hair then. The common answers for troublesome boy's hair were either a thick hair tonic to hold it in place or a flattop hair cut. Even if you got a flattop though, as Bobby Hughes did, you had to tame it with Butch Wax, which was a glob of pinkish material with the consistency of warm candle wax; it came in a small jar which could be carried in a jean jacket.

At that age, I loved *The Little Rascals*, *The Bowery Boys*, *The Three Stooges,* and Dean Martin and Jerry Lewis. Yes, it hurts to tell the truth about that, but that's the way it was. I also loved *Francis the Talking Mule* movies with Donald O'Connor, and Ma and Pa Kettle movies.

Also, in 1955, I was deeply in love with Pamela Ray, and I couldn't see straight for it. She was beautiful, smart, talented and the best dancer ever. Did we date? Well, after a fashion. We went to some movies together, went to several dances together, and we were always great friends. I was very shy then and I would get worse before I began to get better. I started getting teased about Pam by other boys and even some girls and my shyness eventually overwhelmed me and we just drifted apart. Also, ultimately I didn't think I could compete with other boys for her beauty.

I was always shy, but when I was younger and had Donna as the type of friend she was to me, I never thought twice about asking her to go to a movie. It wasn't a date though; it was just two friends going somewhere together. We each paid our own way and made our own decisions about what pop, candy and popcorn we would get. It might be just the two of us together or we might have one or more other kids with us. But it was very easy; just a stop by her house, or usually Jessie's boarding house across the street, a simple, "Wanna go to a movie?" and we were off.

Sometimes she stopped at our house and asked me. Later the rules would clearly spell out, "**WARNING**: Girls do not ask boys on dates," except for Sadie Hawkins day.

But in the early years it didn't matter since we were friends, and the concept of boy and girl friends would come later. In fact, I remember one of my grandmother's friends asking me, "Where's your little girl friend?" I was mortified that she would think I had a girl friend. Our English language does not do as well with this concept as do other languages, where the idea of gender is clearly spelled out and I can say "amigo" and specify a male friend while "amiga" means a female friend. In English I have to go through that, "I have a friend, who is a girl, but she is not my girl friend..." In Spanish I can say "novia" if I want to specify that she is my girlfriend. Donna and I were never boy and girl friends though, just friends. That's our story, and we're sticking to it.

The movie, *East of Eden*, was released in 1955, but I don't know if it actually played Pawhuska then. It was the first starring role for James Dean who was killed, September 30, 1955, in an automobile accident. James Dean was a strong influence on our generation, as the girls were romantically involved with him and many boys wanted to be like him. I still have a red jacket like he wore in *Rebel without a Cause*. He made only three movies, *Rebel without a Cause* and *East of Eden*, both released in 1955 and *Giant*, released in 1956. My mother was about thirty-three then, and she couldn't stop talking about him; he certainly caught women's attention. He had an intense and nervous acting style that gripped movie audiences.

The scene from *Rebel without a Cause* that captivated most boys was when his Jim Stark character and rival, Buzz Gunderson, raced to the edge of a cliff in a game of chicken. The sleeve on Buzz's black motorcycle jacket became caught in the door handle and he plunged to his death while Jim Stark jumped free. Not realizing that Buzz died in the crash, Jim walked up to the group of kids staring over the edge with stunned disbelief and asked, "Where's Buzz?"

"Down there," a boy replied in a flat tone.

The entire scene captivated us, from the cars lined up on each side with headlights on to light the race path, to Natalie Wood standing calmly between the cars and giving the signal to start the race. There is one touching moment when Natalie Wood, as Judy, seems to make a peace offering to Jim.

A few other movies released in 1955 were *Abbot and Costello Meet the Mummy, Bad Day at Black Rock, The Last Command, Love Me or Leave Me,* and the classic *It Came from Beneath the Sea* (just kidding about it being classic, and yes, I saw it.)

We played some form of chicken, but it was usually on bicycles since none of us could drive then anyway. One boy would call another a chicken, which was the worst thing you could call another boy, because it went directly to his manhood of which we had none. But we thought we did. Once called a chicken you responded with the timeless, "Am not!" which got, "Are too!" until proof was demanded, and one of the boys came up with a test. It might be riding as fast as you could on a bicycle to a wall and stopping before you hit it. Then the other boy did the same, and the rubber tire marks were measured to see who was the closest to the wall. The closest was the winner and the other boy was a chicken and held that title for about the rest of the day; and it was soon forgotten.

Secretly, many of us were afraid that we might be chicken; so we did some really dumb things to prove that we were not. Sometimes it might be jumping from a high place and sometimes it just might be a fight. Somewhere in my adult life I learned that it takes more courage to say no and not be concerned about being called chicken or yellow than it does to react to the challenge and do something stupid. As young boys we often did the dangerous and stupid thing, and sometimes one of us got hurt.

The worst case though, was if a boy had words with another boy in school and one of them said something like, "We'll settle this later. Meet me after school, and we'll find out who's the toughest. And if you don't show, you're *yellow.*" Since you did not want to be yellow, you spent the rest of the day worrying and hoping that the other boy would come to his senses, especially if you knew he could whip you. So, if this challenge happened early in the school day, you had all day to be sickened with worry. I actually made one of these challenges and had friends encouraging me the rest of the day, because they wanted to see a fight. I think we got together and worked it out though, because we did not fight.

If you actually went through with it, and showed up and the other boy was not there, then you could go to school the next day and say something like, "Where were you? I was there and you never showed up, so you're *yellow.*" This caused the whole thing to start over again. If you did go, you did not go alone. Two or three of your friends would go with you, ostensibly to keep the other boy honest, but probably to make sure that they saw any fight that might actually happen. These were not World Boxing Association events and sometimes fight meant that one boy hit the other, he cried, and it was over. Sometimes they threw a few more punches, and sometimes they ended up wrestling on the ground. At Union that might mean getting into the goat heads which usually stopped the fight prematurely.

Once in a while there was a serious fight that lasted a while and had a lot of punches exchanged. These tended to result in a long term grudge, but most fights were just misunderstandings.

Bobby Hughes and I had a fight once in which we came out about even and both of us went home crying. Later, he showed me how to clench the hands to make a fist, and he had learned to put his thumbs inside of his fingers; I can't imagine that Gordon taught him that, but it didn't take much experimenting for me to decide that my thumbs belonged outside of my fingers when I made a fist. I think Bobby was crying that day because he had hurt his thumbs badly hitting my face with those thumbs wrongly positioned. But that fight was much earlier, when we were in the second grade. We averaged one fight every two years until the last fight.

I mention some of the movies of 1955 only to give a reference point of the time. Movies were important in our lives then, and going to see them with a friend or friends was a great part of our social life.

I was influenced by movies, even when I knew that something was not real. I had gone with a friend to a movie about paratroopers, and paratroopers and frog men were at the top of my list. I always wanted to be one, which led to my having a pair of rubber flippers and an underwater mask. When I got home from the paratrooper movie, I got an idea since my grandmother had a heavy, black umbrella. Our white house was actually a duplex with the back half being the residence of another family. Our house was very tall but the back half had a low roof, probably no more than twenty feet high. It was a perfect place for a test jump. I climbed it somehow, though it wasn't easy. Once on top, I opened the umbrella, extended it over my head and with both hands firmly gripping the handle, I yelled, "Geronimo!" as they had done in the movie, and I jumped. Barely had I cleared the propellers on the giant Fairchild of my imagination when the umbrella folded straight up, due to my weight, and I plummeted hard to the ground; roman candled, as they said in the movie. I didn't break anything, except the umbrella, but I did manage a mild injury, and I cried. I cried worse when I looked at the umbrella.

Courageously, I explained to my grandmother that I had accidentally broken her umbrella, which she had never used in all the time that I had known her. I did not tell her how I broke it.

One thing that I did not like about the movies was the cartoons with the follow the bouncing ball section. My mother loved them, and there I sat, beside her, embarrassed, my red face hidden by the relative darkness of the movie theater while she sang, along with most of the audience, songs such as *Let Me Call Your Sweetheart, Glow Little Glow Worm,* and other such songs while a small white ball bounced over the musical staff displayed on the screen.

My favorite year was also the year that Jay Lynn Hurt got me to join him in the Boy Scouts of America. I had a Boy Scout's shirt and white web belt, while some of the senior boys had full uniforms. We had meetings at one of the churches, and there was a weekly routine in which we said the Scout's Oath and the Scout's Code, did some exercises and ate cookies. The cookies were the best part. I remember being a Tenderfoot and getting a few merit badges.

I still have my Boy Scout's hand book from that year, and as an adult, I've used it a number of times. I was charged with writing a code of conduct for work and I went to the Bible and my Boy Scout hand book. My boss said that it was a very fair code of conduct. Of course, it was written by God and a great American organization.

There was a Boy Scout jamboree that year, in Bartlesville, in the baseball stadium. In a jamboree many scouts come together and put on a display of the skills that they have been learning and have a competition and receive rewards. I was working with Jay Lynn and other scouts and eagerly looking forward to participating when one night, I missed my step and fell out of the tree breaking my arm. So I attended with Jay Lynn, but my cast and I sat in the stands with my mother and Jay's mother, Juanita Hurt.

My mother had volunteered to drive us to Bartlesville

in her wonderful but unreliable old Chevrolet coupe, and homeward bound, it broke down on a dangerous curve. Jay Lynn and I were sitting in the back on the rumble seat while my mother and Juanita were in front. A man stopped to aid us, and he asked the ladies' names. Juanita said, "I'm Mrs. Hurt and she is Mrs. Payne." He replied, "Well, I saw trouble, but I didn't expect to find a Hurt and a Payne." Juanita reminded me of that in 1987 when the 1962 class had our twenty-fifth reunion anniversary in Pawhuska.

This was the year that Marcus Haynes came to Pawhuska. He was a famous basketball player who had been with the Harlem Globetrotters. We had seen a movie about them shortly before then. I still have the program from that game though, and the team was actually the Marcus Haynes Magicians which he had formed after leaving the Harlem Globetrotters.

Jay Lynn was chosen to go out on the basketball court with Marcus Haynes. Marcus took Jay's jacket, took out an imaginary whisk broom and cleaned a spot on the floor to place the jacket and then put the real jacket on the imaginary clean but real dirty floor. Jay took a free throw and his other friends and I were quite proud of him, for he was playing with the greatest.

And Jay went to Union School.

THE GREAT BICYCLE RACE

Many of us had bicycles and, of course, we all thought we were pretty good at riding them. We each thought that we were the fastest thing on two peddle-powered wheels. One of my friends told us that there was going to be a bicycle race and the prize was a new Western Flyer bicycle. We were all plotting and planning and talking about winning the prize when Roy Mitchell told us to forget about it. Roy said that Jay Hurt was serious about winning and had been practicing a lot. Of course, Jay had an English racer which was what everyone wanted because they were faster and also, with the gears available, you could actually climb Flanagan Hill on the bicycle, no small feat. The organizers felt that an English racer gave a boy an unfair edge, so English racers were prohibited from the race; we pointed out that flaw to Roy only to have him stun us with the news that Jay had traded his English racer for a standard bicycle. That told us that he was either serious or nuts.

There was a bicycle race the year before, although I didn't know about it. The boy who won then was Jack Sweeden and Jay traded his illegal English racer to Jack. In return, Jack gave up the bicycle that he won in that race.

So, in this race, Jay Lynn was riding the prize from the previous year. The race was to be at the Osage County Fair Grounds on the horse track, which meant it was dirt. Dirt isn't the bicycle racer's friend.

The race was a fund raising event for the Lion's Club and local businesses paid a $5.00 entry fee to sponsor the boys who raced. I don't remember that there were girl's races, but a clipping from the newspaper stated that over seventy boys and girls competed in the event. It may have been sixty-eight boys and two girls though.

I don't know how Jay practiced, but I thought we rode enough that we didn't really need any practice, which shows how much I knew about racing then. Most boys went to a store and asked to be sponsored, but somehow I had missed that piece. I was one of the orphans that got picked up by a kind sponsor. Truthfully, one more time, my shyness kept me from asking for a sponsor.

I remember riding in only one race although, in order to make the race manageable, there must have been heats to reduce the number of boys riding. The newspaper clipping said that there were nine sections in addition to the finals, but it did not specify if they were all on the same day. I just remember that I rode as fast as I had ever ridden a bicycle and finished pretty far back so my bicycle racing days were over. Jay found himself in the finals.

The announcer called us with, "Get ready boys." Then it was, "Boys, on your mark, get set, START!" and the race was off. I prefer the time honored, "Start your engines," but we were the engines. The pack began to thin out, and Jay Lynn surged forward, gritting his teeth, every muscle straining, all of his training and determination driving him on and he finished—second?

Wait.

There were two age groups and it was 1954, so Jay Lynn was ten years old and in the race for boys ten years and under and...the first place finisher was in the wrong age group. He was eleven. He was disqualified and Jay won The Great Bicycle Race for our age group. And we were quite proud of him, being a Union kid and all.

The race for eleven and twelve year old boys was won by Maurice Roberts who went to Booker T. Washington School.

The newspaper clipping said that this was an annual race held on Pawhuska Day during the Fair's run but I remember only that year. I was glad that I had participated no matter my finish.

JUST FOR THE BEANS OF IT

There are some foods that I believe should not be eaten as soon as they are cooked. They require sitting in the icebox overnight, aging and collecting their own marvelous flavor. These are: spaghetti, chili, macaroni and cheese, stew, new potatoes and pinto bean soup. They are good when they are fresh, but the next day, they take on a flavor that is unique and absolutely wonderful. My grandmother was a marvelous cook; my mother was not. In fact, my mother did not learn to cook until after my grandmother's death, when she *had* to learn to cook. My grandmother had a magic touch with fried chicken even though she fried it just like anyone else. Still, it took on something from her that cooking alone did not produce.

She liked to make a pot of pinto beans now and then; when she did, it was a huge pot, slowly cooking on a burner on the stove. One day a neighborhood friend, Jerry Traylor, and I happened to come by our house when my grandmother was cooking pinto beans. Jerry was about two years younger than I was and had more toys, so he was a great play friend. As we entered the house from the front door, the aroma of the beans reached out and pulled us into the kitchen.

We had planned on getting something anyway, perhaps a bologna sandwich or a peanut butter and grape jelly sandwich when we made the decision that maybe a bowl of beans would be nice instead. "Is it all right?" he asked. "Sure," I told him, and we got down two bowls and scooped out the beans, filling the bowls to the brim. We were hungry and the aroma was feeding our hunger. But you can't eat beans alone. You have to have corn bread or something to go with beans, and there wasn't any corn bread. But there was a loaf of bread, white, Rainbo and a big tub of butter so, we took the bread and butter into the dining room and began. The thing about really good flavor is that you can eat more of what is producing it. We both ate a bowl, and then we had a second bowl and then a third. With each bowl of beans we were consuming about three pieces of bread laden with rich butter by dipping the bread into the beans to absorb the soup so, around the end of the third bowl of beans, the bread was gone, especially with two of us consuming it. It had not really dawned on me to wonder where she was with the big pot cooking, even boiling a tad, and no one watching it.

Like the three bears, after eating that much, we were ready for a nap; so Jerry went home and I turned on the television and took an unintended nap. My grandmother must have been next door for a brief visit, one that could turn into a longer visit, and she returned to find her beans that she had planned for something else mostly gone. My grandmother was seldom angry at real people, although she reserved a special hostility for people on television and especially politicians and dirty wrestlers, which we called "rasslers." English has always been a problem for me.

She was disappointed that so much of the beans was gone but not really angry at us. There was not enough left for her party so she put the remains in the icebox, where they become a wonderful lunch for Jerry and me the next day. I don't know how she rescued the evening.

THE MARBLE KING

One day, Bobby Hughes came to the door. "We're moving Stevie." It was startling news, and I thought he was joking. It was true. Gordon's father gave Gordon a farm in Perkins, Oklahoma, and he wanted to try his hand at farming. He leased all of the businesses that the Hughes family had, leased the house on Seventh Street and Prudom and moved away. For some reason, it had never come up, and this was my first news about it.

Soon, another family moved into the Hughes house, with a boy my age, a younger sister and a very young brother. I became great friends with the boy my age and spent almost as much time in the Hughes house as before. Jerry Clinton Moyer was a fun, jovial kid with a special talent. He was the greatest marble shooter I have ever seen. He played a lot and he gambled, often putting up his best marbles. He was very serious about it and had an agate, called an aggie, for his main shooter.

He kept his marbles in sacks and cans and had them all over his room. Jerry never lost his marbles all the time that I knew him and there was speculation as to just how many marbles Jerry had. Fortune smiled upon us one day and we found an old odometer that had been removed from a car. We played with it but had no idea how to really use it until someone suggested that we count Jerry's marbles.

We took turns taking marbles out of one container and moving them to another one, so that we did not double count any marbles. As we did, we gave one turn to the lever on the former odometer, now a marble counter. It took most of the day, and we would take breaks which required peanut butter and grape jelly sandwiches, glasses of milk, and other things. Now and then, his mother would come by and ask how we were doing, which we found interesting.

We weren't parents though, and it would be much later before we would understand that she was operating on an important economic principle: If they are doing this, then they can't be getting in trouble doing something else. She left us alone to count Jerry's marbles. I do not remember if the number was one thousand or ten thousand, but it was one of those and more marbles than I had ever seen. I proudly spread the news on Monday that Moyer had that many marbles, and most boys were in awe of him; I was.

Some boys had a marble called a steely which was a ball bearing that had been removed from a car's wheel. Some of them were larger and called a giant steely; again, it was a ball bearing that had been removed from a wheel, usually that of a truck. If you polished and oiled one, it was a very good shooter, and some games would not allow a steely since it gave you an unfair advantage. I had one or two steely marbles but never a giant steely. Most of my marbles were those purchased at the T.G. & Y. Store, which was said to stand for Toys, Girdles, and Yo-Yo's; probably not.

My lack of athletic skills extended to marbles as well as games with a ball, and I never developed the skill that Jerry did so, unlike him, I did lose my marbles—sometimes. In fact, one time I lost all of them and had to start over. At Union, we usually played marbles behind the steps in back and furtively because some teachers would not let us play; they thought we were gambling. We were, but just for marbles. If you won, you won the marbles in the circle; if you lost, whatever marbles you had put up and were in the circle were lost.

Roy Mitchell was the next best marble shooter I knew, but Jerry Clinton Moyer was the undisputed Marble King.

J-DAY

One day after school, Jerry and I came home, to the Hughes house, and turned on the television. A flash came on the screen with J-Day and the announcer said, "One month until J-Day." We could hardly wait till J-Day, whatever it was. The advertisements were persistent and always showed just after school so it had to be something for kids. Each day, each week, we watched the countdown from the Moyers' television, "One more week till J-Day," and then, one day: "Tomorrow is J-Day. Don't miss it."

After school, Jerry, others and I rushed home to the Moyers' television, waited patiently and then: "It's J-Day. Yes, now you and your friends can enjoy Jax Beer in Oklahoma. Brought to you by the Jackson Brewing Company, New Orleans, Louisiana."

IT CAME FROM OUTER SPACE

But the reason we fell for J-Day was because we had been set up for it. Richard Carlson, an actor who played Herbert A. Philbrick in the popular television series, *I Led Three Lives,* was going to be in a movie called *It Came from Outer Space.* Each day when we came home from school, and stopped at the Moyers before going home, we saw advertisements for the movie. Richard Carlson spoke, telling us about this important movie and urging us to see it. Then they would drop little scenes and..."*It Came from Outer Space* is coming to a theater near you....soon. So don't miss it." The advertisement got better and better and, we wanted to see what the creature looked like so anticipation was fueling imagination.

That was what it was always about for boys our age, seeing what the creature looked like.

Then one day, the Ki-He-Kah's monthly schedule arrived and...there it was. We watched the advertisements and checked off the days until it was time. A large group of us went to the movie and sat together and waited. We saw humans that the creature had taken over, making them a bit like zombies. We saw crystal traces, space foot prints that the creatures left behind. We heard their mechanical voices with an echo and watched Professor John Putnam figure them out, talk to them and try to protect his girl friend but....no creature.

Finally, John Putnam insists that they show him what they look like. If he is going to help them, he has to know what they look like. The spokes creature finally agrees, telling him that they are so different that they will appear horrible to a human but....well, you asked for it John Putnam.

The music rose, an eerie sound like a variable rheostat came on, and John Putnam began to slowly back away saying, "No, no, no," and then shielded his eyes as he screamed. This was a popcorn moment. We were on the edge of the seat, leaning forward, holding tight to the wooden elbow rest and...

I could have made a better creature with the tools I had. It didn't seem to have arms or legs, it moved clumsily forward, and it seemed to be a giant tub of Jell-O with a single, eerie eye.

J-Day had to be better than that.

Jerry Moyer's family lived in Pawhuska about two years and then moved to Bartlesville, where I visited him sometimes. They later moved to Ponca City, and I visited them on the farm when I visited my cousin, Jack Hardy.

I saw Jerry Moyer in Lubbock, Texas in 1984, when I was participating in an oil show. He was the same kid I remembered only older; still jovial and fun. No marbles that time, but we did play a game of golf. We did not count his golf balls.

FIRECRACKER SUMMERS

Firecrackers were not legally to be sold within the city limits of Pawhuska, but just at the edge of the city limits, in almost every direction, was a firecracker stand. My mother's friend and coworker, Vida Welch, operated one just beyond the bridge over Bird Creek on Highway 99 south, and that is where I bought my firecrackers.

Firecrackers began to show up in June and everyone soon had some. Most of us bought Lady Fingers because most parents didn't see them as harmful. Lady Fingers were very small, and hardly made an explosion, so we could hold them in our hand, and explode them without much damage; it produced more of a tingling effect than any real danger; it brought lots of laughter. The next size firecracker was about one inch in length, often in blue, red or green starry wrapping, and packed quite a bit more charge. I accidentally had a few go off in my hand, and I had blood blisters for some time; I also became more careful.

The Baker brothers, Bobby and Billy, were walking by our house one day, and Billy was wearing a sling and had his fingers wrapped, rather professionally. I asked him what happened.

"Bobby dared me to hold onto a firecracker as long as I could, until he told me to throw it. I lit the fuse and held it and held it, watching Bobby. He just never told me to throw it so it went off in my hand." Someday, Billy will get even with him.

We looked for the bigger and more dangerous firecrackers, which included cherry bombs, TNT and Two-inchers. We could do more damage with these. The cherry bombs were a favorite, as we could get them to go off underwater, and they were pretty destructive.

There was a rail road trestle next to Vida Welch's place, and we took some tin cans and put cherry bombs in them. They exploded underwater after we dropped them from the bridge. Also, we would load a paper sack with small rocks and put in a cherry bomb or TNT; we thought it was great fun to drop them from the bridge and watch the explosion in the water.

We were not supposed to shoot them in town, but, of course we did. Even the very best kids had to try that. It was routine to be reported, and for a police car to drive by and warn us. However, as soon as he left, we were soon shooting them off again. On the actual Fourth of July, the police gave up, as almost everyone in town was shooting them off. And, many families went to Sunset Lake and had their celebration there.

It was fun to set off firecrackers, one at a time, or tie several together. But, once in a while, some boy would take an entire package, strip the outside paper from the package, and set the entire package off at one time. That was fun to watch, and we would all laugh at it, as it seemed to be very funny.

Then the boy who had sacrificed his string of firecrackers would try to bum firecrackers from us.

Fat chance.

RIDING IN CARS WITH GIRLS

Being friends with Bobby Hughes had one interesting benefit; beautiful women. I don't mean women—or girls —our age, thirteen, although there were those, but Kay and her many beautiful girl friends. So, Bobby and I were often surrounded by some very attractive, but older women.

Sometimes, Gordon Hughes would tell Kay to take us with her. I think Kay liked that, sometimes, if it were a boy that she did not want to spend much time with, for he quickly found some reason to return us home. Sometimes, we were the last thing she wanted on a date.

One evening, a boy who drove a 1954 Chevrolet coupe, retrieved Kay at the Hughes home and Kay *asked* us to go with them. Our presence did not improve his mood which was not good to start with.

Bobby was in a really good mood, as he liked riding with the older boys in their own cars, so he was telling joke after joke, most of them about the Little Moron. He also told a few that had Kay saying, "Bobby!" I was getting in what jokes I could and Kay kept talking, so it was a very noisy car. The boy did not seem happy though and we could tell that he wanted to dump us but couldn't figure out how.

We arrived at the house of the other girl, as they were supposed to be on a double date, and we pulled into a short drive-way behind the house. It might have actually been the back yard but, there we were. The house was on south Ki-He-Kah Avenue, just beyond the parking lot behind Irby's Drug Store, and a beautiful girl named Patsy Lozier lived there. Kay left the car to get Patsy and the older boy spoke sarcastically and almost rudely to us; he did not want us along. Patsy got into the car, moved next to the driver and Kay sat against the door. By then, the driver was even angrier and he jammed the Chevrolet into reverse, popped the clutch, and the car lunged backwards.

Bobby yelled, "There's a kid behind us!" and the driver yelled something back at him, not nice or nicely and—ka-wham! We hit him and heard him go rolling away from the Chevrolet. The driver shouted, "Oh, my God! I've killed a kid!" and jumped from the car and ran to the back.

Bobby and I looked over the back seat and saw him standing, leaning against the trunk lid and ghostly white. He stayed that way for a moment and then walked back just a bit and bent low. He stood and raised an old 55-gallon drum that was the Lozier's trash drum and rolled it to the side.

When he returned to the car, he was still shaking, and he assured us that it was only the trash can that he had hit, and not a person. Still, it had shaken him to his core and he became quite contrite. He took Bobby and me to the Dairy Queen, where he left us, and the three of them drove on to pick up the second boy. I don't remember the boy's name; perhaps I didn't know it. Kay said that he remained humbled for the rest of the evening.

Patsy and Kay do not remember the boy's name but the evening was certainly memorable for Bobby and me. That was my only date with Patsy.

Several of Kay's friends knew us, and if they saw us downtown, or uptown, I never knew which was correct, they might pick us up, and take us for a ride around town. Sometimes we might go by the Pig Stand or Gordon's Drive-in, and there was always a lot of hooping and hollering. Most of the older boys who drove the cars just took us along without any problems. My grandmother would probably have fainted had she known how many cars I had been in, and some of the rides that we had had. Some of the boys drove pretty fast, which we thought was really fun.

We missed the attention when Kay went off to college.

THE SMARTEST BOY I KNEW

Not every story ends happily or with humor.
About the same time as I met the Red Avenger, I also met the Smartest Boy I knew, and I met him in the same place; the park on Seventh Street and Prudom. If you didn't have a friend around, and you went where other boys just might show up, you often met someone and just played together. Sometimes you made a new friend.

He was older than I was, and he knew everything so I would see him and ask a question or he might just start talking. He knew about movies, baseball, war, bicycles and many other things and it was always fascinating to tap into his knowledge for I was woefully ignorant but hungry for knowledge. I found him fascinating, and we were close friends for some time.

I do not know why, but we change. All of us change, in different directions and at different rates. Perhaps I was making friends with other boys who were now letting me play baseball with them, and The Smartest Boy was not a very good athlete. Smartest boys often are not athletes. If they want to be athletes though, and their friends are athletes and good ones, smartest boys begin to feel very left out and often friendless. I know that he felt some of that. I would see him and wave, and we talked sometimes, but we continued to drift apart, not through the fault of either of us. It was just the nature of the changes we were experiencing; growth in two different directions.

A friend said that the problem was that he really was The Smartest Boy only he was smart in a testy, showing off way, an "I'm smarter than you so take that," way. Maybe it was because he had few friends, and they were becoming fewer. I always looked at him and thought how smart he was, and I expected him to be another Einstein. He got in a negative spiral in high school, became confused and left school before he graduated. He enlisted in the navy, and I followed some of his career in the newspaper. One story was about him meeting actor Cliff Robertson during a movie in which the smartest boy was an extra. I thought that he was getting his life together.

After the navy, he returned to Pawhuska, and he seemed to have started using drugs while he was in the navy. He seemed to just get worse and started getting into more and more trouble. I don't know if he could hold a job. I only thought about him now and then, sometimes when I saw him or someone who reminded me of him. The last time I saw him, we were in a store, in the purchase line and he was in front of me. I wondered, should I speak to him? And I agonized about it until, finally we were almost through the line and done. "Teddy?" I ventured. He turned and looked at me, his eyes hollow, almost unseeing. "Do you know who I am?" "Yes," he said, offering a weak handshake, a faint hint of a smile crossing his lips. We shook hands for a moment, and he turned away. I did not know what to say to him; he had said all he wanted to say to me.

I read in a newspaper that he had died, found dead, I think it said. All I could think was; what a waste. He had so much potential as a child. He was so smart; he really was, yet he lost his way and never got back.

I wonder if the rest of us had been better friends with him, seen past his need to show off his smartness, and helped him join us, would it have made a difference. I don't know. I had similar problems and left school early. The navy saved me; it didn't seem to help him and may have been where his real troubles began. I do not have an answer. I only regret that his potential was lost and that none of us could help him.

50 YEARS; 100 YEARS

In 1957 I was thirteen years old and the great state of Oklahoma was fifty years old. Semi-centennial celebrations abounded throughout the state, but I do not remember a major one in Pawhuska.

My uncle Lynn Payne and my cousins lived in Oklahoma City, and my mother and I visited them during the celebration. The Paynes had a Payne on the police force, and he was working security for the celebration. He got my older cousin Jerry Payne and me into the television show *Today* when NBC made a broadcast from the Oklahoma City fairgrounds. All that was required of us was that we sit quietly and watch or we would be dismissed from the show. It was probably the longest I was so quiet in my life; I didn't even ask Jerry any questions.

We sat just a few feet from the legendary broadcaster Dave Garroway and watched the entire broadcast. It was my first experience with television, other than watching it, and I was surprised at how many feeds came in from somewhere else. I guess I had expected it to all be there in the studio.

I spent several days at the celebration and spent a lot of money on rides, cotton candy and other things. I set a goal then to come back to Oklahoma City for the centennial in 2007. Of course, I thought I would still be thirteen years old but fifty years later of it. That means that I thought I would be physically the same and still be able to do all of the fun things that I did then, and I honestly thought that I would have the same interests.

Age sixty-three provides different realities but it's still enjoyable to contemplate going to the fairgrounds, standing on the same soil that was there and contemplating how far Oklahoma and we have come in fifty years. I will probably forego the cotton candy, taffy, and other things that I had then. I will consume a centennial Coney Island as a sort of commemoration to one hundred years of being Oklahoma.

I had hoped my son would be able to join me and let me share some of my memories of it with him. He would have been forty years old. He, perhaps, would not want to hear the excitement of a thirteen year old revisiting it.

Somewhere, I am registered to win a 1957 Plymouth, which was buried in a time chamber. My cousin Jerry and I thought that it was in Oklahoma City but my research has so far been able to find only the Tulsa buried Plymouth. As we contemplated that Plymouth, fifty years later from 1957, we did not know that we would still be using gasoline. There have been many changes in automobiles, but if you had a car then and had kept it, basically, it would still be running with the technology that we knew and used then. If I win the Plymouth, I will still be able to use it just as I would have then, with the only difference being that I could afford gasoline then.

THE GREATEST MAN I HAVE EVER KNOWN

One day, we were no longer at Union, at Franklin, and the other schools. We didn't have a graduation ceremony, and we did not get diplomas, just a regular end of the school year. But it was different. We were going to be seventh graders, and we were going to the new building, new to us, for it was built in 1918. I had been in it for a few things in the auditorium, but it was a giant puzzle to me.

I was excited and scared to death at the same time, and I did not want my summer between Union and Pawhuska High School to end. Of course, I was going to go out for football and be a great player. I would be playing with Butch Daniels, Jay Lynn Hurt, Bobby Hughes and others that I knew, so nothing was changing except that we would all have uniforms. I forgot that our dreaded rival, Franklin, would now have its players on our team, and we would be one.

An interesting thing happened towards the end of sixth grade. The high school band teacher, C. G. Arnold, came to Union with a written test and talked to us about band. Band was the last thing that a great football player would want to participate in so I scoffed at the test and my interview with him was probably just as silly, but, he was a pleasant man and didn't seem to hold my attitude about band against me. I scored well on the test, and he told me that I had a future in band, should I change my mind.

In seventh grade, we were divided into three groups, called 7-1, 7-2, and 7-3, a pretty complex nomenclature that may have been developed by the CIA. Choir was 7-1, band was 7-2 and anything else seemed to fall into 7-3 so as a star football player, I started in 7-3. I attended our first football meeting and listened to Dr. Loy talk about physicals, and I reconsidered my football career. I expected to be hit playing football—heroes have to bear some suffering— but the idea of physicals was intimidating to me. And, I had taken a good look at the kids that had come in from Lynn Addition School. I don't know where they had been kept before and why I had not met them but this was a rough bunch. In a word, I was scared.

Band began to look good to me, so I checked with Mr. Arnold and, even though I was starting late, I could switch to band. At my first class I was far behind and wondering about choir. The other students had chosen and received their instruments, and they were tooting, screeching and banging away to their heart's content, and I had not yet chosen an instrument. A friend from Franklin, Ernest Daughtry, actually had been a strong influence in my choosing band. Ernie played the snare drum and that was pretty interesting to me. My cousin, Jack Hardy in Ponca City played drums and had a trap set so, why not?

"What do you want to play?" Mr. Arnold asked me, in front of the rest of the class.

"Clarinet," I blurted out, and to this day I don't know where that came from.

"Clarinet?" he asked, seeking confirmation.

"Yes sir," I replied and my mother bought my first clarinet, a Bundy.

We rented it from Saied Music Store in Tulsa paying out a few dollars a week. It wasn't bad, but obviously it was a starter horn. I was very bad those first days; a clarinet, without good mouth control and too much force of air can screech like a Halloween horn. I know mine certainly did. Being new and bad, I automatically went to last chair, and that's where I started. But there was no physical and no one was hitting me, although at times, I felt Mr. Arnold wanted to.

It turned out that I became pretty good with the clarinet, and I soon moved up and occupied an upper chair. In fact, the clarinet was the second thing in life that began to give me confidence in myself.

I had had some good teachers, and Mr. Arnold was one. But he was more than a teacher. Most teachers were with us for one year or one course. Mr. Arnold was a coach, just like the football and basketball coaches. We had him in seventh grade, and those of us that stayed with band for our high school career, had Mr. Arnold each year. Unlike the football coaches, he did not have an assistant so whenever we had band, we had Mr. Arnold. Unlike a teacher that finally figured us out by the end of our term with them and hoped that it was the last they would see of us, Mr. Arnold had years to really know us. When we returned in the eighth grade, he knew us better, and he knew more what to expect from us. He also knew how to make us better at what we did and what we were supposed to do.

He wasn't easy, Lord no! If you botched a piece in band, he listened carefully and you got to play a solo, all alone, for all of the band—and him—to hear. I noticed once, that he usually did this on Friday and he asked you, "Will you be able to play that piece on Monday?" "Yes sir," we automatically replied. We were smart enough that we were not going to say, "No sir;" not in front of the whole band and Mr. Arnold. So, we went home Friday night, took our clarinet, horn, or drums and worked until our fingers fell off and our lips turned inside out. If I happened to be the sinner, then I went in Monday, prepared and patiently waited for him to ask me to play the piece. We would start with our general session, fifteen minutes, work on a specific part of the band, cornets, trombones or something, another fifteen minutes, have a written test, another fifteen minutes? "When is he going to ask me to play my piece?" And none of us was going to fight for the chance to play it; we were going to wait to be called on.

And he never did. His goal, I finally understood, was not to embarrass us but to motivate us. And it usually did.

Mr. Arnold had a few axioms that he used. He would say, "Please play that section after the first bar," calling a student by name. "I can't Mr. Arnold" brought forth "Can't can't get his pants on. Now play it," always said with a smile, sometimes even a laugh, and we all laughed. It sounded dumb; it stuck—for fifty years.

But the one that has made me better all my life was: "The enemy of the best is just good enough."

We would practice, a lot for being kids, but we had a tendency to say, "That's good enough." It was ubiquitous, and he did not like or tolerate it. If he heard you say, "It's good enough," he drug out, "The enemy of the best is just good enough."

He explained that when people have quality and they are the best, if they don't do their best, they sell themselves, and everyone else, short. It grudgingly made me a better clarinet player. It made us a better band. We earned first division awards in our class each year in marching and then again in concert. We earned number one awards in quartets, sextets, solos and other things and David Meriable won the student conductor award. We were, literally, The Pride of Pawhuska, The Pawhuska High School Marching Band, and we felt it as well.

After seventh and eighth grades, we were ready for the big time, the high school marching band. Only we didn't know how to march. Somewhere in the summer between eighth and ninth grades, we met for extra classes and we marched. We lined up in rank and file and heard our first, "Band! Attenhut!" We learned how to forward march, stand at attention, assume parade rest, perform right and left flanks and other pony tricks. Then when school started, we did it all over again, this time with the sophomores, juniors and seniors.

Band was only ½ credits, but I worked harder in band that I did in any other class. We came to school early, which Bobby Hughes hated because he rode with me often. That meant he had to arrive early and sit, which is probably where he developed his great story telling ability. We went to the field and we marched for an hour, learned new routines and then went to the band hall and practiced and learned for an hour. At night, I took my clarinet home, and I practiced from one to two hours and on the weekends I practiced four to five hours. Most of my food tasted like clarinet reeds.

We had practiced so much that we were getting cocky. We thought we were pretty good. But we had practiced wearing our school clothes, no hat and with an empty stadium, except for an observer or two. Friday night arrived, and we met at the band hall, fell in outside wearing our black and orange uniforms with hats and were inspected.

The uniform was heavy, had brass buttons and braid, and it was hot sometimes. The hat was heavy but it made the uniform complete, and we all looked alike, somewhat. The drum major wore a white uniform with black braid and a high, furry hat; the twirlers wore an abbreviated uniform. Then we began our march from the band hall to

Ormand Beach Stadium, a drum cadence, da-rooty-toot-toot, da-rooty-toot-toot, metering our stride. We paused outside the stadium, did a right minstrel turn and marched inside to the grounds. Ronnie Coday, tall and authoritative, was our drum major in our freshmen year. We played The Star Spangled banner and the game began. We played a few marches and fight songs during the first half, and then we began to get ready for the half time marching show. Except for being on the field to play the anthem, we had been in the band section, playing as required but out of sight. Now, we filed into our positions and headed towards the field. We had trained, learned, drilled and practiced, but nothing could prepare us for what happened next.

We formed on the field and Ronnie Coday called us to attention for our first, official half time show. Then he whistled us, three sharp blasts, into motion and the announcer said, "Ladies and Gentlemen, the Pride of Pawhuska, the Pawhuska High School Marching Band." And to "Men of Ohio," we began our march down the field. We had not expected the cheering that rose from the stadium. All of our practice had not prepared us for that. We focused on playing and on marching a thirty-inch stride, hitting the notes, keeping the rhythm and following Ronnie's commands, and we survived. But the truth is, most of us were weak in the knees. We did not expect to be weak in the knees, but it happened. And we played through our first performance with a few mistakes but overall, we did well. Each week we got better, and it got easier but I found that, in spite of my experience, the first time out, every year, when we heard, "Ladies and Gentlemen, the Pride of Pawhuska, the Pawhuska High School Marching Band" and thunderous cheers and applause, my knees went weak. The people of Pawhuska were a marvelous audience.

Memory can be illusory, and I found myself telling someone about the size of our band then. I said that we filled the field six ranks wide, ten files deep and that would make us a band of sixty. Was I exaggerating? My 1961 Wah-Sha-She (the school annual or year book) has each band member listed by name; I counted eighty-two names. The band was a formidable organization in 1961.

I said earlier that there are ways in which you can reposition yourself into other classes. I did not graduate from Pawhuska High School as I left school in my junior year, 1961, and enlisted in the United States Navy. I returned to high school at the completion of my four-year enlistment, and I graduated from College-High School in Bartlesville in 1967 as a member of the class of 1966. Two things helped me get through, first boot camp, the schools and finally my enlistment: "Can't can't get his pants on and "The enemy of the best is just good enough."

My favorite day with him was April first. He knew it was going to happen and those of us with prior experience knew we were going to do it so there was no surprise. Yet, every year, he named the selection, we placed the sheets on the music stand, he raised his baton, and everyone in the band played something else; few of us playing the same music. "April Fool, Mr. Arnold," someone shouted. He laughed, acknowledged our genius, and we went back to work on the real music. We never tired of it, and neither did he.

One day, a boy stopped by his office and said, "Hi, C. G." Mr. Arnold turned to him and said, "If you ever call me C.G. again as long as you are a student, I'll bust your butt." Years later, a man appeared in the door way and spoke to him. Mr. Arnold looked at him, puzzling, struggling to identify him when the stranger said, "The last time I called you C. G. you told me that you would bust my butt if I ever did it again." A smile broke out on Mr. Arnold's face as he said, "Johnny Lawless."

I called him C. G. a few times when I saw him at The University of Tulsa. I was older then and I might have thought I had become a man and an equal. Later I shifted back to Mr. Arnold as it didn't take much more breath to say, and he has earned being Mr. Arnold with me. I can never be his equal.

Over the years, the subtle influences that Mr. C. G. Arnold exercised over me slowly became apparent. I was in a program at the University of Oklahoma when our instructor asked each of us to define greatness and give examples. A student started with Richard Nixon. (We all have our cross to bear). Someone followed with John F. Kennedy. Then a woman said her mother was the greatest person she had ever known. The professor then broadened the definition saying that fame was not necessarily required to be a great person, man or woman. When it was my turn, I named C. G. Arnold, and I explained his influence and his axiom. So, Mr. Arnold's name stayed on the board as a Great American for the rest of the day. I told many people that I thought he was a great American, and I often said how much he meant to me. I never told him though. I made my best effort to do that though when I wrote a letter trying to express my feelings about him. It isn't easy; it is worthwhile.

I began college at the University of Tulsa in 1973 when I was twenty-nine years of age. In my first year, I completed thirty-nine hours of study with a 3.9 GPA while working forty hours weekly. My overall GPA remains at 3.8, and I hold two Associate of Arts degrees in Spanish from Tulsa Community College with a 4.0 GPA. Of any success that I have had in life, I owe much to C. G. Arnold, the greatest man I have ever known.

BOODA

C. G. Arnold inspired students to be the best that they could be, and Booda was the best drum major I ever saw. He had graduated by the time we entered the marching band, as he was in the class of 1958 so we did not get to march for him. But we did get to watch him, and the majestic Ralph Farris was the one that most looked the part. To see him in his school clothes was to see just another student, but when he donned his uniform with its towering white Busby hat and brought the marching baton to position, he took on a field marshal's presence.

He strutted and glided in front of the parading band and added his unique magic to its performance. He was called Booda, which many of us thought was for the stoic character he showed as the drum major. It turns out that he was given the nickname because his sister could not say baby brother and it came out as baby booda. Booda stuck. Automatically, I had spelled it as Buddha and continued my misconception about his nickname until I talked to him, and he told me the baby booda story. He was a delight to watch when he led the band.

IENNOR SNEVAH

Though it sounds like something from a Harry Potter book, there was and is such a person and my greatest friend. But like the Mirror of Erised, you have to look at it backwards. I don't remember why but one year, we started spelling everyone's name backwards and pronouncing it, as best as we could. Mine was easy, for if you use my high school moniker of simply Steve Payne, it becomes Evets Enyap, odd but pronounceable. So, to my friends that were in on the joke, I became Evets.

It was through band and Ernie that I met Ronnie. Ronnie played cornet and sat a ways from me in band, but he and some others were forming a club of some kind and invited me to his house. Actually, it was not to his house but to the garage loft behind the house, where they had a club house. I'm not sure what kind of club it was to be, but I wanted to impress them, especially Ronnie, so I told them that I could get them all of the cigarettes and whiskey that they wanted. First, it was a boast and meaningless as I might have been able to sneak out a pack of Luckies now and then, but that was it. I was twelve and even what I had learned in the Boy Scouts had not taught me how to get all of that; later, the navy would teach me how.

They didn't invite me to join because of that, and I felt bad about it; but over time, and not a very long time either, perhaps they decided that I was just boasting and wasn't a bad kid after all so I was invited to join, and I did. I'm still not certain what kind of club it was, but it was benign. We did nothing rebellious, nothing dangerous, nothing anarchist.

I have thought a lot about Ronnie, for different reasons, since I first began to write this, and I realized something important to me: He and I have never had a cross word. We have had moments when our friendship cooled and we were not together as much, but there were never words of anger in it. Even the best of friends, including husbands and wives, need a break now and then.

Besides being in the Seventh grade together and in band, he and I had many things in common. We loved building models of everything. We built ships, airplanes, tanks and cars. We built them together as we would buy a model kit and go to his house or mine and work on them together. We loved *Mad Magazine*, and we shared each issue. We would call each other and read a section and the other would join in with his opinion. Then we might get together and go over the same magazine again. We found it very funny.

We loved motorcycles, and we both got copies of Floyd Clymer's *Cycle Magazine* and shared our experiences with that. We enjoyed the same movies, and we had adventures together.

We had many things in common yet, we were very different. He lived on The Hill, I lived in town; he had both parents, I had my mother and grandmother; I had never met my father. Ronnie had an older sister; I was an only child (with three brothers). I think we had similar intelligences, with his being a little stronger than mine, but we had been educated very differently. I am not speaking of the differences between Union and Franklin but the differences between polite society and the rest of us. My grandmother had taught me the manners of saying please and thank you.

I knew to always open a door for a lady, to stand in the presence of a lady, to offer my chair and to be as polite as I knew how to be.

Ronnie had more social graces than I did, and it always made me nervous being around his parents. His father seemed older and he had more of the Judge Hardy demeanor about him. I never quite knew how to behave around him, but almost all adults intimidated me a little. Judge Havens intimidated me the most. Yet, I was able to learn a great deal from him. He talked about books that I had not read and did not read until I was an adult. I remembered many of the books that he had spoken of, and I read them and I missed being able to talk about them with him.

In spite of any differences, Ronnie and I developed a solid friendship. One Saturday, we were together and in an adventurous spirit, we hiked. We started somewhere downtown and walked almost to Senior Hill, and from where we paused we saw a rock ledge in the distance and took off hiking for it. It was miles away, on the side of Williams Park. But being our age and poor judges of distance, we thought it was closer. So we walked—a long distance. We had neither food nor water with us, and we became exhausted, hungry and thirsty. We finally reached our destination near Williams Park and soon, Judge Havens appeared in his Buick, a very upset man. Ronnie and I both got a lecture as he had walked very far looking for us and was very worried. I felt that it was my fault and from his tone, I was afraid that Ronnie and I would not be allowed to remain friends. But it was over later in the week, and Judge Havens was treating me the same as before.

Ronnie and I did not want that to happen again though, so we struck upon a plan to buy binoculars so that we could judge distance better. Also, we could spy on someone although I'm not sure who it was supposed to be.

At that age, we were inventive, fanciful and naïve. If it

had two eye pieces, it was a binocular to us. He and I ventured into Lowry's store, where we had seen two identical sets of binoculars. We made a deal with the sales person where we would make a down payment and then pay $.25 weekly until they were ours. They were really opera glasses and not the best either, but he let us pay them out and each week, we went in together, paid our $.25 and eventually, we had our binoculars. The man never asked us what we wanted them for.

We used them mischievously sometimes. Next to the Packing House Market was a building in which we could take the elevator to the top floor and then walk up to the roof top. One day we bought plastic pea shooters and what's a pea shooter without a place to use it? So, we went next door, to the Worten Building, took the self-service elevator, walked to the roof top and looked for suitable targets. Just across the street was the Western-Auto store, a business similar to OTASCO. Soon a man walked outside and stood at the threshold for a moment and...a perfect target. I don't remember which one of us had the audacity to try it, and I didn't think either of us had the skill but with the right amount of lung force and the right size pea. "Got him!" the shooter cried as we ducked behind the protective wall, remaining unseen, laughing. The target rubbed his head and looked around. It could have been a fluke though. It might have been an insect arriving just as we had shot. To confirm it, one of us tried again and got a second target. We were having fun but experience had taught us that there is a time to quit and unusual for us that day, we retired, not only for that day but from pea shooting generally.

Also common to both of us, we developed guilty consciences easily.

Ronnie and I had a scientific bent that we shared, and we thought we could make a workable rocket engine. And, as boys always know when they are doing something wrong, we tried to hide it. We bought a box of .22 calibers, long hollow point shells and took them to the railroad tracks behind Bacon's station, which was on Main Street and Lynn Avenue. We used pliers and removed the lead bullet, then poured the powder into our vessel and lit it off, somehow, without burning either of us or setting the place on fire. We had very little success with a rocket engine as we had not considered how to control it. We did obtain liftoff, of a sort, but it was generally unsuccessful. It was a financial consideration that caused us to abandon the project though because a box of .22 shells was too expensive to continue to use for rocket fuel; if we had only know about liquid hydrogen then, who knows where we might be now.

A HORSE GOES INTO A BAR AND SAYS...

We were not bad kids, generally, though there were a few among us who turned out to be more difficult customers. A few of them even saw the inside of prison.

When we were very young, we told Little Moron jokes and that is making fun of someone. Most of us would not do that today. As we became adults, we told some variation of those old jokes, perhaps Aggie jokes, Polish jokes, Cowboy jokes. Most of us told racial jokes, and I'm sure that most of us would not do that today; we know better now. The truth is, we knew very few people of different races, so we saw no harm in it. Once we began to know people, and saw the harm in what we had thought were innocent stories, we stopped repeating them.

Humor is a very important part of human life, then and now. Perhaps we can find humor outside of making fun of a particular group of people but, I attended the University of Tulsa, so I feel I can tell stories about TU students, if I really need to. And then, there are always Klingon jokes to be told.

I was running with some men one day, a large group of about eighteen men, and I decided to try a Klingon joke.

Two Klingons meet each other as they are walking

down the street and one Klingon says to the other, "If you can guess how many buerferxiles I have in this sack, I'll give you both of them. The other Klingon responds, "Three?"

From the back of the group rang out, "Hey! My grandmother was a Klingon."

So, I am left with University of Tulsa jokes.

"Did you hear about the power failure at the University of Tulsa last week?"

"No, what happened?"

"Well, the power went off in the middle of the afternoon and thirteen students were stranded on an escalator for over three hours."

So, if I have to tell one, I just stick with jokes about University of Tulsa students—and lawyers.

THE HOSPITAL SHIP, USS HAVEN (AH-12)

I built models, and I was very serious about it. I tried to get them to be as accurate as possible, and I used paint to finish out the details. One of my most challenging, and my favorite, was a model of the hospital ship, USS Haven.

My grandmother allowed me to set up one of her card tables in a corner of the dining room, and it was marked off and protected, even from Rosie, the woman who helped her clean house. I recall that I worked on the Haven for twelve weeks, often five or six hours a day. I painted each life boat, inside and out, and each plank of the deck. I used sewing thread to make line for my flags, which were paper with a tiny hole for thread to pass through, and I installed every detail that was provided by the maker of the model, Revell.

When it was finished, it was the pride of my work with models, and it went on a special display stand and was put, rather permanently, in a glass display case under the stairway of the old white house. I would study it and think with pride of all the work I had done on it. When any one who had been around ships visited, they would admire it and compliment me on the fine job I had done with the Haven. These were adult men, and I felt a lot of pride from their praise.

Later, when I was stationed in Long Beach, California, aboard the USS Point Defiance, I learned that one of our former officers, a man I liked very much, had been assigned as commanding officer of the Haven. He was a lieutenant, with double bars on his shoulder, which is equivalent to a captain in other services, and he had been a former enlisted man. I had a good rapport with him, and he had mentored me some aboard the Point Defiance, so I decided to visit him aboard the Haven.

I went aboard and stated my business and was told that he would see me, but it would be about thirty minutes. There I was aboard the real USS Haven, so I decided to look a bit and see how much I knew about her. I walked around the first deck from the starboard side and looked at the life boats that I had worked so hard to make perfect, then to the port side, and then aft to the stern. It was as though I was walking on a ship I had built; I knew her, at least all of the details on the exterior. When I met with Lieutenant Cloninger, I told him about my model and how I knew the Haven from building it. It was, for me, an oddly fulfilling moment, something that had been brought from my childhood in Pawhuska into my reality in the navy world.

THE CREATURE FROM FRIDAY NIGHT PREVIEWS

I loved movies when I was growing up and I still do. I saw through the mind of a child then and now I see through the mind of an adult, one with a lot of experience and also a lot of bluff. I want people to think I am knowledgeable and sophisticated and that I know what I am talking about when I really don't. If we are asked why we like or don't like a certain movie, we reach into our bag of tricks and try to justify our opinion and the more we know, the more we can lay smoke. The truth is that I like certain movies with out any reason, such as *Always* (Steven Spielberg, 1990), and I'll probably never really know why. Perhaps with *Always* it's the vintage airplanes as I would probably go see a movie about airplanes with absolutely no plot. With *Always*, it could also be the clever dialogue or the relationship between three friends or even the humor of the movie. Then again, it may be the mystical appearance of Audrey Hepburn in the movie. And just maybe, it's the magic created by the combination of all of those things combined. In any case, it's one of my favorite movies; it was unsuccessful commercially though. Many of my favorite movies are not commercial successes.

I can tell you all kinds of things about movies to make

you think I know them better than I really do. I've learned some tricks as I have been on the Universal Studios lot in California twice, and I have seen a little bit of movie making. I attended a taping of the television show *Dharma and Greg*, and I've read too much about them, about techniques and how some previously mysterious things were done. In some cases, I have been able to talk to the actors, and they have told me how something was done or created, so some of the absolute mystery that movies once held for me has been taken away.

I miss the mystery.

For example, I have been on the street where *Leave it to Beaver* was filmed and right up to the front lawn of the Cleaver house. I watched a movie with car chases through the urban neighborhood, and I counted four separate tours past the Cleaver house. I might never have noticed that had I not been at the Cleaver house and, yes, it ruined the movie for me. But, I don't think it was very good anyway.

When I was between certain ages, perhaps between twelve and twenty, I thought some movies were great and today I'm ashamed to admit that I saw them. Also, I hold the knowledge of others who saw them with me as a tool that I can use for blackmail in the future should they ever try to get uppity. I'm talking about the old horror movies, but I can also include the hot rod and motorcycle movies and the teen-aged musical phenomenon discovery movies such as *Go Johnny Go*. I think that one of the movies that we went to see was called *Motorcycle Gang* and starred John Ashley and Steve Terrell, but it's been a while.

At one time, the Ki-He-Kah Theater had Friday night previews; the movie started late, perhaps 10:30 or 11:30 PM. It has been many years, and I am uncertain of the time but it was certainly later than normal and after the good movie went off. Some of those gems were *I Was Teen-aged Caveman, Earth vs. the Flying Saucers, I Was a Teen-aged Werewolf, The 4-D Man* et al. And then, for a while, around

1959 perhaps, the Ki-He-Kah showed movies on Thursday night for $.15, so a lot of us went and formed large groups that sat together. We were too raucous and disturbed those few people who really came to see the movie. Why would anyone come to see this movie?

Often they were old Tarzan movies or Abbot and Costello movies and even some worse. We predated *The Rocky Horror Show* by quite a few years as we shouted at the characters on the screen—we didn't throw things though—and much of the time, the dialog was bad and invited our teen-age comments. Bob Hughes was funny, and he was one of the best at coming up with clever but not always respectable lines for the movie. One that I remembered and probably can repeat was during a Tarzan movie with Johnny Weissmuller when Bob stood on his seat, in the balcony no less, and shouted "The vine Jane, the vine!" His cry mimicked a joke that had been going round which was very funny to us, although not good for Sunday school, and we all joined in with some line of our own and the laughter encouraged us. Mr. Brewer invited our entire row not to come back for two weeks, but he quickly forgot about it, and we were back in the theater within a few days. I suppose that the regular movie fare multiplied by twenty or so plus a large Coke and popcorn, a Dill pickle, two hotdogs, a bag of Milk Duds, a box of Good N' Plenty licorice, two Hershey with almonds bars, Bit-O-Honey, M&M's, and a Mr. Goodbar over ruled his good sense. Or he may have just said, "Boys will be boys" although some of us were girls and, what else would a boy be besides a boy?

Mr. Brewer was an executive not just a theater manager. It was a good job then, and he always wore a tie and nice clothes and he looked like an executive in them. He lived in a substantial house on Grandview Avenue on the hill so the trappings made him look successful to us. His assistant manager was a woman who was attractive but grouchy. I saw her smile once, but I don't remember what caused it.

Mr. Brewer could greet you with a nice smile but when we were too noisy or had our feet on the chair in front of us and some of the other things that we did, he could be intimidating, especially if he was threatening to take away the only entertaining thing in our life. Yes, there was television, but that wasn't social in the same way that the movies were and especially the cheap movies, for we went to be with other kids more than to see the movie. I remember him being very angry when he banned Jesse Tomey from the drive-in theatre for life; something to do with a cherry bomb.

A word about sitting in the balcony at the Ki-He-Kah and why it seemed so special to us on Thursday night: Years before, some friends and I had tried to go upstairs into the balcony, but Mr. Brewer caught us and told us that we were not allowed in the balcony. It was reserved for black people and that was not the word that we used then. If we referred to a black person, we usually said colored. In fact, the bus station of Pawhuska then had two drinking fountains with the legend "white" and "colored" near them. Also, the restrooms were labeled for "Men," "Women," and "Colored." The buses had a section at the back that was reserved for black people and white people sat at the front of the bus. Restaurants, like the fabled Manhattan Café did not allow black people to sit in the same section as white people. In fact, I don't think black people were allowed to eat in the Manhattan. However, if you went through the kitchen, several black people worked in the kitchen and prepared the food.

Many people used another word for black people which I have chosen not to repeat; I do not want to further its use, but I note it here as a word of the times. Pawhuska people had many advantages because of the town being small and having a lot of basic trust not only in each other but in what we often called American values. For the most part, they were good values, but they did not apply equally to everyone. There were several separate races: White, Indian and Negro or colored. There were many people, such as myself, who were products of marriages between Indians and whites, but very few between whites and blacks.

Discrimination existed, even in a small American value based town, against both blacks and Indians. My grandmother was Indian and experienced discrimination sometimes but not often, not while I was growing up around her. I have read about the experiences of Indians in earlier years, and the discrimination that existed. I'm sure my grandmother experienced it as much and as often as other Indians. She never made much about it, and she even had her own biases. When we said Indian then we meant Native Americans, not someone from the Indian continent, and it was easily understood that way. I grew up with the word Indian to mean my family, and I feel that I am being affected when I say Native American, which I will use when I feel that it is what everyone expects. Among friends and family I use the word Indian and so do my relatives.

Several times while I was in school I brought friends home and introduced them to my grandmother, to find them surprised that my grandmother was an Indian. This happened once with a girl friend, and it seemed to bother her. At some point, she had to realize that I too am part Indian. Almost everyone I knew was part Indian, and I accepted that as given; so I was surprised when I met someone who said that they did not have any Indian blood. It is an awkward feeling, to be part something and to have it be identified that way. We seem to like a well clarified identity so that we can say, "I am French," or something. Growing up in Pawhuska, certainly in my family, we were told that we were part Indian from very early on, and we accepted it. We have some European ancestry, and it is probably French, but the records are not easily available and not many of my family have ever really cared or we would know. But we do know that we are Indian and for the most part, what tribal connections we have; we just don't know our European lineage.

What I have written here is neither to defend nor to criticize the practices of citizens of Pawhuska but only to describe them. I was guilty too. I don't think anyone I knew was exempt from some degree of bias. We were products of the times and of our family, city, county and state culture, and it was an imperfect culture. It would be an error to write about the times and not admit that these things existed.

But back at the movies, since the Thursday movie was only $.15 we could buy more Cokes, candy, dill pickles and popcorn, and that's a combination that can lead to some interesting things. One Thursday night we were sitting downstairs in the middle section close to the front and watching a very bad movie. Thankfully, I have forgotten what it was, but there was one long scene in which it got very quiet, and one of the two men on the screen looked at the other—with one of those doomed looks—and asked "Do you hear that?"

The actors were looking out at us and it was almost as though the question was directed right to us. As soon as he stopped speaking, it got quiet and a moment later, as though answering his question, a boy just a little older than I, who was sitting on the left hand side just a few rows back from us, farted—the loudest heard anywhere, anytime and by *everyone*. Laughter erupted throughout.

The theater was crowded, but somehow those around him were able to move just far enough away, in self defense, for everyone to have a clear and unmistakable view of the guilty boy and then... At that moment, the screen became bright enough to see who and where he was. And, he was the only one who wasn't laughing, so there was no secret to save there. The actor looked at the camera—at us—and asked, "Do you smell that?" and the laughter rose in unison.

The guilty boy stayed for the rest of the movie, which I'm not sure I would have done—no, I would have slunk out, and I won't say tail between my legs here, but from then on, it turned into a comic horror show.

I've always wondered if the boy, when he became a man, remembered; if he lived it over and over again, died a thousand deaths, and went on to become a criminal master mind—or worse. Maybe he's lost in the south China seas somewhere now, a modern, nomadic *Lord Jim* and constantly asks, what went wrong? Maybe he went on to a redemptive and fulfilling life somewhere in the Peace Corps trying to make up for his past sins. We can only hope. (After I had first written that, someone called me and told me that he became a minister but was then defrocked for misconduct, so it seems both possibilities became real.)

Why do I remember one silly incident like that from more than forty years ago? While watching television one day a year or so ago, I happened to flip by *Teen-aged Millionaire* with Jimmy Clanton in it and watched about thirty minutes of it. I suspect it opened some memory channels in me. I also saw *Earth vs. the Flying Saucers* on television, or at least part of it. Being a kid then and going to the movies and being with those other kids was a fun time.

I don't want to relive it because, I know now that they weren't good movies at all. Maybe I knew that then but I wouldn't admit it to myself. We only had one theater then so our options were limited, and we saw whatever was on the screen. But I'm glad I had it as an experience. It's just one of the things that helped to shape us as a generation and maybe prepare us to know when a movie is good today, if not to stay out of Cuba. My wife and I saw *Down With Love* a few years ago, and it would have made a good $.15 night movie, sad to say because it had two of my favorite actors in it, Obi-wan—I mean Ewan McGregor and Renee Zellweger. See how much I've learned about movies?

THE POPCORN INCIDENT

I went to a movie that I was very excited about seeing, and some of my friends say it is the greatest horror movie ever made. I don't think so, or I would not have gotten in trouble. The movie was a Vincent Price thriller called *The Tingler* and the premise was that, at the moment of death, one was so frightened that the body created a beast attached to the spine and this was the Tingler, or something like that.

It had a few moments, but it was also very slow. It's the slow moments that get you in trouble. A girl, younger than I and whom I barely knew, sat in front of me. She had returned from the concession stand with a soft drink and a large bucket of buttered popcorn. She and her friends were wearing dresses while my friends and I were wearing jeans. Dresses would come later during the draft in the Viet Nam War. Intent on the movie, she had decided to shift positions and had sat with her legs crossed beneath her.

I will never know why but at a moment, slow yet building to suspense, I simply reached up, rubbed my hand in her hair and went "Buhhhhhhhhhhhhhhh!" very loudly and she shrieked, around one hundred and sixty decibels, and with a single gesture, threw her popcorn bucket forward into the next several rows.

The boys in the rows in front of her were not happy but, when they saw it was a girl, and this girl, angry though they were, they forgave her. She never implicated me—but it was close.

THE STATE THEATER

The first movie theater I remember was the State Theater, which has been gone a long time. I miss it in spite of its flaws, warts and all, and it had plenty of those. The State Theater was on Main Street at the foot of Grandview hill on the west side of the street across from city hall. City Hall was also the police station then and the Osage County Court House was and still is mid-way up the hill. The building that the State occupied had an upstairs and apartments in it, possibly some offices.

The State was not as elegant as the Ki-He-Kah, but we were kids so who knew. We were looking for action, not elegance. I saw some good movies, and I saw some very bad movies there; but my taste for what is good now was reversed then. My favorites were the Saturday matinee double features. It didn't cost any more yet we saw twice as much movie plus a serial feature and a cartoon. The movie cost ten cents, a drink a dime and popcorn was a nickel, so a quarter could buy a lot on Saturday. That price is fixed in my mind because one Saturday, I had only twenty cents.

I had spent my dime to get in, and I was going to get my fix of a Coke and popcorn. When I discovered only a dime remaining, I had to choose between the Coke and the popcorn, but Jay Lynn Hurt came to my rescue by offering to lend me a nickel if I paid him back a dime on Monday at school. I reluctantly agreed to that, and I did pay him back on Monday as I was afraid not to. That was second grade, and Jay had not been with us too long; so I did not know him well, but I knew he was supposed to be tough. Paying him the dime seemed easier. Yet today, I can be grateful because it did fix historical prices in my mind. And of course, I've forgiven him long ago for getting that extra nickel out of me: Right.

I loved the serials although I was also frustrated with them, as they never ended and that meant we *had* to come back next Saturday to see how our hero or heroine (usually a hero) got out of that burning car as it plunged over the cliff. I still remember a few of the serials by description, if not by their titles. My favorite was Commando Cody in *Radar Men from the Moon*, and I tried to emulate him, damaging my grandmother's vacuum cleaner in the attempt to use it as my rocket engine. Commando Cody was a tough but good guy, who had a rocket that he wore strapped to the back of his black leather jacket. It had control knobs on the front, and he wore a helmet that looked a bit like the business end of a bullet with places for eyes and mouth. When he left on a mission, he would don rocket jacket and bullet helmet, turn the knobs in front resulting in a low humming sound. Then he would run and jump forward, often out of a window, as though his jump caused a kick start of the rocket engine. He often did this from the top of a high building, and I was scared that it wouldn't start, and he would crash and die, like my grandmother's vacuum cleaner did with me. It didn't start on the jump. The first time I shared this story in writing, a Pawhuskan wrote me back and told me that after one of the movies, he tried to impress two girls next door and did the same thing with the same result; he didn't fly. He said that he was very embarrassed and slightly injured and learned not to do that again. I was very glad that he shared his experience with me. Now I know I was not the only one who did stupid things after seeing a movie.

When I was so young I did not know about actors, and I thought these things were *really* up there on the stage in front of us. I don't know how I thought that all of that happened in so small a space, but I believed it, which caused a serious argument between one of my older Hardy cousins and me. Finally, Barney helped us sneak behind the screen and showed me that there weren't really any people back there. He also let me touch the screen and, up close like that, I could see that it had little holes in it and even some tears of which some had been sewn or taped for repair. Behind the screen was an unexpected world for it was used as storage and it was untidy and cluttered. I looked to see where the sounds and pictures came from, but I couldn't find them.

Later, Barney explained the projection booth to me, and after that I spent some of my time looking up at the projection booth, trying to see the characters in the beam of light coming from there, but all I could ever see were particles of dust. I don't think I knew that they were dust particles though.

The Commando Cody feature was twelve episodes long so, for twelve long weeks someone had to take me to the movie on Saturday. An episode was about fifteen minutes long and first, they had to show us how Commando Cody or his girl friend had been saved the week before, and we always felt stupid for not seeing it, as it was so obvious. Then they had a fist fight, someone knocked over a drum of gasoline, then a lantern was thrown or someone shot a pistol and hit the gasoline. The music rose in volume and intensity and either our hero was trapped in a burning building, a crashing car, a crashing airplane, a crashing speed boat or some variation of that.

George Wallace was the actor who played Commando Cody, and one of the villains, who had his weekly fist fight and shoot-out with Commando Cody was the actor Clayton

Moore, who went on to play The Lone Ranger. When Commando Cody was flying, he was always prone, looking straight down and he kept his legs straight back and his arms out front, just as though he were lying on a table or something. We heard the wind whistle by and the noise from his rocket. I think I remember him taking his pistol out in flight and having a shoot-out with villains in an airplane.

Something else that was different then was that we always wanted to sit on the front row closest to the screen and the small stage.

I don't sit at the very back now, but I sit a lot closer to it and wonder how anyone can sit up front in a theater. Actually, it was progressive. We started out on the first row with no seats in front of us, so we could cross our legs, walk around each other without stepping over each other and even have a fight now and then. We had a lot of freedom to move.

As we got older we moved back a few rows. Actually it was a defensive tactic, because there were the Movietone news reels, and at the introduction a row of seven or eight cameras were shown facing us and panning the audience. Movietone news reels had their own music and baritone voiced announcer. One of the older boys said that they were taking our pictures, and if we did not want to be in the next news, we had to drop down below the seat backs in front of us out of view of the Movietone cameras, and we could not do that on the front row; so we moved back.

The announcer gave us enough warning to get down in time, but I had peaked through the crack between the two seats a few times and saw them panning toward us. I felt that I was safe there though. Since I never did see us on the news, it seemed all right to me. Once the cameras were off screen, we could sit back up and watch the news, which we did sometimes. We weren't mature enough to really watch the news then, but sometimes it was fun and there was always an intentionally humorous piece in it and being playful with it as we were doing, made it pass more quickly. Going to the State was a social event, and I never went to a movie there by myself; not out of fear but because it wasn't done; you didn't go to the movie by yourself. A man told me once that you fish by yourself, but you don't go fishing alone. It was like that.

I remember that The State had some carpet down in the foyer and there might have been curtains. Most of the seats were well worn, and they were in their last hurrah. Unfortunately, The State was not the cleanest theater either and fortunately, I don't remember anything about the rest rooms.

But, about the serials: What happens next? Why, you have to come back to find out, of course.

CURSES! FOILED AGAIN!

Although *Commando Cody and Radarmen of the Moon* was my favorite serial there were others that I found exciting.

My second favorite was *Crash Corrigan and the Undersea Kingdom* and I remember a scene in which Crash was tied to the front of a tank-like vehicle, while the villain lectured him on values and perhaps tried to get information out of Crash. The most impressive thing to me about Crash Corrigan was the credits; he was listed as played by— Crash Corrigan! I had begun to understand and accept actors, even in my young mind, and here was a real person being himself, so that meant—to me, at least—that he wasn't an actor, and I was just very impressed with that.

Although I've seen Commando Cody since I've been an adult or a person over thirty, whichever comes first, I've never seen a full show of Crash Corrigan, only brief clips in programs that tried to cover the history of film or show us how bad the movies really were. They were fun for young boys though.

There were other serials and one was a Superman series with an actor named Kirk Alyn, who I understand asked for too much money for the movie *Superman and the Molemen*, so George Reeves was contracted for that. I saw that movie at the State Theater, but I don't remember if it was a serial or a whole movie. Most of the other serials were cops and robbers in chases and shoot outs, which were quite exciting. One of them may have been Dick Tracy, but I'm not sure today.

One movie that I saw at the State Theater haunted me well into my thirties, when I finally got to watch it late, one Saturday night, on television, and get most of the demons out of my mind.

The movie was *The Thing,* now sometimes billed as *The Thing from another World.* I think I was just too young to see it, and I was with my cousins Barney and G. A. Hardy, who convinced me that it was a true story. Barney even pointed out that the credits listed The Thing as played by....???? which didn't help me any. The Thing was actually played by James Arness, who went on to television fame as Marshall Matt Dillon on *Gunsmoke. The Thing* was the scariest movie I had ever seen or would see until I saw *The Illustrated Man.*

The Thing was the pilot of a space ship capable of interplanetary flight, and it crashed in the North Pole area. Kenneth Toby, a wonderful actor who never permanently escaped B movies, played an air force captain in charge of the group and they excavated, or escabated, as I said then, the space ship out of the ice and recovered the pilot, who they believed to be dead as he was frozen. (Stand by for the punch line).

The soldier assigned to monitor the ice block couldn't stand looking at the gruesome creature—they were all creatures to us then, so he put an electric blanket (plot device: Will The Thing escape?) over the ice block, and warmed it to the point that The Thing, somehow, escaped.

He was never shown in a way that we could see him but only in shadows and half-shapes to the point that our minds began to form him, and my creation was scary. Then his arm was cut off in a door, and the arm began to move and come alive. I was ready to leave then, but I was forced to stay because I didn't know how to get home and Barney wouldn't let me leave. One of the scientists studied the creature's arm, with a microscope, and then thoughtfully announced that the creature was actually a vegetable, closely akin to carrots. Hmm, a frozen carrot from out space; holy Birdseye, Batman!

After the movie was over, I went straight home and hid under the bed until I heard people looking for me and I felt forced to come out of hiding. I didn't sleep until I enlisted in the navy though, so it left that fear in me that I had to remove by seeing the film when I was grown. And then I understood why I had been so scared all of those years.

It's OK; I can handle it now, as long as I leave the lights on in the hallway.

I saw a wonderful and classic movie at the State though, and that was *The Halfback of Notre Dame*: What? What's that you say? Sorry, that's *The Hunchback of Notre Dame*. It's the other one that has Ronald Reagan in it. Charles Laughton played Quasimodo, the Hunchback, and I remembered for years the scene where they stripped his shirt and showed his awful hunch and then beat him. I don't think I ever felt sorrier for anyone than I did for Quasimodo in that scene. I have never named a child Quasimodo. I also felt sorry for the Frankenstein monster, even after he threw the little girl in the well. He didn't understand, so how can we blame him? I wish it would have worked for me in the first grade.

The movie ended tragically for Quasimodo but happily for the girl, Esmeralda (who was played by Maureen O'Hara) and her lover Gringoire, who was played by Edmund O'Brien. Yet, I never forgot the forlorn look that Quasimodo had as they were beating him; it was heart breaking. I didn't know that he was an actor in makeup. When I was in school, I was stoop shouldered, perhaps due to an accident, and some people called me Hunchback; and when they did, it hurt, of course. It always brought that image of Quasimodo back to me. I've never been able to watch the film again so far, but maybe I will now. Writing about it helps to understand it.

THE STATE THEATER AS PLAYGROUND

The State Theater was that all right, a theater but it was more than that for us as young boys; it was also a playground. The State was located at the foot of Grandview hill and just behind the old building that housed the State was a boy's field of dreams—a rocky hill with caves and other hiding places. The hill was laden with large rocks of different sizes and shapes, and in at least one place, these formed the cave. It wasn't really a cave but it had been dug out by dogs and boys and nature so that it seemed to be a cave, and we accepted it as such. You could talk to another boy about the hill behind the State and mention the cave. Any boy who had been there knew exactly where you were talking about.

It was on this craggy hillside, which probably belonged to Osage County, that we had some of the finest post movie shoot-outs that ever were, for one group of boys could get on the high part above the hill and fire down upon the boys in the area where the cave was. Those in the cave could lean around the naturally formed shelter, keeping their masked faces just out of sight and fire up the hill at the opposing gang. I'm not sure who the good guys or the bad guys were or if there were any such divisions, but those that were wearing their bandanas pulled up over their noses must have been outlaws. Perhaps it was just all good natured shooting, but the unmistakable sounds of rifles rang out from the versatile range of sounds of gunfire, both rifle and pistol, that a small boy can make with his mouth as he imitates the sounds he has heard from the movie or almost anything else. The rifle and pistol sounds were peoughhh! peoughhh! with the rifle sound having a bit longer echo, and sometimes even the thffffffft sound of arrows could be heard.

More fun than shooting the other gang, whether they were the posse or the outlaws, was being shot yourself for then you could clutch at your chest, give out your finest "Arrggggggggh, they got me Roy!" and fall, rolling in your best dead man imitation; the more rolls you got, the better it was.

Some boys became exceptionally good at it, stumbling first, reeling forward in their final steps, as they looked for the right place to fall—a place that let you die convincingly but kept you from getting really hurt and avoided tearing your new Levi's, so that you wouldn't really die when you got home. And I doubt if any mother would have accepted the explanation that her son had been shot and killed by that dastardly Cave Gang while he was protecting the town.

I don't know if we gave much thought to the school teacher or the widow then. We were more interested in preventing the stage coach hold up, even if its wheels did turn backwards. I suppose we must have pretended that the robbery was to take place somewhere else; for none of us ever pretended that we had a stagecoach there on the hill. I'd like to think that I became pretty good at dying because I practiced it a lot. I even studied with a couple of masters.

The masters were older than I was, and they had had several years of falling and dying before I had even begun, although Bobby Hughes and both of the Mitchell brothers were pretty good. When you did well though, they would shout encouragement to you, make suggestions and even teach you new sounds beyond the simple "Arggggggggh."

Of course, we were handicapped because we couldn't bring our guns to the State Theater, so we had to use our fingers as pistols and we wore imaginary holsters with imaginary belts and lots of bullets in them. I don't think we wore our cowboy hats, as they probably weren't tolerated in the theater, although I certainly had one that I wore to school.

In the photograph, taken on the back stairs of Union Grade School, of our first grade class, my round, fat face can be made out under the black cowboy hat.

One of the older boys got me on a technicality one day. I had shot at him some forty or fifty times, and he told me that I couldn't do that because I only had a six-shooter and he had counted when I had run out of bullets. I dutifully threw my imaginary pistol at him then, which he ducked and then he shot me, but he only winged me. I had learned that from Roy, for as good a cowboy as he was, now and then he was winged. If you were just winged, you weren't completely out of the game, so if you could get another pistol, you could keep right on shooting. Getting a pistol was easy if you had partners who understood, who had seen the same movie you had, and who wanted to keep you in the game. You just yelled "Toss me a gun!" and they would toss you an imaginary pistol.

Sometimes though, as they did, they might lean out too far and get shot. I never really understood the rules of how someone knew if they got shot for sure, as it was an honor system. If the other boys had a clear shot, and they told you that they got you, well, usually that was enough. Once in a while someone wanted to protest and say, "You did not! I got behind the rock in time." Then there would be a little discussion, but nothing ever got ugly because, dying with a good drop and roll was as good as shooting the other guys. Of course, once you were dead, you had to lie there and be a good actor. Twelve years and under don't do that very well, because we all wanted to get back into the shoot-out as quickly as possible. Somehow, the leaders always sensed this and a new game would begin.

There was another wonderful thing about the hill, and it was in spring when the grass was new, thick and green; and it was slick. We would go down town to the trash bins (clean trash) behind the furniture stores, Oklahoma Tire and Supply Company (OTASCO), and Firestone and get old cardboard boxes and take them to the hill above the rocks just outside of the courthouse building and make slides out of them.

We sat on the cardboard box and pulled the bottom up to make a sort of combination handle and steering device, and then we took off, headed down the hill across the slick grass. The hill was in two parts, the high part, short and steep, and then it leveled off and was nearly flat for a ways; then there was a second slope. If you had a good box, if the grass was slick, and if you really knew how to cardboard slide, you might get all the way to the top of the rocks, which was the goal. But it was dangerous there, and you could go right off of the rocks and over the cave. I never saw that happen, but I was scared some times. I saw one of the older boys dive off just at the edge and let his cardboard box continue on over the cliff. He was congratulated on his courage and his luck; he admitted how frightened he had been as he skidded nearer and nearer to the edge and certain death—certain something anyway.

But all of that was public and visible. Ronnie Havens reminded me of another, darker aspect of the State playground, and I found that he and I had similar experiences—but not together. We had not yet met.

The floors above the theater, that had once been apartments and perhaps meeting rooms were off limits but—behind the building was an old, exhausted iron fire escape and once we had reached the bottom rung, we could climb it, and go into the building. It had a Hardy Boys mystery sense about it, first, because we weren't supposed to be there and then, the old rooms were abandoned but with furnishings left behind. Our minds quickly suggested that someone had died there, and perhaps still haunted the rooms.

One room held some kind of old medical device, perhaps a brace or crutch used by someone who had been crippled. It stood in a corner and seemed ghostly, bidding us to leave, reminding us that we did not belong there and then, there was always a noise from somewhere that was sudden, unexpected and caused one of us to shout "Let's get out of here!" We would take off running, desperately searching for the fire escape. I went there more than one time, always with the same result, and then I think a policeman saw some of us and gave a half hearted chase, yelling and waving his cap. I didn't know their names then, except for Frank Heskett, the Indian motorcycle riding Chief of Police, but that was enough for me. It was my last time in the apartments above the State. It was just a few years ago that I finally realized that the ghostly and ghastly noises we had heard from the floors above were probably some of the older boys, who lay waiting for just such gullible boys as we, and they are still laughing somewhere.

I don't remember when the State closed, but it was being torn down, brick by brick, in 1958 when Keith Webb was one of the men I saw working on the old bricks with a crowbar. Keith, although only about fifteen then, was a working man because he had quit school and married my friend Donna; they were expecting a baby, and he needed to work.

Perhaps it closed in 1954 or 1955. In spite of it being older, less elegant, narrower and dirtier than the Ki-He-Kah, I grieved for our loss, for the death of the State Theater.

It was a good friend and a wonderful place to

experience things out of time, for the world was already moving on, at a faster pace than we might like; but Roy, Gene, Johnnie, Lash, Crash Corrigan, Superman, and Commando Cody made our world a little better for a little while. I only wish that *The Thing* had met one of them.

THE GREAT DUNCAN HOTEL

Downtown, at Main and Ki-He-Kah, was the hotel. It sat on the corner, across from the bank building and kitty corner to the Triangle Building, and it seemed elegant to me. I never stayed there but I spent time in the hotel building. A series of steps led up to the lobby, and on Saturday evenings, these steps were occupied by older men, who sat and smoked and told stories. I think they were just retired and that was their social life; they weren't really bums. Most of the time, they were well dressed, often in suits, and they seemed to always wear hats, something my generation did not. As kids, we went in sometimes to use the restroom. The restroom was done in oak with tile floors, and it kept that same elegant theme of the hotel.

The stalls inside of the restroom were operated by putting a dime into a coin slot and turning the handle. If you didn't have a dime, you were in trouble except, the stall door was raised above the floor and at that age, most of us could just slip inside from below the door and open it from the inside saving the dime. Once the door was able to be opened, then you held the door and let the next boy in. If we went in and an adult was there and especially if he was eyeing us suspiciously, we actually put the dime in and then followed the standard practice of holding the door. I'd seen adults hold the door for other men and save the dime, so I didn't feel bad about that. If we were getting watched too closely, or especially if he said something to us, which happened sometimes, then we all paid the dime. I don't think our failure to fill the hotel's coffers resulted in its ultimately facing hard times.

We had a few out of town relatives come in for the tribal elections and they sometimes stayed at the Duncan Hotel, so I did see in a room a few times. I think that they were standard rooms. But the lobby was elegant and comfortable. It always seemed a bit dark, and it was shaded and cooled by its distance from the street.

Later, my mother worked there, but that was after the hotel had declined some.

I was driving through Pawhuska on the way to oil field work in Elk City, when a policeman directed me around fire fighting activity. When I reached a safe point where I could see, I realized that the Duncan had burned and I felt very sad for having lost a great building from my childhood. It was a center piece of Pawhuska.

THE SONG

When we were kids of the 1950's, we had our parents' music—still: Perry Como, Dean Martin, Eddie Fisher, Frankie Laine, Rosemary Clooney, Frank Sinatra, Gale Storm, et al. There was nothing wrong with them for they were stellar performers; it just wasn't *our* music. We listened to it and even bought some of their records although we were still missing something: Then came *the song*, and with it—*the singer*.

Would the song have existed without the singer? Would the singer have become what he became without the song? Sometimes everything just comes together, and we get magic. There is no other word for it since it can be analyzed, it can be studied, and it can be evaluated: It can never be understood. The sum is greater than the parts.

We cannot recreate it, neither in a laboratory nor in a computer. There was the singer and the song but still, he and it needed two more things: The audience and a catalyst. We were the audience; the catalyst was the changing racial conditions in the United States.

Of all songs, this struck me most, to the point that I can remember the first time I heard it and how I felt. I remember when, where and what I was doing as though that moment was frozen in time. It was the first record that I remember having the feeling that I had to have it, and I was so excited that I couldn't wait to hear it again. The radio station may have been KAKC, broadcasting at 970 AM. I was twelve years old in 1956.

My mother had a 1941 Chevrolet coupe that had only front seats (no back seat) with a split portion, not quite bucket seats but still far ahead of its time. The passenger split folded down to let you into the back area, which was flat and covered with a cheap rubber mat; that is where we loaded from two to four eleven and twelve year old boys. She bought the car in 1955, from Cotton Taylor, for about $150.00, paying it out at $5.00 a week. It was the first car she had owned and she was proud of it as was I. It was standard gray for the 1940's era, not very pretty, standard shift with the shift lever on the steering column and the gears locked up regularly. We had to stop and someone had to dislodge the gears before we could drive again. I didn't know how to do that then, but I would learn later, when I bought a worn out Chevrolet pick-up truck. My mother, Bettie, didn't really know how to drive, but she was learning. She took her driver's test over and over until she finally passed it. Perhaps he passed her out of kindness. Perhaps he just got tired of seeing her each week.

Now she was licensed but not very competent and two moments of fear stick in mind for all time; going up the hill at the low water bridge over Bird Creek and going up Flanagan Hill. Both hills allowed the car to get up enough speed that a gear shift from low to second was required, and my mother never mastered it. She never got into second gear quickly enough to prevent the car from slowing and requiring a shift back to low gear; this sent the car rolling down the hill backwards. So, she put on the brakes and stopped in the middle of the hill. She also never mastered starting in low gear on a hill and going forward. She would race the engine, let out the clutch, slowly, then pop it and kill the engine. She never made it up Flanagan in that car so she would go across town, to Tinker and Main

Streets and over West Avenue to 15th to get to the hill. We spent a lot of time backing down those hills to get a second chance at it, as she was determined but unsuccessful. If she had enough speed and no one slowed in front of her, we could actually get up Ki-He-Kah hill. But once in a while, someone ahead of us would want to turn left over to Grandview Avenue and would stop in front of her. We would begin the long backwards path down the hill and again, our circuitous route to The Hill.

We were in that old Chevy on the way to Cedar Canyon where I had close friends, Chuck and Mackie Carnagey when I heard the music. Sometimes I was allowed to go out and spend the week end with them, which I loved doing for we were great hunters and fishermen. I'm not sure I could find Cedar Canyon today, but it was familiar then and Chuck, Mackie and I had even made a pilgrimage out there on our bicycles. It was to the west, a little south and about seven miles from Pawhuska and felt much further, especially on our 1950's bicycles with, balloon tires, heavy frames, and a single speed.

As the old Chevy topped a hill on the way to Carnagey's and the reception on the radio cleared, there it was, from the top: The song. I couldn't pronounce his name when the announcer said who sang it; I could barely grasp it: Ebus?

He must have been from Ethiopia or somewhere, the way the name sounded. And with laughter today, I realize that I didn't understand a word he sang. But I felt the song, down deep inside of me, its rhythm, its pulse, its soul. It was bleak, lonely and dark with the tinkling piano, the sound of brushes on the drum head and then the pounding of the guitars as they mimicked the mournful, desperate sound of the singer.

I had to have the record, and I asked my mother for it. She capitulated quickly, and as soon as I was back in town I raced to Greer's Sporting Goods, our music store with a dollar in my hand, and tried to describe what I had heard, since I had not caught the song title. The young lady, older than I then, got the idea for I had been only one of all of the teenagers who had stormed Greer's and gobbled up the last records about the bleak and lonely hotel. New ones were in though, and she gave one to me to try in the test booth.

I looked at the funny name on the record: Elvis Presley, the Ethiopian or whatever he was. I sat it gingerly on the record player and heard the beginning of the song, the bluesy feel it had and then he began to sing. That was it, the song I had heard on the way to Cedar Canyon, and I bought it. And I played it—a lot. Bobby Hughes and I played it, at my house, at his house, at everyone in the neighborhood's house. And when our parents heard it, well—it wasn't your father's Bing Crosby.

If you were a performer then, how did you know that you had made it? You were invited to the Ed Sullivan show.

Ed Sullivan was on Sunday evening, and one night I was at Bobby Hughes's house watching on their television, bigger than ours; we enjoyed each other's company while watching so television was more fun there, sometimes. We could talk about what we saw and understand each other. When we watched at their house, we were usually on the floor in front of it, so his parents could see over us. Sometimes we forgot they were there, and we said what we thought, which got laughter and once in a while a rebuke.

There was Elvis, the first time we had seen what he looked like, singing *Heartbreak Hotel*. Elvis not only sang different, he looked different, *so* different from anyone I was used to; different from Pat Boone, from Tennessee Ernie Ford, from Perry Como. Elvis didn't just look different; he *was* different.

His hair was dark and long, and he had funny looks and different skin. He flashed a mischievous, quirky smile from time to time, teasing us. And there was the lip that impersonators would master, a single rise of one side of his mouth in a sarcastic, challenging way.

He sang in a way that made your blood run cold. He moved in a way that made your body jump, against your will, certainly against your mother's wishes. He moved in a way that could never be forgotten. There I was, present at the birth of something new, not something I would read about in a history book and wonder about without not really understanding. I was there, feeling it and sharing it with my friends. And I don't think I understood it in a way that I could explain it to any one else, neither then nor today but, oh, it was real. It was special, and it was ours; our music, our beat, our dance, our time. A young man, not much older than I, stepped onto the stage, looked into the camera, and changed the world—forever.

And we helped just by watching and buying his records.

THE CONCERT THAT WASN'T

I was very shy then and often afraid to try new things, at least of certain kinds. I was fine trying a new trick on a bicycle, climbing a new and higher tree, most physically daring things and creative challenges. I had an Erector set, a chemistry set and an art set, and I built models. But socially, I was backward. Time and experience have helped me to overcome most of that, but sometimes, I have moments of shyness and old fears surface. I can still get my feelings hurt once in a while when I think someone doesn't like me.

Remember; Paranoia is not a country in Europe.

My social awkwardness was pronounced then and prevented me from doing some things. But it was coupled with my boyish enthusiasm at coming events; so that I would get very excited about something coming and then start getting fearful as it approached. These were things like a school play in which I wanted to play the romantic lead, and I would have visions of winning the princess, for it was always about a princess then. Reality dictated that I would be one of the pajama clad Chinamen who shuffled onto the stage and had a minor part, rather than the prince who won the heart of the princess. Jay Lynn was usually the prince.

But I forgot about that each time, however and so, apparently, did my mother, ready to forget and forgive me for my performance meltdown at the last event.

Shortly after hearing Elvis, buying two of his records and then seeing him on television, we learned that he was going to be in Tulsa, at the Pavilion on the Fairgrounds, April 18, 1956. I had never been to a concert beyond something at the high school, if even that. But as soon as I found out Elvis was coming, I got excited and asked my mother if I could go. I did not necessarily mean that she would take me, and I did not know how to buy tickets, where to buy them or how I would get to the concert. Of course, she answered me in standard parentese: "No."

I was disappointed, but I understood. In fact, it seemed impossible to me but we were kids, and it was our duty to ask the impossible. It was the duty of parents to say, "No." Then both parties entered into the classic bargaining position of begging and making promises that child seldom kept while parent extracted demands and reviewed past failings of said child. These negotiations could go either way and often resulted in said child bursting into tears, sometimes from genuine emotion, sometimes from being spanked for being persistent.

Since I didn't really expect to get to go, I did nothing so I was surprised when my mother asked me if I would like to take a friend. "We're going?" I asked. I don't know how she got the tickets, but she did; she had acquired several of them.

We were going to see Elvis Presley in person.

I had only seen singers perform in church and a few around Pawhuska so a large audience to me was what it took to fill the Baptist Church, maybe a few hundred people and these were familiar and at home. I invited Bobby Hughes who shared my excitement. He also shared my fears. As the date grew closer, he began to talk about all of the things that were bad about going. As the date of

April 18, 1956, grew closer, we became more excited until—"You're not going?" I screamed at him, panic overcoming any good sense I had. "No," he said and started down his list of reasons.

I was stunned. I had never been to anything like this and having a friend go would sure have helped. I could still have gone, but I listened to him, and I let him talk me out of going. My mother asked me one last time, and I sadly declined, feeling guilty for having put her to so much trouble.

My mother had the tickets though, and she wasn't going to waste her hard earned money so Kay Hughes, Bobby's older sister, Cleva Jo Hurt, Jay Lynn's older sister, my mother and Juanita Hurt, went to see Elvis Presley. They went in the old Chevy with its two front seats so I suppose that the girls sat in the back. My mother seemed to enjoy the music, perhaps even the live performance but several days later, in the Manhattan Café, someone asked her what she had thought of Elvis's performance. "He was nasty," she said, summing up her assessment of rock n' roll and Elvis.

Elvis returned to Tulsa in the 1970's, when he was King again, and I tried to buy tickets for my wife and me. They were sold before the line officially opened.

I never got to see Elvis.

EB

The second song that impacted me was one that I heard, not on the radio, but from the speaker system at a roadside café. The café was located just east of the bridge over the Arkansas River by Ponca City. My mother and I had been in Ponca visiting my cousin, his parents properly, but my visit was with him. She and I had stopped to order a hamburger and a drink, perhaps a milk shake. I said café, but it was closer to a dive. It was small, noisy, weighed down with neon signs that advertised beer and soft drinks and served a rough crowd that it entertained with honky-tonk music, much like the old Pig Stand in Pawhuska. They made a decent hamburger and probably did their part to contribute to the legend of the greasy-spoon café in American culture.

Still, I was a teen-aged boy, and there were really no bad hamburgers, especially if you were hungry. And I was a teen aged boy, often hungry unless I had just eaten. Normally we had some kind of parting meal when we left the Hardy home (Their surname being Hardy), but, somehow, we had missed it this time and found ourselves needing food before the long journey home. It was just a little over forty miles, but it was over such a rough road that when Duane Eddy recorded *Forty Miles of Bad Road*, I thought it had been written it about the Ponca City-

Pawhuska road. Then it was only two lanes with lots of cracks and breaks and with weeds growing up through the surface; it was a road of sharp curves and lots of them. It passed through Burbank and Shidler, which it now bypasses saving time, gasoline and frustration. It took courage to travel it, and food provided courage; at least root beer did, or maybe milkshakes.

Growing up in Pawhuska, I was bothered about a part of our Oklahoma image whether it applied to us or not: Hillbilly. We had radio stations that played Hillbilly music, and there were always things around that suggested it such as the bars that Pawhuska had. Some bars had signs that billed them as a tavern but, again, dive was the word that always came to mind. Even at eleven or twelve I had been able to go into a couple of them, not as a customer, of course, but perhaps on an errand or with someone. It seems odd to me today, that we could do that, but it happened. Some of my relatives, cousins and aunts and uncles were hillbilly; I can find no other word to describe them. Some of my friends had met a few of the Hillbilly relatives and I was embarrassed.

The song I heard that day was definitely hillbilly in my mind, yet there was something about it that caught my interest. Perhaps it was the twang of the guitar or the downbeat. I didn't know anything about the singers, of course, because it was the first time I had heard them, but I made some judgments; I assumed them to be older, perhaps in their forties, very old, and with bib overalls and straw farmer's hats, fat of course, with few teeth and not very good looking. Still their song captivated me, and by the time it was over, I was hooked. It was the beginning of a love affair that lasts for me today, although one sided for they know nothing of me. I am just one of many fans, but still loyal, and I still buy their music when I can find it.

The song was *Bye Bye Love*, and they were Don and Phil, the Everly Brothers, who would become so well known that they often are recognized just by their EB logo. They were not much older than I was, as it turned out. That was, again, one of those records that I had to have. I still have it, along with my original 45 rpm copy of *Heartbreak Hotel* by Elvis—and a few others.

I saw the Everly Brothers on Ed Sullivan, and I was stunned by how good looking and how young they were, not quite the hillbillies that I had envisioned. It was somewhere in this time that we began to call this music by the new name: Rock n' Roll. Alan Freed, a disc jockey (DJ) in Cleveland, Ohio was playing a lot of music by black singers and some of the records were marked rock music and some were marked roll music. He took both terms, put them together and voila! We had a name for our music. It was hard to say what Rock n' Roll was, and if anyone asked you to define or describe it you usually fell back on examples, citing an Elvis Presley, Ricky Nelson, Little Richard, Fats Domino, Jerry Lee Lewis, Jimmy Clanton or Gene Vincent song. It was difficult even for professionals to define it. It could be characterized by a beat, a motif, a key, a four or five note structure, repetition or any number of things but for us, we just knew when it was Rock n' Roll—and when it wasn't. Some of what came to be Rock n' Roll had been hillbilly and blues and jazz and bluegrass and country but somehow, it all melded together to form the new music; the devil's music some said. I didn't take that very seriously, as I couldn't understand most of the words anyway. I think it was something else, something more primitive that pulled or drove me to it, something deep within me that was matched by the rhythm of the music.

A young preacher during the 1950's said, "When you ask a kid today to explain what attracts them to Rock n' Roll, they will say "the beat the beat the beat the beat." Maybe it was the beat. But I think the sum was greater than its parts. I think if you took out any element it weakened the piece and it wasn't Rock n' Roll anymore; it was watered down. And it wasn't what we wanted. The devil's music never led me to do anything particularly evil just by itself. Some of the songs were supposed to have lyrics that were sexually explicit, and if you listened very closely you could hear them, but only because you wanted to and worked at it. For the most part, no one could actually understand what words were being sung anyway. Other kids were a more pronounced influence on me, but I think it was hormones and being teenagers, not Rock n' Roll music that influenced us.

THAT'LL BE THE DAY!

One might conclude that my favorite singer was Elvis Presley and for a time he was. Anyone who has known me very long soon learns that my favorite singer was, and remains, Buddy Holly. His true name was Charles Hardin Holley, and Holly supposedly was a misspelling that he allowed to remain. I was accustomed to the startling good looks of Pat Boone, Elvis Presley, and Ricky Nelson, so I was surprised the first time that I saw a photograph of Buddy Holly. He wore thick black glasses, had wavy, almost curly hair and was not as good looking as we expected, not with the standards we had then. Time changes perceptions, and we get used to how people look as we grow, both older and wiser.

It was his voice that drew me to him; his childish, mocking voice with a hiccough in it that was difficult to imitate; it was truly unique. And a lot of the songs he sang fit my life too so I felt a kinship with him that I did not feel with Elvis, even though Elvis was a better singer and a greater influence on our generation. When my best girl and I broke up, I listened to *An Empty Cup, A Broken Date* repeatedly and made myself more depressed. Fortunately I also had *Rave On.* which always brought me out of depression although I have injured my fingers snapping them to it.

My first Buddy Holly album was called *The Chirping Crickets*, and I still have it, with the original album jacket. I rarely play it now, but that is because I have the same album in a compact disc (CD), and I can play it when I walk, run, ride a bicycle or drive. I bought the album for one song, *That'll be the Day* and I only liked a few of the songs to begin with. As I played it again and again, other songs grew on me and became favorites for me. *Not Fade Away,* at first, is a strange song, and it wasn't easy to listen to. It is one of my top favorites now. I divide his music into rockers and ballads. My favorite rocker is *Rave On!* My favorite ballad is *It Doesn't Matter Anymore.* In the movie *Pleasantville*, there is a scene in which a boy plugs in the jukebox, and it begins to play *Rave On!* The teens cannot keep their feet still as the beat moves them to move; that's the way it was.

Buddy Holly was killed, February 3, 1959, in the crash of a small chartered aircraft near Clearlake, Iowa. In the aircraft with him were Ritchie Valens and J.P. Richardson, known as The Big Bopper. It was one of the saddest days of my youth.

Like all humans, I have been asked what my concept of Heaven is. I reply that it's a front row seat at a never ending Buddy Holly concert. I have modified that, since 2003, to say, "It's a front row seat at a never ending Buddy Holly concert with my son Stephen playing lead guitar."

That'll be the day!

THE NATIONAL ANTHEM OF ROCK N' ROLL

One of the songs that was the favorite for many of us has been called The National Anthem of Rock n' Roll, and it certainly seemed to sum up music for us. When I first heard it on the radio, it opened with a clattering, rattling sound that reminded me of a herd of wild crickets stampeding across a flat tin roof. It might have been castanets; then a cow bell pealed twice, then came a falsetto voice with a yi-yi-yi-yi [pause] yi-yi-yi and then a tenor broke into *Little Darling.* It is difficult to listen to it without doing something with your hands and feet for it defies sitting still. The rhythm is pronounced, repeating at regular intervals, the harmony is blended, and it makes no sense whatever. We only know that he has found his true love, he loves her, then he has been untrue, and then, he wants to hold her little hand. At a critical moment we heard a forgiving, la-la-la-lah, and then a deep bass voice broke into a spoken part while the tenor sang background. To my chagrin, I did not acquire a copy of the record. Unexplainable and yes, unforgivable, I know. Somehow, I just missed getting one. Over the years I have heard it played, and I've worn out many cowboy boot soles to it.

After I had taken several seminars on goal setting and

achieving results, I set a written goal to get a copy of *Little Darling* by the original group, The Diamonds. I was so successful that I now have more than twenty recordings of it. La, la, la, lah.: Cha-cha-cha.

Johnny Otis and the Metros released *Hand Jive*, which was another song that one can not listen to and sit still. Miss Whitsitt did not teach the Hand Jive, and I never learned it then, but I did learn it later at Studebaker's in Dallas, Texas. I'm slow at some things.

OTHER SONGS

Some of the music was deeply spiritual and not just Rock n' Roll. Some might say religious, but I prefer spiritual. Frankie Laine released a powerful song called *I Believe* that made me shudder when I listened to it. It also helped me understand why *I* believed so deeply in some things; it helped me to recognize simple pleasures in the nature that surrounded me. *He* was a deeply spiritual song. *He's Got the Whole World in his Hand* was a popular hymn and since it was easy to sing, many of us did. Not every song is easy for the rest of us.

I loved some traditional hymns too: *The Old Rugged Cross, In the Garden, Onward Christian Soldiers* and others.

There is a story of the little girl who, after Sunday school, asked of her mother, "Momma, who's Andy?" "I don't know," her mother replied. The child repeated her question each week until her mother asked, "Where is Andy being talked about?" "It's in the song," the little girl said. "What song?" "You know, momma, "Andy walks with me Andy talks with me…"

We did not have a plethora of radio stations nearby, and there were none in Pawhuska. I say that for two reasons: It was true, and I have always wanted to use "plethora" in a sentence.

I recall KVOO and KAKC in Tulsa as the most listened to stations. The music was eclectic and not specialized as it is in 2007. KAKC played Rock n' Roll, but we also heard Johnny Ray, Kay Starr, Johnny Cash, Ferlin Husky, Kitty Wells, Ray Price, et al.

Most people had a radio at home, sometimes a very good and expensive one but most of the radio then was AM (Amplitude Modulated). Most people had a radio in their car and if a choice had to be made between air conditioning and a radio, it was going to be a hot summer.

Our first new car had an AM radio with five push buttons, to which you could set your favorite stations. I once set all five to KAKC and since my mother did not know how to set them she thought the radio was broken. I reset them and she very nicely asked me to never do that again.

Cars did not come with FM (Frequency Modulated) tuners and there were only a few FM stations available. FM stations were noted for playing music that would put you to sleep in the middle of an old western movie shootout, so we didn't feel that we were missing much by not having an FM tuner. We called the FM music Longhair Music.

RICKY

Sometimes we don't see things well when they are happening. But given thirty or forty years to think about them, we see them better. Ricky Nelson is one of those. First, I was jealous of Ricky; I didn't like him, but it wasn't because of anything he did; it was because of the girls. He was good looking and young. I was good looking and young. He was on a television show; I watched television. He could sing and play a guitar. I could sing. But when I added those up, he had more points that I did. The only thing I won on was that I lived in Pawhuska and he didn't.

He could sing all right. In fact, he could sing well and had many hit songs, some of which I liked in spite of myself. My favorite Ricky Nelson song is *There'll never be Anyone Else but You.* Ricky was everywhere. He was on the weekly television show, *The Ozzie and Harriet Show*, and on the radio and other shows, and he was becoming a pain in the neck. There were other things besides Ricky Nelson but if I went to a girl's house, soon she would say, "Do you like Ricky Nelson?"

I didn't want to offend anyone, especially a girl so I would mumble, "Yeah, he's okay." She would "Ooh," and "Ah" and "He's so dreamy, and I love his hair. He has the cutest dimple, he blah, blah, blah..." until I was sick of him. I wasn't the only boy who was sick of him; we all were. We were competing with him for the attention of a girl that didn't even know him. He certainly didn't know her. I tried to comb my hair like his, or like Elvis's. They had duck tails; I had duck feathers.

But I was also naïve; I didn't realize that *he* wasn't combing his hair. It was a staff of professionals that combed his hair, put on his makeup and generally dressed him. And, if they made a mistake on camera, they did a retake, sometimes up to five or six takes. When we saw *Dharma and Greg* being taped in 2001, each scene was filmed a minimum of three takes, any with obvious errors four or more.

I only had one take each day, and it was a print no matter how it came out. I was alone at home, before seven in the morning, with poor lighting, and either Brylcreem or Vitalis as my hair dressing, myself as a hair stylist, and the word "coif" was far in my future. But I didn't know to say that to a young girl, who would probably have said, "Oh, you're just jealous." I was.

As young boys, we did not understand that the girls didn't really "love" Ricky; they were only looking for communication tools and Ricky and others were common ground, something that we both could see and share together. We boys had bicycles, dogs, war movies, cowboy movies, .22 rifles and motorcycles as our communication tools. But because we did not understand that and could not process it with mature feelings, we sometimes became jealous, just as if Ricky *did* live in Pawhuska and just down the street. It was lucky for him that he didn't.

Later, in high school, there was a good looking young man, Jimmy Rector, who looked a lot like Ricky Nelson. I noticed the similarity so I'm sure a lot of girls did, but I was never jealous of the real Jimmy Rector like I was of the fictional Ricky Nelson. Jimmy wasn't on television though.

Boys also had ideal girls such as Sandra Dee, but we

usually were content to just say, "Sandra Dee." "Yeah...." And let unfinished statements speak for themselves. We rarely spent much time extolling specific attributes of a movie girl whereas the girls studied magazines such as *Seventeen* and learned everything about the world's Ricky Nelsons.

Ricky Nelson had just introduced a new song on the Nelson show, and it was soon to be a hit. Bobby Hughes and I were walking from my house to his, north, along Prudom Avenue when a girl we knew was intersecting our path as she headed towards town. When we were just a few feet away, Bobby, who had been quiet and thoughtful for a few moments, a rare state for him, suddenly blurted, "Do you like Ricky Nelson?" Before I could answer, she stopped, turned to face us and, with her hands on her waist spat out, "Like him! I don't even know him."

There was a strange and silent moment as I waited for him to say one of the many things he might have said and then she, red with embarrassment, turned and walked away from us. "What made her think I was talking to her?" he asked. "Dunno," I mumbled. We laughed, and then generally forgot it. I did not know her name but I knew her by sight. She was younger, a cute blonde with a perpetual pony-tail. But she could never look me in the eye after her *faux pas*. It didn't matter as it was minor compared to most peoples' and too many of mine. I saw her in Bartlesville once, twenty-five years later, and I started to speak to her, just a sign of recognition that we were both from Pawhuska. She looked at me, just for a moment, and then I could see her reliving "Like him! I don't even know him." Without a word, she reddened and walked away. I wish I could have found words and helped her over a silly stumble, but I failed.

HEY ABBOTT!

I was in the seventh grade and walking home after school. We lived one block inside of the defining line for taking the school bus, so I had to get to Pawhuska High School on my own. I walked, rode a bicycle or caught a ride. This day, I had stayed late for something in band, and Bobby Hughes had gone ahead. I found myself walking alone this day and worse, I was feeling friendless. I do not know why, but it is likely that I had got up the courage to ask a particular blonde out and she had shot me down. That always did wonders for our fragile boy egos.

I sensed that there was a boy walking behind me. I would like to have walked with him, but I didn't know him well. I knew of him, as we said. I knew his name, knew several girls who had a crush on him, knew that he played basketball and that he was good looking. Good looking is a relative term for seventh graders, and it is only when we get older and are reminiscing over the high school annual and see our back then photographs that we want to burn all of them. But, for a seventh grader, he was good looking; several girls had told me that.

We may have been fifty or so feet apart, and I was feeling very bad and wondering why I did not have any friends, why he and I couldn't walk together when I heard him call, "Hey, Payne! Wait up man."

I stopped, and he ran up to me saying, "Man, I've been walking fast trying to catch up to you. I thought you didn't want to walk home with me." We were both carrying books and I a clarinet case. He took some of my books and carried them and we walked until our trails diverged, talking, joking and laughing. He was an athlete, and I a musician; our paths seldom crossed. Yet when they did, we were always friends and had wonderful talks together. As with Ronnie Havens, the boy and I have never had a cross word. But I have never had the courage to tell him how much he did for me that day by calling to me and sharing the walk home. He lifted me from a depression and made me feel that I could be liked by others at a time when I was feeling, and telling myself, that I just wasn't likeable. It is for that simple gesture fifty years ago that Gary Abbot has always had a special place in my heart.

THE REVARDS OF PAWHUSKA

I have not lived in Pawhuska for many years so I am not known by people who more recently moved to Pawhuska. When Pawhuskans learn that I am from there, I am often asked, "Are you related to the Paynes that live on ___?" "No," I tell them. My mother met my father when he passed through Pawhuska on a motorcycle, so my Payne family was from Rush Springs, Oklahoma and other places.

As to my Pawhuska relatives, I am a Revard. Revard is a variation of a French word, rêve, although there are other spellings, and it usually means dream. My grandmother, Louisa Victoria Hardy was a child from the union of Emily Bell Revard, an Osage, and William Hardy of Newkirk, a Kaw. Louisa had a brother, Ray Hardy and two sisters Julia and Geneva Hardy.

When I was growing up, I often called my relatives Aunt Ola Mae, Aunt Roberta, Uncle Revard, etc, but learning more about genealogy, I think that they were cousins. It has made some things confusing, but I think that happens in most families. Sorting it out now, after many of them have passed on, is more difficult.

My cousins were Candy Cooper, daughter of Ola Mae, and Mackie Moore, Eddie Zaun, Carrie Zaun, Cathy Smith, children of Roberta. Ola Mae, Roberta and Revard Davis were siblings. Also, there were Barney and G. A. Hardy, sons of my uncle Ray Hardy. I had other cousins in Ponca City and Newkirk under the Hardy flag.

None of my Payne family lived in Pawhuska, so I had no uncles and aunts my mother's age there, but there were my Uncle Ray Hardy and aunts Geneva and Julia from my grandmother's side and a generation older than my mother. Aunt Julia had a daughter that I knew as Pan and sons Kenneth and Bennet Griffin.

Pan is a beautiful and exciting woman who has lived her own life. She actually had little schooling but she educated herself and learned to be the best person she could be. Pan's name is actually Emily Bell, after my grandmother's mother, but someone nicknamed her Panhatchipie and the shortened, "Pan" has stayed with her all of her life.

Bennet Griffin, a decorated soldier in General Patton's army, was killed in Europe during World War II.

My grandmother, Louisa, who was known as Louise to most people, married Max Harris from Oklahoma City, who came to Osage County looking for an Indian girl. My mother was produced by their union. My mother was named Bettie Louise Harris. Max and Louise adopted my mother, Bettie but Max was also her real or biological father from an affair he was having with her mother. My biological grandmother was a Cherokee Indian, to the best of my knowledge and according to the family lore.

My grandmother later married Chuck Lessert, and she was known in Pawhuska as Louise Lessert, the name I knew her by.

My mother often talked about growing up in Oklahoma City in her early years, and she talked about not celebrating Christmas. I didn't question that for she used an interesting word that was not in my Pawhuska vocabulary. She said that they went to synagogue, and I simply accepted that.

Years later the lights came on and I realized that she was being raised Jewish. The reason was that, Max Harris, my grandfather, was a Jew. Is the grandson of a Jew a Jew also? It depends on if being a Jew is genetic or religious or cultural. I was raised as a Baptist mostly, because my mother let me go to church across the street so my upbringing has been Christian and early on, it caused some conflicts between my mother and me because I was trying to make her my first convert. If it is indeed genetic, then I indeed, am, as my cousin Pan says, one-quarter Jew.

I read of a man who did not know of his origins who contracted a company in Houston to determine them. He and other family members took simple mouth swab samples which were analyzed for genetic markers, and he learned that he and his family were Jewish, a secret kept by his grandfather. If it could be determined by a genetic marker, then there is a genetic aspect beyond mere culture that makes one Jewish, and so I may be as well. Shalom.

When I understood some of the difficulties she had gone through with this dual identity as she grew up, I understood better. It had resolved itself long ago though, and it was not an issue for us later in life. The issues then were that I, as a son, could not visit my mother without her trying to feed me and get me to take home two or three baskets of food; a typical mother and son issue as they try to mother us in our forties.

My family then, is Revard, and I am a Revard but not by blood. So, is that my family? Marcy Loy Williams was adopted by her father Dr. Bill Loy and his wife, two of the most respected citizens of Pawhuska, and she is a Loy as I am a Revard. Your family is who raises you, not who gave you birth, especially if that is the only family you know. Marcy agrees with me on that, and she has never felt a part of any family but the Loys. I am the same about the Revards, except that I am also a Payne

One of my friends, who never questioned his family membership, was told one day, by a stranger, that he was adopted. He was nineteen years old when he learned it, and confirmed it with his parents; it was a stunning blow to him because he had always accepted that he was a _____. It didn't change anything about him except that he was not blood related to his mother and father; still, that was his family.

THE HILLS OF PAWHUSKA

The hills of Pawhuska, unlike the Revards of Pawhuska, are not a family but literally hills. Pawhuska seemed to me to have four levels with one or more hills rising to the next level. The first level was across Bird Creek from my aunt Julia Griffin's home. The hill rising from the low water bridge brought you up to the main level where down town was; it was also the level that we lived on and where Union School was. The next level was generally known as The Hill and could be reached by a number of paths. Hills on 11th, through 18th Streets as well as Ki-He-Kah and Grandview hills, gave access to The Hill with 11th Street hill being the steepest. By the time you reached 18th Street, near the hospital, the slope was gentler and the hill a little longer. It was easier to climb for some cars, such as our old Chevy, than the steeper hills. Ki-He-Kah hill was steep and long with a gentle curve in it, while Grandview hill that ran in front of the Osage County Court House was steep and straight. The fourth and highest level was the one above The Hill, where Williams Park is.

All of the hills can be named by the street name, such as 11th Street hill, except for three. Technically, there is Prudom Street hill but no one calls it that; it was always known as Flanagan Hill and anyone who has been in Pawhuska soon learns its location. It is the hill between 10th and 11th Streets on Prudom. It is short, only three hundred and twenty-five feet long, but it is steep which worked to our advantage when the streets were icy as the police department closed it to traffic, and we sledded down it. The hill on Grandview Avenue that leads up to Williams Park has usually been called Dial Hill, although there is no posted street name for it. And, there is Castle Hill. When I was growing up, most people knew about Castle Hill, but I have found, in mentioning Castle Hill today that many people do not know about it or call it by that name. Castle Hill rises along Matthews Avenue north of Main Street and passes behind the Indian Agency buildings. The ice plant was on Matthews Avenue.

At one time, there was a house shaped like a castle tower on the west side of the hill, and some people just called the hill after that. Also, I have been told that the house was built by a family named Castle. When I was in the first grade, I became friends with a boy that lived in the house, and we visited him several times. His father and mother showed us their business, which was broom making. I don't think that they were doing well with it, and he moved away during the first grade year. I really enjoyed him, and I missed him.

My first motor scooter was built by Cushman to be sold as a Sears & Roebuck model which meant that it was inferior in quality to the model sold by Cushman dealers. It had an automatic, centrifugal clutch with a single speed and had only 4.8 horsepower so it did not have the capability to climb steep hills. I would start at the bottom of Ki-He-Kah hill, and if I did not get a good run at it, the motor scooter just could not make it up the hill without help. That meant that, with the engine running and pulling the machine, I would have to get off and push to assist it up the hill. I had mastered a few techniques, such as an indicated stop at the bottom of the hill and with some luck I might make it, at reduced speed, over the top of the hill. If I thought that I would not have enough speed, I turned eastward at the short hill on Tenth Street in front of The Virginia, and took another route. Of course, it was embarrassing to have to turn off in the face of superior machines so I tried to be alone. Once defeated, I would go out Lynn Avenue to 18th Street and go up by the side of the hospital. It was a longer route but gasoline cost $.29 a gallon, and I got forty miles to a gallon so it was not a factor. I could get enough of a run there to make it. And, there was always the very long way around via Tinker and West Avenues to get there. It could not make it up Flanagan Hill.

THE HILL

Every city and town has social levels and places where people live that may indicate one's place in society. Pawhuska had The Hill which was the level above downtown and where the Kiwanis pool and most of the great houses were. The Hill was loosely defined though, for there were families with wealth, but also families with less wealth. Along Grandview Avenue, where the great houses were, and east of it for several blocks, was clearly The Hill. As one moved closer to West Avenue near the cemetery, it was less clearly defined.

My mother, grandmother and I lived in an adequate house, but it was not on The Hill. On the other hand, when we first moved to Pawhuska and were experiencing our most dire financial straits, we did live on The Hill; we lived in a small house, perhaps a shotgun shack, known as Labell's. Over many years I have told people that we lived at Labell's, and they responded with, "We lived at Labell's too." There is a nice house there today, at the corner of 15th Street and West Avenue.

A common question, "Where do you live?" was answered with, "Oh, we live on The Hill." That might get a positive response, or it might get a jealous or skeptical response. But not everyone who lived on The Hill lived in a mansion, nor was everyone there wealthy. The closer to the cemetery, generally, the less wealthy and extravagant the home but, it was still on The Hill.

Kids who lived on The Hill went to Franklin but the dividing line for Franklin and Union was broad. Jon Horn, who lived on Tinker, was just about equidistant between the two schools and went to Union while someone a few blocks north of him might have gone to Franklin. Ninth Street was a clear divider, for if you lived on the north side of ninth, you went to Franklin; if you lived on the south side, you went to Union. When school started for our class, some kids who had lived across the street from each other and played together found themselves in different school systems.

I knew only one Franklin kid before the seventh grade; after seventh grade, most of my friends were from Franklin, and that could have been because of band. Once in the band, we spent a lot of time together.

Where did I live? I lived on the Non-Hill.

THE STREETS OF PAWHUSKA

The streets have changed little since I was a boy in Pawhuska, but there have been a few important changes. For example, the intersection of Ninth Street and Lynn Avenue was a four way stop then. The influence of old habits was demonstrated to me, when *I* almost caused an accident, by stopping on Lynn Avenue as I reached Ninth Street; the car behind us narrowly avoided colliding with us. The protest of screeching tires and The Hawaiian Good-Luck Sign that he raised in the air spoke his displeasure.

"Dad, what are you stopping for?" Stephen asked.

"There's a stop sign Stephen." I replied.

"No there isn't."

"Stephen, there has been a stop sign here as long as I can remember."

But it was gone.

One block further south, I found that 8th Street no longer continues eastward as it had always done. I remember it well, for it was there that the Chevrolet ran over me and my Cushman Eagle.

Chevrolet: 1
Eagle: 0

East along Eighth Street was the armory building and down the street was the poor man's Whiting Hall. It was a small building known as the Round-Up Club, and there were often dances there. It was a building shaped a little like the neighborhood groceries and may have been one at one time. My grandmother went there sometimes and listened to music and danced. She and other women spent a lot of time sitting and fanning themselves with the small, Japanese fold out fans.

I was with two men she knew once, and one of them asked the other man to go outside and discuss something with him; I went along. When they got outside, one of them took out cigarettes and they lit them and began to smoke. The other man took out a bottle of whisky and they passed it back and forth between them taking sips and rubbing their eyes. I watched in awe. As the contents of the bottle grew fewer one of them said, "Ready to dance now?" and they went inside. I stayed outside and watched others come out and repeat the same routine. It was before Oklahoma passed its liquor reform laws of 1957.

Also, somewhere far down Eighth Street, there might have been an old swimming pool but if so, I barely remember it; it was already dilapidated and not a factor in our fun.

Main Street now continues on to the east and connects to Highway 99. Then, Main Street stopped at Lynn Avenue and the City of Pawhuska had a maintenance department that occupied the space. Also, a red light was suspended above the intersection of Lynn Avenue and Main Street. The light blinked both directions at the same time to notify travelers that this was a stop. There were STOP signs posted on the side of the street as well. Then, in a trek to Tulsa, or anywhere south, one drove the long and slow way out past Ward's Salvage yard, Adolph's tavern, the county hospital, the drive-in theater and the fairgrounds; it took a while, adding precious minutes to the trip to Tulsa.

Many streets had a small metal STOP bump placed in the middle of the street at intersections. I doubt that it was very visible, and the only reason I remember it so well is that I hit the one on Ki-He-Kah and Seventh Street with my first English racer while I was riding, eating a hot dog and drinking a coke, all at the same time, and my front wheel came off launching my meal and me through the air. I was healing from a broken arm at the time, and my first thought, while still air born was, "Dr. Loy, here I come." But I landed on my hot dog with my nose and most of the right side of my face and protected my arm from damage. The hot dog did not survive. I picked up my wheel and put it back on the bicycle, loosely since I had no tools with which to tighten it. I had enough change for another coke, and I walked my bicycle to the Dairy Queen to get my drink, forgetting that I had catsup, mustard and relish over the right side of my face. I was already shaken and shaking still when I ordered and got the strange question of, "Are you all right?" Puzzled, I answer, "Yes," not yet having learned my lesson. At least she didn't shake me. When I got home and looked in the mirror, I understood.

At least the part in my hair looked good.

THAR'S BRICKS IN THEM THAR STREETS

When I am in Pawhuska and traveling up and down the asphalt covered streets of the hills, I sometimes forget about the enduring and endearing bricks lying just beneath. In my youth, Ki-He-Kah and Grandview hills were exposed brick streets, and so was Ninth street. Having seen them before they were covered with asphalt, I wonder if other streets such as Revard and Rogers are also of brick. I admired the old brick streets and part of me wishes that they were not covered but I also remember that they became slick when there was rain, snow and ice and perhaps that is why they are covered now. Bricks just seem to last forever and the color and shading is beautiful. Flanagan Hill remains uncovered by asphalt and the bricks can be seen there. Perhaps it is too steep and the asphalt won't stick. Then again, perhaps the bricks, with their uneven edge, give those that walk it a place for their shoes to grip. Surely this is the hill that Jack and Jill came tumbling down.

LEAVE YOUR PICKLE PASS BEHIND YOU

I learned the secret to happiness when I was twelve years old, while lunching with my mother in the Manhattan Café in downtown Pawhuska. I was eating tenderloin of trout at the time, and there was a song playing, and the secret was in the song. The song was about a bridge, and I had only two images that came to me when I thought of a bridge: The swinging bridge over Bird Creek and the low water bridge over Bird Creek. Often the low water bridge was actually *under* Bird Creek. I had been over many bridges including the old bridges over Clear Creek and Bird Creek and I had crossed the Arkansas River Bridge at Ponca City many times, in a car, of course.

Yet, if you said "bridge," the image that came to me was one of those, and I know why, though it was not a happy image. When my mother, my grandmother and I lived on Girard Street in Mrs. Armstrong's duplex apartments there were some boys that were my playmates. They were older so they were the leaders of most things. I did not see them regularly, but I did see them sometimes and I liked them and looked up to them. One day, perhaps in 1949, one of the twins drowned. I was not there with them, but the impact upon the rest of us children was sudden and frightening. I was later told that his drowning, and the fear it created for my grandmother, was the reason that we moved to Prudom.

You must remember that I was only five years old, and I had been warned repeatedly about not crossing the swinging bridge for below was the creek and on the other side was another world that I had been taught to fear then. I knew where the creek was, and I was already a little afraid of it, of the steep and grassy banks and of the dark water below. In the long grass and weeds lurked a thousand insects, and I had already been bitten and stung enough to want to avoid the creek.

After the boy drowned, all of the parents in the neighborhood came to collect us children, and I remember one thing more than anything else; the look of fear that I saw on the face of every parent. I think they were all women, mothers, grandmothers, other caretakers, and some of them even whipped the kid that they were rescuing, just for being there, we thought. We were all in a kind of common place between the houses of the apartments. It occurred to me later that perhaps these women knew only that a child was lost, and they did not yet know the name of the child. Perhaps they did not know that the child had died, and they thought he was only missing, that there was still hope. I don't know everything about that day, and I can not clearly remember it all but I suspect that the whole thing put a fear of dark water in me that I have never completely been able to displace. I discovered that again the first time that I drove over the Calcasieu River Bridge at Lake Charles, Louisiana, and I looked for something in my car to hang on to; and I found I could hardly breathe. I made it, each and every time, but the fear never completely left me.

My grandmother was a gossipy and nosy person, and she loved to be an on the scene witness. She did not want to leave me behind, so she took me with her down to the low water bridge where men in khaki pants, string undershirts and khaki work hats were looking for the boy's body. These men had an ashen and fallen look that I remember today, much like I saw on the news clips of people when John Kennedy was shot. That look left an indelible impression on my five year old mind: scared me forever. Today, if that same event occurred, teams of counselors would be rushed in to help the children and their parents learn to cope with it and gain closure. I am not being critical of that but rather praising it. We just had to learn to cope with it, and I'm sure we did but none of us in the same way.

A bridge is a connector and also a symbol for connections. A bridge is how we cross spasms and canyons, and it joins us together instead of keeping us apart. Yet a bridge for me was a symbol of the most ghastly thing in my life. Yet there in the song was the secret of happiness, and I heard it as distinctly and clearly as if you had called my own name. "Leave your pickle pass behind you." Now, if I could only understand what a pickle pass was, I could leave it behind me and find true happiness.

I asked my mother, and got only the blank looks that parents can be so good at. Only children are better. I listened to the song many times, and I longed to know the answer, to find an easy way to happiness. I never did learn that secret but many years later—and the truth is that I had asked many a person, man and woman, what a pickle pass was—I was finally asked, "What do you think a pickle pass is?" and I replied that I had no idea. "Where," then, "did you get this obsessive question about the pickle pass?" "It's in the song," I replied. "What song? Sing it for me." and I did, at least the part of the song that advised me to leave my pickle pass behind me.

The only person who had ever asked the next question, who had ever listened to me on this heard me, thought a minute and said, "Wait! I know what you're talking about!

It's not a pickle pass, it's **a fickle past**." Later, we heard that song by Patti Page together, and she could hear as clearly as I had always heard "pickle pass" and she understood my dilemma. She had solved it for me, and it turned out that I had been looking for happiness in the wrong place for a long time.

There is no secret to happiness as we all have it, and we all lose it. It's a temporary thing at best and we are happy just before Christmas when we haven't yet opened the package, and then it begins to wane after we open it and find out what we got. It's like a roller coaster, where we approach the peak and then for a split second we reach it, and then start down the slope. Its pursuit causes many people to live lives of unhappiness because they never find it because they look for it in a thing or an event. It's in our Constitution, "the pursuit of happiness," and yet it eludes so many people.

I can tell you when I am happiest, and that is when I do something good for someone else, especially when it's unexpected of me. It can be the simplest thing sometimes, opening a door for someone at the right time, giving someone an unexpected gift; I mean a real gift with no strings attached; no expectations in return. There was a single moment of happiness that was the greatest of all, and that was when my son was born. But most of my feelings of happiness, and I'd rather say contentment or satisfaction, have come when I helped someone else. I still feel that way.

THE GREAT POCKET WATCH CAPER

We were finally getting somewhere. We were sophomores, in the tenth grade, and we could see the end in sight; just two more, long years and then, well we didn't know or we would have remained sophomores. Bobby Hughes and I were in a class together for the first time in a while, and there were characters in the class. One of my favorites was a happy-go-lucky Duane Titus. He was always smiling, cracking jokes and I had always enjoyed Duane. But he was about to be an unwitting victim to unfolding events of The Great Pocket Watch Caper.

We had an English class with Ramona Rounsavall, a young woman that we probably made older that year. She was an attractive brunette with shoulder length hair, and we enjoyed her a lot, but we also teased her a lot. Bobby Hughes had a pocket watch that had been given to him by someone close, perhaps his grandfather. Then again, perhaps he was making that up. He had the watch apart on his desk in English class, and it was on a paper towel, carefully spread across his desk. It was obvious that he was not paying attention so, Miss Rounsavall asked him, "Bob, what are you doing." No response. "Bob?" "Yes, Ma'am?" "What are you doing, Mr. Hughes?" When she said Mr.

Hughes, he should have paid close attention from previous experiences. It was nearly equivalent to Young Man. She repeated her question. To my surprise he responded, "I'm working on my watch," and continued as though he was at home on a day off. "What?" "You heard me. I'm working on my watch." If this were a plan, I did not yet understand it, and I silently thanked heaven that I was sitting a good ways from him though it did me little good on that fateful day. "Bring me the watch," she said, and held out her hand as though he was sitting just in front of her. "No," he said. He had me scared by now. "What?" Now you've done it Hughes, I thought. "No," he said. And then, unbelievably, he said, "Look, this is my watch. Go get your own #@*% watch." There were audible moans of disbelief in the class. "What?" she said, much like my mother, when she amazed me asking questions to which she already knew the answer. He repeated it.

"Mr. Hughes," she said, "Go straight to the office and wait for me there."

The office was the office of Mr. Bean, our stoic, balding principal, and now Hughes had done it.

"Does anyone else have anything to say?" she asked in a challenge to her loss of class control. I should have known from the tone of voice, by how she asked the question, to stay out of it.

I should not have and somehow I knew it but, I had to say something in defense of the hapless Mr. Hughes so I did. I do not remember exactly what I said but I think it was my tone, not the words.

"Go!" she barked, and pointed at me with an extended finger to make sure that I saw she meant me. "Go join your little friend in the office."

"Little friend?" I wondered. That was years ago when we were at Union and now we were big, almost adults and someday, with more experience, some degree of luck and a national crisis, we might be adults. But just like at Union, and with me sitting ten seats away from him, once again, he had—like quicksand—pulled me in with him.

I made my way out of class and down to the office, with considerable fear, and joined Mr. Hughes outside of Mr. Bean's office as he was busy with something important and did not have a moment for us.

I later learned that after she had sent me out, she had said, "The next person to make any noise, I don't care what it is, goes to the office with those two clowns, and I mean every word I am saying." Clowns? We finally had a profession.

At that moment, the door opened and in strolled Duane Titus who had been on an excused absence to a doctor's appointment. Silence reigned for a moment as everyone in the class stared at the innocent but unfortunate Mr. Titus.

"What's everybody looking at?" he asked as he smiled. It was too much for her and she turned and shouted, like a mad Lady McBeth, "Out! Out! And go to the office with your friends!" At least she didn't call him Spot.

Mr. Titus joined us where we talked and assured him that we did not know what had got into her. We expected her at any moment but she did not arrive. Shortly before class ended, Mr. Bean came out of his inner office and asked, "What are you boys doing here?" "Miss Rounsavall told us to wait here for her," one of us said. "Do you know why?" "No sir." "Well, boys," he said, "She isn't here, and I don't know what she wanted [she wanted to see all three beheaded at the Guillotine] and it's almost time for your next class, so, why don't you run along, and I'll see what she wanted." We needed no more encouragement to leave. By the next day, she had forgotten about it, and we resumed class as usual, if there were a usual for us.

DANCING QUEEN

A young Pawhuska woman told me that she was awkward, clumsy and without confidence; until she met the Dancing Queen. The Dancing Queen taught us how to dance, but like some of the great men of Pawhuska, and she was a great lady, she taught us more than that. She taught us self confidence by teaching us fool proof techniques, simple box and side steps, spins and dips, how to hold a girl, how to lead and how to be led. She taught every dance, from tap to ballet and in between. She did not teach us The Bop; Chunker did that. But she was a virtuoso dancer of everything else.

Evelyn Whitsitt had her studio along Ki-He-Kah Avenue, near Louie's Hat Shop, and I remember the first time I went. I remember it because I was scared stiff. I wanted to learn how to dance, but it was intimidating; probably the girl part. But I sure didn't want to dance with the guys either. We went once each week, at least those in my class. I'm sure Pamela Ray and others studied more than that. We started with a simple step, learned the basics and when she thought we were ready, she added more and made us grow. Along with physical skills, she tried to polish our social graces.

She topped our learning off by providing a major dance held at the Whiting Hall. For that, we had to ask a girl, which was about as intimidating as being the groom in a wedding later on, and we had to treat her like a lady. She suggested, but did not demand, that we buy a corsage for our prom date; she suggested but did not demand that we behave as adults. We arrived at Whiting Hall, many of us wearing white sports coats, victims of listening to too much Mary Robbins, took our date's coat to the check booth, and then introduced our date, shaking hands with the other boys. We learned the delicate art of small talk, things that the girls could talk about too, except for Ricky Nelson; and we learned to forgive the kids from other schools for not being Union kids.

Whiting Hall

THE LONGEST WALK

Television talk show host Phil Donohue had New York Mets ace pitcher Tom Seaver on his show one day. "The longest walk," Donohue said, "is from home plate back to the bench after you have just struck out." He was wrong.

The longest walk was back across the dance floor at Whiting Hall, after you had just struck out. It was one thing to go with a date, someone you took and who was supposed to dance with you. But if it was a Friday night dance, Ernie Fields and *In the Mood* and you had gone by yourself, it was much more intimidating. The girls lined up on the wall by the widows overlooking Seventh Street, the boys on the opposite wall and somehow, we had to bridge that great gap across the middle.

"The girl over there."

"Where?" "The one in the blue sweater, she's looking at you. Go ask her."

"I dunno man. Are you sure?"

"Yeah, go for it."

"Why don't you."

"I can't dance."

"Okay then, here I go."

And we would begin the long walk across the floor, to the other side. Walking, slowly, practicing.

"Would you dance to like with me? Uh, I mean, would you like to dance with me?"

"Would you like to dance with me?" repeated over and over until, we were there, standing in front of a dream, demur, eyes cast downward, painfully shy and we said,

"Were you at the football game?"

"Think it'll rain?"

"I got to ride in a Corvette."

Anything but, "Would you like to dance with me?"

"Why do the girls dance together?" a friend asked me. It was because most of us were too scared to ask them to dance.

It was a long walk over to the girls; it was a longer walk back if you did ask and were told, "No."

Eventually we learned somehow for most of us fathered children; a much more intimidating prospect.

KING OF THE WILD FRONTIER

F ess Parker, who had appeared in a movie called *Them*, caught the attention of Walt Disney, who cast him as *Davy Crockett: King of the Wild Frontier*. He quickly became my hero, and I emulated him as best I could, even picking up a slight Tennessee accent since I didn't know Mr. Parker was from Texas. *The Ballad of Davy Crockett*, sung by Tennessee Ernie Ford became popular and all of us sang it, over and over and... Soon, coon skin caps, buck skin jackets and Ol' Betsy rifles were selling everywhere, and we were all little Davy Crocketts.

My mother told me that Fess Parker was coming to Tulsa, to my uncle's store, and asked me if I would like to go meet him. Would I? I could hardly wait. My uncle, through my grandfather Max Harris's side, owned a department store called Froug's. Like many of my relatives, I had only met him one time and was told to call him Uncle Froug. Like my Uncle Ray, he was older than Uncle Bud Lessert, but he was a nice man.

The day we were to go, my mother got me up early, and I dressed in my buck skin, fringed jacket, my coon skin cap with tail, my faux buckskin trousers and I loaded up Ol' Betsy and my plastic powder horn. I was ready to meet Fess

Parker. The old Chevy had an unusually productive day, and we reached Tulsa without our customary delay in Skiatook, without visiting the people we did not know but who had taken us into their home and shared sandwiches with us when we broke down in front of their house. We arrived and parked and then went over to the department store where we were to wait for him and...there must have been ten thousand Davy Crockett's dressed just like I was. It was worse than waiting in line to see Santa Claus, and there was only one Fess Parker. My mother asked me, probably with hope, if I would like to just skip it and go to Mohawk Park instead. "No," I declared. "We've come all this way [as though I really thought I had traipsed from Tennessee to Texas to see him] and I ain't a'leavin' until I seen him." I said in my Tennessee accent. Her heavy sigh meant that we would stay, and I would see my first real hero.

    I eased into the line and visited with other boys as we moved along, Ol' Betsy to our shoulders. Talking about the movie and about how we would have done at the Alamo made it move a little faster and soon, I could see him, his coon skin cap rising above a platoon of bouncing Ol' Betsy's. He was tall, good looking and just a turn or so ahead. Then we were moving closer and closer and then, I was only a few boys away from him. I pulled Ol' Betsy up straight, stood as tall as I could and moved up to the next position. Then, I was standing right in front of him, a real movie star—although I didn't have a clue where movies were made—and I was looking up at him, the tallest man I had ever seen.

    "Howdy. I'm Fess Parker," he said in a thick Texas drawl as he extended his hand towards me. I took his hand, looked up at him and froze. I just looked at him, disbelieving that I was standing there, touching him, the man that to me *was* Davy Crockett. He pumped my arm, smiled and removed his hand, ready for the next Davy Crockett behind me, and someone gently nudged the speechless boy that I had become along with the crowd.

PAWHUSKA CHARACTERS

Attorney Bill Hall told me that when he moved to Pawhuska in 1968, the town was colorful and full of characters to him, even though he had grown up in a small Oklahoma town himself. Bill told me that he would go into The Manhattan Café for lunch and he would find cowboys dressed in working gear, even to the point of having blood on a shirt or pants. They might be wearing chaps still, and some might have spurs on. There would be several Indians in the restaurant, and sometimes they would be wearing traditional Indian dress. Pawhuska was full of characters all right.

THE OLD MAN

We called him The Old Man, and if a boy said that, we knew he was talking about Henry Roberts. Henry bought the pool hall when I was about fifteen, and most of us soon knew who he was. He was a bit of a country philosopher and character at the same time. I always thought he was older than he was because he just seemed older. He always had gray hair, and he wore a khaki shirt and pants outfit every day that I saw him. He could seem a little cranky sometimes, but he was very kind at heart and cared about every one of us. A game of pool cost $.25 and sometimes, if we didn't have the money, Henry let us play on credit. As soon as I had enough to cover my debt to him I paid him. He never once badgered me to be paid, and I'm not sure if he kept a ledger; he just seemed to trust us. Keeping honest with Henry was a matter of trust. Thanksgiving and Christmas days, when Pawhuska was all but closed, Henry opened the pool hall for us—unless it was Sunday. Henry closed on Sunday, all the time I knew him. When we spoke to him, we called him either Henry or Old Man. He was more friend than anything else; we treated him as one.

THE BICYCLE KING

There was a family in Pawhuska, and they were often treated poorly by other people. I made fun of them right along with other boys, and I am embarrassed about it today but I can't take it back.

One of the boys was named Walter and he rode a bicycle, just like we did. Only Walter might have been twenty-six or so when we were twelve. He loved his bicycle, and he took exceptional care of it. It was, for the most part, his only means of transportation. I don't know if he worked, probably not at a regular job but years later, I know he did work for the sanitation department in Bartlesville, Oklahoma.

Walter had a 26-inch frame with white-wall tires, black fenders and a basket on the handlebars. He also had mud flaps, several horns, and a long whip, like an antenna, that rose from the back, and he had a raccoon tail topping it all off. It may have been from Walter that we learned to put cards in the spokes to make a motorcycle sound. He was usually friendly, if you stopped to talk to him, spoke loudly, and I think he made up many things. He was faster on a bicycle than anyone I have ever seen, and he rode it everywhere. He could be seen at the Pig Stand and just a little later out by the football stadium completely on the other side of Pawhuska. He loved trucks and would race them pulling down with his arm for them to blast their loud truck horns. I saw truck drivers who smiled and waved at him good naturedly, and I think many of them knew about him and some actually did know Walter. My mother and I were in Wynona one day and when we exited the café, there sat Walter on his bicycle, ten miles from Pawhuska.

We boys often talked with him although none of us became true friends with him. The truth is that I don't know if Walter was slow or just eccentric. Whatever he was, he was a true Pawhuska character.

FOUR ROSES

We took trash out to the alley that was between Main and Sixth Streets and put it into one of three 55-gallon metal drums stationed there. One morning as I was about to discard household trash into the drum, I heard a noise which startled me. I froze for a moment, holding the paper sack suspended above the rim and then on the other side of the drum, where he had been sleeping, a man slowly rose. He was holding his head and moaning softly. "Where am I?" he asked. He smiled faintly. I told him where he was, and we talked a little, then he began to wonder down the alley. He did not seem to be injured, just disheveled and smelly. I was eleven then and disconcerted over my meeting with him, so I told my grandmother about the man. I was still a little shaken, but she seemed calm. "That's Four Roses," she told me. He was a man who drank too much, too often, and was known by everyone. I grew up seeing him make similar ghostly appearances from time to time. He never harmed anyone, except himself. I had gone to the navy and returned and there was still Four Roses. My California wife took some time adjusting to the idea of him, that he was so well known and yet lived the life style he did. One day, my step-father, Art Brave told me that Four Roses had quit drinking. I had seen him go into a bar so I questioned Art, and he told me that Four Roses did go to bars but he only drank soft drinks. He was a decent man and I was glad that he stopped. What was his real name? I never knew and maybe it was Four Roses, but I had always assumed that he got the name from his favorite whiskey, Four Roses.

WINDY

I was in Irby's Drugstore with my mother one day, looking at comic books, and I had picked out a few to buy. As I presented them to the young woman behind the counter, a man tapped me on the shoulder. "Let me get those," he said. He was well dressed, slacks, a nice shirt with a bolo tie and a jacket. A small, tan cowboy hat crowned his head and he seemed elegant to me. He paid for my two comic books and then held out a nickel to me; I accepted it, thanked him and watched him shuffle out the door, humming tunelessly. That was my introduction to George "Windy" Garrett, the great story teller, as some called him. I never heard one of his stories but I heard about them, which is why someone dubbed him Windy. He was one of those men who seemed to be one age. He seemed older that first meeting but he never aged all the time I knew him. He could engage you in a spirited argument, and he got very excited sometimes, raising his voice and drawing attention. The first time I experienced the word eccentric, George Garrett was my mental model to which I attached the word so that I could remember it. Late in life, he backed out of a parking spot downtown and straight in to the Chief of Police, Emil Hunt's, official car. George lost his driving privileges then, and he never forgave Mr. Hunt. One day we saw a frightened lady sitting in her car, a man beating on the roof and telling her, "He took my driver's license! How do you expect a man like me to get around without a car? What's the world coming to?" and on he went. She might have been from out of town. Maybe he thought he knew her, but George had to tell the story and speak to the injustice of Emil Hunt taking his horse away from him. Everyone called him Windy, but he did not like to be called Windy to his face. "Windy!" he would explode. "My name is George and don't you forget it." He was always a wonderful man to me.

LOUISA VICTORIA HARDY LESSERT

I had to look no further than my own family to find interesting characters for my grandmother, Louise, was a character in her own right. Once we had a television, she had favorite programs, perhaps suspect in an Indian woman of her age for she was probably around fifty plus then. She loved wrestling and rarely missed a Saturday match. Her favorite wrestler was a small, athletic man who wrestled as Argentina Zuma. She hated The Great Bolo, as most of us did for he was the evil incarnate then. He wore black trunks and a black ski-mask that covered all but his eyes and mouth and the real issue then was, would the Great Bolo be unmasked tonight? My grandmother was a fiery, emotional viewer, and she would often take her shoe off and throw it at the television.

I was used to it and I would simply go get her shoe and return it to her for the next time Bolo cheated, offering silent prayers of thanks that the television still worked. But sometimes, I would have a friend over and I had not prepared him for her verbal outburst, her favorite word for The Great Bolo—which I will leave out—and the accompanying airborne shoe. It scared whoever was there, at first. Fortunately, she only reached that level of excitement about three times a match. She would be upset for days if Bolo won the match.

I thought it was real too so I can't blame her.

I saw my grandmother as this lady of her age with all the attributes expected of one so I was surprised to one day learn that my grandmother had been a flapper girl. My uncle, Bud Lessert, was visiting and said something about the Charleston, a dance from my grandmother's time, and she promptly stood and performed one to show Bud how it was done.

She was a heavy smoker and smoked only one brand of cigarettes, Lucky. It was Lucky Strike in a red and white package with the famous L.S.M.F.T which supposedly stood for Lucky Strike Means Fine Tobacco. At twelve, we boys had created other things that it might stand for. She bought them by the carton, and at some point I was able to free a package or two and hide them in the tree house behind Chunker's house. Louise was famous for holding a Lucky in one position for so long that it formed an ash the length of the cigarette. That was when she was concentrating on a television program. Ola Mae once asked her, "Aunt Louise, how do you do that?" "Do what, Olie?" "Hold your cigarette like that." And Olie tried to do the same thing, without success. I came home one day from school and caught the distinct odor of a Roi-tan cigar and thought, "Uncle Bud is here." Nay, my grandmother had read that cigarettes were bad for you, so she had taken up cigars in an effort to cut down on smoking. It didn't last long though and she went back to her Luckies.

My Uncle Bud Lessert was her step-son from her marriage to Chuck Lessert, and she loved Bud and his sister Catherine. Uncle Bud lived in Oklahoma City and visited occasionally and almost always unannounced. Perhaps it was after he got off work and drove in but he would arrive late, often after eleven o'clock at night and be treated royally. If Louise was still awake, she would make coffee, sit down with him and light up a Lucky and talk long into the night. I might wake the next morning and find Uncle Bud asleep on the couch, exhausted, and I would barely get to see him before I started off to school. He might be gone by the time I got home or he might stay a day or two. He was always welcome, and my grandmother tried to kill him by feeding him. He told me once, that no matter what time he arrived, she always fed him and not just a sandwich. She might start an entire meal for him and then she always asked, "Did you get enough Bud?" The eternal struggle between grown men and the women who mother them went on then, as it did with my mother and me later.

Louise asked him one time why he was the way he was and he told her that if she would read a book that he had mentioned she would understand. My Uncle Bud was gay before it was fashionable. It didn't change how anyone felt about him, but it was a fact of life in our family. The good news is that every family has someone who is gay or something; some just don't know it—yet.

Louise was superstitious and every meal began with a worried look, and then she threw salt over her shoulder. I threw salt over my shoulder too but just because she had done so. In the days when she would still walk downtown, I would go with her. We never went under a ladder because it was bad luck. A black cat crossed the sidewalk in front of us once and I was kneeling, calling, "Here kitty, kitty," and coaxing it towards me when she grabbed me and told me that we would have to walk the long way round because a black cat had crossed our path. That meant we went completely around the block when we were just feet away from our destination.

After we had the 1956 Oldsmobile my mother was taking us to Bartlesville and my grandmother was with us, in the back seat. As we approached the down slope of the highest hill on Highway Sixty, my grandmother suddenly called out, "Bettie; Stop! Quick!" and my mother came to stop at the side of the road. "What's wrong mother?" she asked. "I ain't driving down this hill. I'll meet you at the bottom." And she did.

Louise loved the comedians of the mid-1950's television and wrote to most of them: She sent Arthur Godfrey and Jackie Gleason Indian cook books and proudly showed everyone the letters of thanks that she received. We waited for months for the shows to exhibit the cookbook, which they did not, but she never lost faith that they would someday. George Gobel was her favorite, and we watched his show faithfully because, she controlled the television.

She was either very shrewd about money or very naïve, and I'm not sure which. She shopped like this: She would call Bivins' furniture store and tell them in a broad way what furniture she would like to see. Two or three men would arrive with furniture, bring it in and place it where she directed them. After moving it around, a piece in, a piece out and so on, she would tell them that she wanted to try it like that for awhile, and so it stayed in the house. If she liked it well enough, she called Mr. Bivins and told him that she would keep it and asked him to charge it; she never once asked the price. If she liked it, it stayed; that was it. When she received her payment, she paid what she could. One time, she called another furniture store and had them deliver new furniture in the same way as did Mr. Bivins. But this store wanted to take her existing furniture in as a trade. She saw no problem with that, and it was a done deal; we had new furniture with the old furniture as a trade—only the furniture she had just traded had not yet been paid for so she had double payments to two different stores. It is easy to see how she got into financial problems now and then. The other furniture store quickly sold the traded furniture, and Mr. Bivins did not know that she was paying on furniture that she no longer possessed.

When someone got something new, she wanted to try it. She learned about air conditioning, and soon we had a new air conditioner; but it was an evaporative cooler, what we often called a swamp cooler. It was a large metal box that was outside of the house, held a large and noisy fan and had fiber pads on the walls that were wetted continuously, usually by a secondary connection off of the house faucet. The fan moved outside air through the wet pads and cooled it. The cooled air flowed into the house, and it worked fine except for the fan noise, which could be compensated for by turning up all sounds that you wanted to hear and talking loudly, and the humidity. Everything in the house gradually became saturated with water. I had a set of encyclopedias which became so jammed in the book case that I could not get them out until the cooling season was over and things began to dry out.

She was generous to a fault, and she loved the Catholic Priest, Father Joe. He was walking by one day, in front of Jessie's boarding house, when she saw him and sent me after him. She was so excited that I was concerned about her, and I transferred my excitement to Father Joe who ran with me back to the house. "Would you bless our house, Father Joe?" That was all she had wanted. Our house had been blessed by Father Joe and other priests so many times that I know it has gone to house heaven and is probably where the Saints live.

As Father Joe knelt in front of her, she saw that he had holes in the soles of his shoes. "Thank you, Father Joe and when you go by the Hub Clothiers go in and get a pair of shoes for yourself and put them on my account." I don't know if he did but she called them as soon as he was out and made the deal for him to get shoes. She was a devout Catholic who rarely went to church but she believed. I was told that she had never been married in the Catholic Church, just in case. I think that Just in Case was the fear that the marriage would fail and she would be left in a state of sin so she just didn't marry there. Her first husband was an Osage named Paul Cedar, and I was told that she dearly loved him. I asked Pan why they separated, and Pan told me that he died. It's hard to make a marriage work after that. She was married to Max Harris, my grandfather, Chuck Lessert and other men.

At my grandmother's funeral, my mother said, "I am so upset." "Why," asked Uncle Ray, Louise's brother. "That woman said that mother had been married thirteen times."

"Well, that's a lie," Uncle Ray said with pride. "She was married more than any thirteen times."

BUT WAIT—THERE'S MORE!

My grandmother was an early victim of television advertising. For weeks, she had seen the advertisement on television for a food preparation tool called The Veg-O-Matic. For a low price, we were offered the Veg-O-Matic, four or five specialized cutter blades which could cut carrots, potatoes, ice cream and a host of foods. The advertisement grew on you. How could it not? It was on every night, late, perhaps during The Tonight Show; it was low priced and came with several accessories to make it better:

Wait—there's more. There was always something special, such as an umbrella, a pencil sharpener, a new Buick, or something and eventually, my grandmother ordered one.

Once the order was in, and it was sent by mail with a check—allow four to six weeks for delivery—we waited. I was not as anxious as I had been when I had ordered a working miniature of the USS Nautilus, a decoder ring, a secret signal lamp, a fort and accompanying toy soldiers, a deed to land in Alaska, and other things from cereal boxes but still, I was a little anxious. One day it arrived, a large box with a photograph of the Ronco Veg-O-Matic on the side and my grandmother opened it, removed the unit, its blades and whatever the extra promised item was.

She was a wonderful cook and liked to make things so, with the available blades for Julianne potatoes, diced tomatoes, sliced cucumbers and a host of cuts, she made everything she could think of. Unlike some things, she really did use this thing, and we all benefited from it. The best thing for me was French fried potato cuts since we usually got those at a hamburger stand.

She believed that anything said on television, or printed in a newspaper, had to be true or you couldn't print it. I fell into that too, perhaps because of her, perhaps because I'm naturally gullible. Over the years, we wound up with a lot of things advertised on television that didn't quite work out; but, those that did were a testament to my grandmother's character and her belief in the American way, even if it included The Ronco Veg-O-Matic.

If I see one today, or an advertisement from the past, even if it is making fun of the Veg-O-Matic a little, it brings back fond memories of my grandmother Louise, a character in her own right.

ROSIE

My grandmother, Louise, often hired an elderly lady that lived a few doors from the Hughes house to help her with her housework. My grandmother must have been approaching sixty then, and Rosie must have been older still.

It was interesting to observe them, for they both liked to gossip and tired of housework quickly. There would be a little dusting, the vacuum cleaner would roar for a bit and be dragged about, and then one of them would suggest a short break. All the time they were on break, Rosie was running up billable hours to my grandmother, but they never rushed. Louise would fix a pot of coffee or tea and light a Lucky while they talked and gossiped away. Sometimes, she would turn on the television and they would watch and enjoy a snack with the coffee.

Thursday was cleaning day each week, and I don't think they got much housework done, but it gave my grandmother needed company of someone about her age. Rosie spoke loudly and had a bit of a hoarse voice. The unusual thing about Rosie was that she was a black woman, or colored lady, as my grandmother referred her, and she lived in a white section. The house she occupied was behind a larger house, and it may have been classified as a servant's quarter.

In the middle to late 1950's, Pawhuska's white and black populations were separated by Bird Creek as it meandered around the south of Pawhuska, and few black people lived on the north and east sides of the Swinging Bridge. I never heard anyone question that Rosie lived there, and that it was all right. I never really thought about or questioned it, and I didn't realize then that the legal system actually supported two Pawhuskas.

Even when we began integration in the Pawhuska school system, most of our black population lived in the same area as before. Interestingly, white people could move into the black area, but black people could not so easily move into the white area.

Rosie became more of a friend to my grandmother than did many of the people she had known longer.

JULIA

My aunt, Julia Griffin, was much like her sister, my grandmother Louise, yet she was different. She chose to live on the other side of the swinging bridge and purchased two lots there. This was in the area called Colored Town and very few white people lived there. Julia was, like my grandmother, an Osage Indian but in this case, she made sure that you knew she was white. Julia used the same methods of shopping by telephone as my grandmother; she and Louise talked to each other every day. Their telephone conversations were long and gossipy, and they probably said the same thing every day. One of their behaviors that I marveled at was the ability to return to an interrupted telephone conversation in the exact spot that it had been interrupted, just as though one had pushed the pause button on an audio tape player. There was never, "Now what was I saying?" or "Remind me what we were talking about." It was a continuation of the conversation at the exact point it had been interrupted.

Aunt Julia was not very trusting and kept a .22 caliber pistol by her side. When ever there was a knock at the door, she rose, picked up the pistol and answered the door with the pistol at the ready. All of her neighbors were accustomed to it, and so was I. My grandmother sent me on an errand to Aunt Julia's one evening when Ronnie Havens was with me. He had never met my Aunt Julia and I wanted to introduce him so I asked him to come with me to the door. I knocked and replied "Stevie" to her, "Who is it?" She opened the door and I looked into the pistol held above my head and I said, "Aunt Julia, this is my friend Ronnie..." and he wasn't there. I looked beyond the car and sheltered behind a small tree that offered little protection was Ronnie. "She's got a gun," he said. After some assurances that this was normal behavior for my aunt, he came back and I made the introductions, but I don't think Ronnie ever went with me again.

Aunt Julia had truly unique furniture for no matter how much money she had, she feared a return of The Great Depression. All of her furniture, except for a couch and a few chairs, was made from wooden crates that were used to ship oranges; she had Soderstrom's Grocery use them to deliver groceries to her house so they had a dual purpose.

THE MYSTERY LADY

I only saw her in a fleeting way as she drove her blue Buick convertible about town. The Buick was often jammed with teen-age boys, and there were unsubstantiated stories about her, but she really did exist, and conversations with others who lived in Pawhuska then have confirmed that for me. Someone probably knew who she really was, and why she chose Pawhuska, but none of my friends knew her whole story; none of us knew the truth either.

She was attractive with long black hair. I never saw her close enough to be able to describe her more than that. Others did though, as she was often at the Country Club sunning by the pool in a tiny swimming suit, the kind that got noticed and commented on, in 1960, by the gentlemen of Pawhuska. One boy said that his father suggested that he not look at her. Right.

I have been told that she lived in a small trailer house near Williams Park in a fashionable neighborhood. I may have seen it then, but I do not recall it well. Stories told of her answering the door in nothing but a barrette and sunglasses, and she was rumored to hold wild parties where the boys attended and drank beer.

I could never get an invitation, so I can't speak to the truth.

I don't think she was employed, and her Buick, a four-door convertible, was about a 1954 model so it wasn't new. The trailer house that I saw was of medium size and not fancy. She may have had an independent income, because she seemed to have adequate to surplus free time.

She seemed to have arrived mysteriously, lived there, and then left just as mysteriously, but she certainly fueled rumors and conjecture while she lived in Pawhuska.

PAYMENT

It is difficult to write about my grandmother and Pawhuska without mentioning payment. Someone from Pawhuska and especially from the time of the 1950's and 1960's knows what payment was. For those who are not from Pawhuska, payment deserves a brief explanation.

In 1906, federal legislation divided the mineral rights of the Osage Tribe between the existing 2,230 members of the nation. My grandmother, Louisa Victoria Hardy was allottee #1289 and listed with the name of Louisa V. Hardy-Panther. As oil production was developed within the Osage lands, the members of the nation were paid quarterly from any income that the nation received. That became known as payment.

The economy of Pawhuska, and indeed Osage County, was influenced by the payments to members of the nation and most Pawhuska businesses allowed Osage members to pay their debts at each payment of every three months instead of weekly or monthly.

One of my cousins says that her family often lived "payment to payment." My grandmother did too only, my mother's income from a regular job working for Bell Telephone Company supplemented my grandmother's income and was really what got us from week to week.

TELEVISION

We didn't have a television for some years but, fortunately, we lived directly across the street from Jessie Garcia, Donna Poulton's grandmother. Jessie owned a large rooming house and was one of the first in our neighborhood to get a television. I remember many things about the television in a general way. It was a large wooden box with a very small screen. The world was black and white on it and with considerable fuzziness. You could tell who had televisions then just by driving down the street and looking up to the roof to see the television antennas. I suppose that someone could have bought an antenna and installed it just to make people *think* that they had a television, but there was probably not much of that.

Donna and I and Bobby Hughes were great friends and we did a lot of things together; we could sometimes be found in front of the television. It was difficult to watch it because of the small screen and there were certain favored watching places in the room.

Jessie bought a magnifying glass stand to put in front of the screen and that was Jessie's and one or two other honored people's place to watch it. I tried it once and learned that you had to sit right in front of it to see the screen without distortion. I preferred the floor. We didn't watch television all week but only on some nights and then someone made a large batch of popcorn and everyone shared in it. Something called Jiffy-Pop came along then with an aluminum pan and an expanding cap that spiraled upward as the corn popped. A lot of the popcorn was burned, because people didn't want to miss a minute of things like *I Love Lucy* and failed at the constant shaking required and just let it sit there and burn. Sometimes we ate it anyway.

Television programming wasn't good but we had channel 6, KOTV, and channel 2, KVOO from Tulsa. Channel 8, KTUL, was out of Muskogee then and came in weakly so we barely had three stations. This was the early 1950's and television had an odd character about it in that it wasn't on all day—and all night, as it is now.

There were broadcasts in the morning, preceded by a test pattern that I watched without understanding what it was for. Test was a dirty word for me with only one connotation, and I didn't know if we could fail the pattern test or not. Sometime later in the day television went off and did not come back on again until later in the afternoon. The news was on in the evening, and then television went off with rather dignified announcements from the golden throats of stentorian male announcers. "KOTV now concludes its broadcasting day..." and a lot of information that none of us understood followed. Later all stations concluded with Glen Miller's *Moonlight Serenade*.

The news was delivered by just one person then, and one more did the weather, perhaps both sports and weather. Today it takes four to five people to give the same report. I loved early television as simple as it was. I can't remember accurately all of the programs I watched at any given time as they are mixed in my memory. But from those early days with Donna, *Science Fiction Theater* was my favorite and no matter what kind of fight Donna and I had had, I always made up, no matter the cost, to be able to watch it.

Later we got our first television, and I remember

watching *Boston Blackie, The Adventures of Superman, The Lone Ranger, The Cisco Kid, The Mickey Mouse Club, Dragnet*, and my share of cartoons on Saturday morning. I watched *Sky King* and *Fury*. A few times I was stuck home sick during the week, and I watched some soap operas when they were the only thing on in the afternoon. I wasn't sophisticated enough to watch and fully understand some of the great television of the time, the Playhouse 90 type of shows. I watched some but not all of them.

I don't know if things are better today but they are different. We have satellite television with a TiVo receiver, and we have available one hundred eighty stations. Once, in the middle of an arthritis spell that left me unable to do much, I searched desperately for something to watch and finally settled on a movie that I had seen several times but loved so I watched it anyway, intermittently. Was it worse having three stations with difficult choices or one hundred eighty with poor choices? I'm not sure. Maybe if it were all new to me, as it was then, I would think it just as great and mysterious as it was then.

On the other hand, I went to my computer, logged into http://www.lefigaro.fr/ and read the news about France in French straight from the horse's mouth. I could not have done that then. I did not speak French then, but neither was the technology available to access a French news program.

That's not television although I have to recognize it as a kindred cousin. There are several French and Spanish newspapers that I can access and for learning, I go to www.cnn.com and find a popular story and then to the Spanish page and pull down the same story and print both so that I can check my translations and learn more. It's a marvel; yet in some ways, I miss Dave Garroway and J. Fred Muggs and all that went with them. Maybe that's what the test pattern was about after all.

I learned not to read a book all at once. I learned that there is no sin in reading a chapter today and one tomorrow until I have finished the book. When we went to a movie, we didn't have that option. We watched the entire movie, sometimes even paying attention to it, and then went home.

With movies on television, I continued to do that. If I started watching a movie at 10:30 PM, I watched all of it so it became a habit. One night I was watching John Wayne in *She Wore a Yellow Ribbon.* I had started it late and as I began to nod and drift and miss parts of it, I realized that I was recording it on a VCR. I set the timer to shut off and then went to sleep. Even though I could do it, with the technology, it took me a while to break the habit of watching a movie, beginning to end, no matter how tired I was.

EAT OUT OFTEN

Pawhuska had a number of restaurants then with the stellar restaurant being the Manhattan Café. I think it was only two stars and a half on the Michelin scale, but on the Stevie scale, it was four stars.

The Manhattan was downtown, on Main Street and next door to Irby's Drugstore. The front had a white sheltered entrance with a door on the west and east sides before the main door. This protected diners from cold winter winds; when I lived in North Dakota, I often wondered why restaurants there did not have a similar entrance. It was colder in North Dakota.

There was a counter with the swivel stools that I thought were so much fun, and then there were tables with some against the wall next to Irby's. If I couldn't sit at the counter, the tables at the wall were the next best place. Behind the main dining room was a room reserved for the Cattleman's Association and private parties, and it was used for the football team on Friday nights after the ball game.

My favorite meals there were tenderloin of trout and breaded veal cutlets, which I got on special occasions as it was probably the most expensive restaurant in town.

Gordon Hughes had a drive-in called Gordon's that was on Main Street just across from Roy Adkins' garage.

You could go in and order, but most people just drove through and a car hop came out, took your order and returned with the food. Bobby Hughes and I worked there together for awhile, which must have been fun, usually bussing tables and washing dishes. Kay told me that she had to work there because it was her job.

Jessie and Joe Garcia had a café on Ki-He-Kah Street that was next door to Mr. Clements barber shop, and I probably ate there more than I did at the Manhattan. My mother encouraged me to, probably due to the lower prices. Jessie once had her restaurant in her boarding house, and Donna and I would eat there together. Jessie often gave us tortillas—her version of hush puppies—to keep us quiet and out of trouble. My grandmother would ask why I wasn't hungry. Jessie had a juke box in the restaurant, and it was there that I heard Conway Twitty sing It's *Only Make-Believe* for the first time. I remember that because, in his famous opening, he sounded at first like he was going to throw up. I had just eaten a large chicken fried steak with brown gravy, mashed potatoes with brown gravy, and cherry pie with ice-cream; it was excellent but too much, and I did not need encouragement from Mr. Twitty.

There were the Pullman Café, the Crystal Café, Rancher's Café, Brown's Café, the Dairy Queen, the Tastee Freeze, Sally's and Andy's so there were enough restaurants. There was also The Greek's, as everyone knew it, although that was not its official name, and later, Mrs. Looney would add the Red Bud Restaurant on the west side of town.

PIG STAND BOOGEY

The highway out of Pawhuska and towards Ponca City might have been one of the worst roads in Oklahoma. It could have been in the contest. There was a bridge over Bird Creek that was old and narrow and further west, over Clear Creek, was a bridge that made the Bird Creek Bridge look safe and modern. In between the two bridges was a slight jog in the highway and there was the Pig Stand. It was a small drive-in and a teen age hangout before the Dairy Queen became one.

There were always a lot of cars, and a young lady came and took your order and delivered it to you at your car window. If you had a convertible, you parked there, with the top down and played music loudly. It wasn't so bad as most of Pawhuska listened to the same radio station so it was just sharing. The Pig Stand served beer and there were often entertaining fist fights between some of the boys.

The main course was just known as a pig; it was a chopped bar-b-q sandwich on a round hamburger bun with a lot of flavor. It was spicy also, and I loved it; but I sometimes paid for eating two or three of them.

When the new highway was built, some fifty years ago, the Pig Stand moved westward to the end of the four-lane but remained in business. Chunker Brunger honors the original by playing a song that he calls "The Pig Stand Boogey."

EVERYBODY GOES TO THE GREEK'S

In California, a navy friend and native Californian once asked me if I liked Mexican food. "Sure," I told him. "We eat it all the time where I come from." He looked at me, puzzled and said, "I thought you were from Pawhuska, Oklahoma." "I am," I said, proudly. "What Mexican food do you have in Oklahoma?" I quickly enumerated them. "Well, we have chili and tamales." "And...?"

I lived just a short distance from The Greek's and ate there often. It was officially called The Bar-B-Que Inn, but if you asked someone to meet you at the Bar-B-Que Inn, they probably wouldn't understand. Ask them to meet you at the Greeks, and they knew what you meant.

Tom Javellas was The Greek and ran the restaurant, which was next to the telephone office. On Friday and Saturday nights it was where everybody gathered and parking was at a premium. You often had to circle the block or drive around a bit before you could get in. Tom served chili, with or without beans, and with an abundance of oyster crackers. He always had clear glass cruet bottles, with glass stoppers, on the tables. The cruet was filled with vinegar that we used on the chili to thin it a little. Some of the jars had garlic resting in the bottom.

Against the back wall stood a Wurlitzer juke box, with songs $.10 each or three for a quarter. We usually took the quarter option, if we had enough money. I think a bowl of chili was $.65 then; one of my larger friends always had two bowls which left us less money for the Wurlitzer.

My standard for chili came from The Greek's, and it is still the only chili I really like to eat. In North Dakota, chili was served with kidney beans and the first time I ordered it in a restaurant, I pushed it back from the table and the waitress asked, "What's wrong with it?"

"What's wrong with it? It's got kidney beans in it."

"Sure, that's the way chili is made," she said, with a warm smile. I always asked after that and was told, "Sure, that's the way chili is made." My first bowl of chili in North Dakota; and in Montana, South Dakota and Wyoming, was my last. When I was transferred to Texas, the first thing I did was find a restaurant that served chili, a la The Greek.

Tom also served hamburgers, eggs, steaks and other meals, but to me, and almost everyone I knew, it was the chili that kept us coming back. Next to the Pig Stand, I saw more fights just outside of The Greek's than anywhere else.

One evening, Bobby Hughes, Melvin Irvin and I went into the busy restaurant and sat at a booth against the wall and close to the Wurlitzer. Tom came over and told Melvin to leave and I regret to say that he called Melvin something. Bobby stood up and said, "If our friend Melvin goes, then we all go."

Melvin was, and still is, a black man.

Tom shouted, "All of you get out and don't come back." And Tom would not let me back into the restaurant again until, one day, in 1961 when I attempted to go in with someone while wearing my dress blue navy uniform. Actually, I had to be talked into trying it again, and I was afraid and uncertain what would happen. But Tom shook my hand and said, "I'm so proud of you and you can come in my restaurant any time." Tom was a kind man, very sentimental with a rough exterior. He remained my friend from that day on.

THE DAIRY QUEEN

The Dairy Queen was important, not just for food and drink, but as a major part of our social life. The Dairy Queen began as just the small white cinder block building that it was and served only ice cream and drinks. It did not have food service, and there was no inside service. We just placed and received our orders at the window. There were two park picnic tables outside for seating.

Mrs. Alma Hutson opened a trailer behind the Dairy Queen, DQ, as we knew it, and served hamburgers, conies, corn dogs and Frito Pies from there. Later, another section of cinder block with large windows was added and the food service moved into that. A Wurlitzer was added, and the Dairy Queen became a teen age hangout.

The driveway entrance was on the south side and you could continue out through the alley or make the semi-circle and go by the window to see who was inside and then out of the north side. Many times I would be sitting inside and see someone I knew pass through. They might stop and motion me out, or I just went out. We would talk a bit, see who knew what, where something might be happening, and we might spend a good part of the evening together. Sometimes, you might get picked up that way two or three times in an evening.

There were friends that we spent a lot of time with in a

car, but we did not know where they lived. We had never been to their house; they had never been to ours. We would meet at the Dairy Queen or the pool hall, or Whiting Hall, and go from there.

If you ordered a Four hundred, you got chocolate milk; an eight hundred was double chocolate milk and a suicide was just about everything in one cup. A suicide had Coke, Dr. Pepper, Pepsi, and 7-UP and the flavor varied from pretty good to yuck depending on how it was mixed.

To attest to our relatively good driving skills at the time, most of us made the trip around the Dairy Queen without hitting another car. It was a small driveway, and cars were parked anywhere that a car could be parked so it was a narrow gauntlet that we ran. Few of us made it up and down both drives without at least bumping the rear of the car on the concrete slope of the driveway.

Bill and Helen Simpson ran the Dairy Queen for most of my high school career. When I was stationed in Long Beach, California, they moved there and were very supportive friends for me; a home away from home with a lot of Pawhuska connection.

THE TASTEE-FREEZE

The Tastee-Freeze was built after the Dairy Queen and was on Lynn Avenue and 12th Street, so it was close to the school. It served about the same fare as the Dairy Queen, but it was smaller. It rescued many of us from cafeteria food.

One day a boy who was a junior had his 1956 Ford parked on the north side. He had his feet up and the driver side door open and was listening to his radio as he downed a hamburger and malt when a boy on a bicycle came down the hill yelling for people to get out of the way; his chain had come off and he had no brakes. He turned to miss a group of girls and ran into the blue Ford knocking the driver's door off of the hinges. He created a very stunned angry junior that day, but he survived since it was an accident; it was a close call.

GABE'S

The official name was the Husky Grill but we all knew it as Gabe's. It was a small café just across from the high school on Lynn and 15th. It was open for breakfast, and I had a few coffees and rolls between band sessions then, but lunch was the major event. Gabe started preparing in the morning with two stainless steel containers that he filled with hamburgers wrapped in aluminum foil. One held hamburgers with everything and the other hamburgers without onions. We crowded in, yelled our orders and exchanged our cash for hamburgers and a drink. There were no diet drinks then; just Cokes, Pepsi, 7-UP and a few other drinks.

What was always amazing was how many students Gabe served in such a short time. Gabe was ahead of his time and heralded the fast foods of McDonald's later to come. He was too busy for us to get to know him then but years later, when he had gone back to work at Reda Pump Company in Bartlesville, I did get to know Gabe, Gabriel Villaseñor, and found him to be a really funny man.

HENRY'S

There was a bar-be-que café, which served the best bar-b-que in the world, just south of the bridge on Highway 99,. The structure was small, made of cinder blocks, and had little space for parking, but it didn't matter. We didn't go there for the atmosphere, but for the food. The black gentleman with gray hair, who cooked and served was friendly, always smiling, and often gave you a discount on what you ordered. It had the atmosphere of his personality, but what he did with food was an art form. I liked his chicken best, and sometimes ate more than I should have. It was difficult to stop once you got started on his chicken. The old building remains, but the aroma that wafted out and onto the highway, pulling you in is long gone.

SALLY'S

No reference to the restaurants and cafés of Pawhuska would be complete without mentioning Sally's. If her small café along Ki-Hi-Kah Avenue is not an institution, then Sally certainly is. She began working in the café in its early years, purchased it as her own, and for more generations that most of us want to be known, has been feeding the people of Pawhuska. At an advanced age, she still goes in and makes her signature tamales.

I stopped in one day because my brother's truck was outside, and I needed to talk with him. I introduced myself to her, only to find that she remembered me from the days on Prudom, when her daughter Andy visited Grandpa Murphy and played with the children in the neighborhood. Sally's Café is small but mighty; witness all of the great cafes now gone while she is, literally, still cooking.

THE NEW CARS ARE HERE!

Pawhuska has no new car dealers, and it may be difficult for young people living there today to think of Pawhuska as once teeming with car dealers. In the 1950's, next to the post office was the Ford dealer and directly across the street was a dealer who sold Plymouth, Dodge and Chrysler cars and Dodge trucks. On the corner of Main and Leahy Streets just east of the Packing House Market was Shook's Cadillac and Oldsmobile dealership and just down the street south was Ira Lemaster's Pontiac dealership. Just behind the Safeway store was Eddie King's Buick dealership. Next to the Phillips 66 station that was once leased by Felix Lawless was a Quonset hut building that sold Lincoln and Mercury cars and Ford tractors, and on west Main Street was the Chevrolet dealer who sold Chevrolet cars and trucks and GMC trucks.

Pawhuska was booming in the 1950's, and my friends and I were boys of about eleven years of age when we became interested in cars as we planned for our future and what we would drive. Of course, driving age was still about five or six years off at the time, but that didn't discourage us. And we were thinking of new cars; few of us were going to have a new car at sixteen.

We always knew about cars, something about them, but at a certain age our thoughts had turned to them in dreamy ways. Cars in the early 1950's were still influenced by the end of the Second World War and just before the 1950's began, cars usually came in one color and were still a little boxy and uninspiring. That wasn't true of all cars, but it was in a general way. Cars might not have been safe but they looked safe. The 1950's brought new paints and painting techniques so the colors were improving, and more colors were being offered.

Ford Motor Company introduced the 1964 ½ Mustang during the middle of the year and that changed how new car models were introduced. But before that, the new models introduction was a celebrated event, not just in Pawhuska but virtually everywhere. It was a standard release date and all of them were pretty close to each other if not on the same date.

Each September brought to Pawhuska not only a new school year, but the introduction of the new car models; we awaited them as eagerly as many of our parents did, perhaps more so for they had learned patience. We had not. It was a special time as most of the dealers brought the new models in under canvas and unloaded them in secrecy at night, so that the first glimpse the public had was a major event.

Mike Avery and Bobby Hughes and I were particularly eager about wanting to see them and one of us would call the other or go by each other's house. We would march down and try to find out as much as we could. Bobby was more aggressive, perhaps because his father, Gordon Hughes, had some inside information because of his law enforcement duties or maybe Bobby just bugged the dealer.

He was our best informed conspirator though, and he would call me and tell me that the Fords were coming in, and off Bobby and I went. He was correct but too early because the Fords were in but still under wraps. The delivery trailer was backed up into the alley that ran beside the Ford dealer and a man was backing one of the cars off; they had lifted the canvas and pinned it up for the driver to see and the only thing visible was part of the door; the driver leaned out as he backed the canvas hidden car down the metal ramp and into the alley. Even then we could smell the undeniable aroma of new car.

One of them shooed us away with a laugh, and we retreated to the post office grounds and watched as much as we could from behind a small hedge. We could smell the new paint of the engine as it slowly roasted while they maneuvered the car around, and then it was inside the garage and the door was closed.

By that time several other boys had joined us, and Mike Avery arrived on his bicycle, dressed in his black motorcycle jacket a la Marlon Brando. We talked excitedly and speculated on the shape and style of the new Ford. Someone said that they had seen it, and there were hardly any changes. This was the 1956 Ford model year, and he was right that year. The obvious difference between the 1955 and 1956 Ford was the shape of the signal and parking lights on the front and minor changes on the tail lights. The paint and trim were slightly different too, but the car was largely unchanged.

That didn't take away from our excitement as hearing about it was one thing; seeing it was quite another, and we had to see it for ourselves. The last car was unloaded and the transport moved out onto Sixth Street and drove away; the men who had unloaded and stored the cars began to drift off a few at a time until there were only one or two left. The lights were still on inside and Bobby got the idea of trying to look inside through the garage windows so he, Mike and I drifted over, actually we sneaked over, to the large garage door and I bolstered Bobby up to the window where he could see. My turn would be next. It was getting late, and we were getting nervous because, although we weren't doing anything wrong, it *felt* wrong. Bobby began to ooh and ah, and Mike and I were both asking him, "What? What is it? Can you see a car? What's it look like?" "Yeah," he said, "I see it, they've got the tarp up." "Let me see!" Mike called and jumped high, trying to see through the glass and hit the door with his body.

I became very nervous and dropped Bobby who fell against the wooden door and slid down it—his face did—as he shouted things I won't write here.

There was a clamor inside, we heard a man shout and there were footsteps, and as the door began to come up, we did what all boys that age do when confronted with a situation. We ran.

Mike jumped on the bicycle and peddled north through the alley, and Bobby and I ran as fast as we could, in front of the post office, down the street past the funeral home and to his house, frightened, yet laughing as we ran, in that "we got away with that one" way that boys have.

We were scared and breathless when we arrived and his mother asked us if there was a problem. We still had that guilt about us and we said no without satisfying her suspicions. Bobby and I lay on the floor for a while in the Hughes front room as we watched television; then the phone rang and I was asked for, so I went home.

With Bobby and me, we never went home as neither of us seemed to have a sense of time so there was always the phone call, "Would you please send Bobby/Stevie home now?"

It was late, not news late yet, but late enough that I was exhausted; and I slept the night through, scared or not. Bobby called me the next morning and I met him at his house, and we walked to school together, still excited about the cars. I had a hundred questions for him and he teased me with glimpses of what he said he had seen although he had a great imagination, and he might not have been telling me the whole truth. I was ready to kill him anyway.

We were still concerned that we might be in trouble for we knew that the men had seen us while we watched the cars unload, and they probably knew who we were. We did not yet realize that we were unimportant to them.

Mike Avery brought it up again as he said he had heard things, and we were very nervous; Mike liked to exaggerate. My grandmother had a stock answer to any bad behavior, and that was that we would be sent to Stringtown. I didn't know where or what it was but she had made it sound so ominous that it was one of my worst fears. It had a sobering effect on me, and now Mike was saying Stringtown too.

There was a man that we were more afraid of than any other and that was Mike Poulis, who was the town constable. There were the city police, the highway patrol, and the sheriff. But Mike had a special role that we thought was to pick up truant boys, and he seemed to harass and threaten us more than any one else. Mike was older, heavy set and gruff in nature. He always seemed particularly tough to me, and he would tell us that he was going to catch us someday and put us in jail.

That was on a good day when we were just hanging around The Greeks and not really doing anything. When I was older and could look at things differently, I decided that Mike was probably a good man and was just teasing us for the most part. But he was the one we were scared of then and the one we did not want to see after the new car caper. Between going to class and having fun at recess, we watched out for Mike who usually did drive by Union once a day.

By the end of that long school day, we had not been picked up and sent to Stringtown. One of the boys had told us that Ford was offering *free* coffee and doughnuts to come by and see the new Fords, so we forgot our danger and off we went to see the new Fords.

We did not understand that they probably meant the

doughnuts for paying customers, who could *buy* a new Ford but, free coffee and doughnuts, well—who could refuse that?

Decent, God fearing adults probably only took one doughnut each but eleven year old boys took you at your word when you said free coffee and doughnuts so, Bobby Hughes, Mike Avery, Butch Daniels and a few others and I met at Ford where we took them up on their generous offer. I was not addicted to coffee then so I drank just a little coffee, and I treated it with real sugar, six lumps, please, and a half jar of half and half cream. But this was special because we had doughnuts and the coffee was for dunking, not drinking so it didn't matter how much coffee I got.

There were no adults with us but we were all experts in automobiles. Butch Daniels was the automobile expert *par excellence* and to demonstrate that, he began to kick the tires on one of the new floor models. I had great respect for Butch and his knowledge of cars so I kicked a tire or two; and then Butch was under the hood of one car, and he told us that it had a Thunderbird engine. I was very impressed by that although I had no idea what it meant, but it sounded good. We had all seen a Thunderbird but we didn't really understand engine size and some of the technical aspects as well as we would later.

With sticky hands from sugary doughnuts we each sat behind the steering wheel of the new car and then loaded ourselves up with brochures about the new Fords and we left, still talking about the Thunderbird engine and how fast it could go. We knew it could go fast because the speed indicator said 120 and several of us still believed that it meant exactly that. We had been in a Chevrolet earlier where the speed indicator said only 110 so we knew that the Ford was faster than the Chevrolet. The smell of the new cars was exotic, and it was not only in the cars themselves but all over the showroom and new car fever was in us; we became grand little sales people for the new Ford.

Of course, as soon as one of the other dealers had us in for coffee and doughnuts and loaded us up with brochures, we became sales people for that dealer too. I think I remember Ford's generosity more than others because it was the next closest dealership to Union and easiest for us to get to after school; the closest was Eddie King Buick, but I don't think they let us have doughnuts. I'm sure that the other dealers offered some reward for coming in, but I don't remember it so well. I do remember having new automobile brochures from every dealer in town, and I even had a place where I stored all of them so I was an expert on cars. The whole process of bringing in new cars drug out over a week or more and soon, we had all seen each of the new cars and the excitement had worn off a little, though never totally, and we moved on to other pursuits, as eleven year old boys do.

But I remember one day that year sitting on the front porch of the Hughes house as Bobby and I watched one of the new cars make the turn from Seventh Street on to Prudom, and we got a good glimpse at it in motion.

Bobby said, "You know, I think they have gone as far as they can in car design, and there won't be very many changes from here on out."

"I think you're right," I said.

That was the wisdom of two eleven year old boys in late 1955.

CHARACTER OF CARS

Tulsa of 2007 has many excellent roads, and it is generally quick and easy to get across Tulsa. Tulsa of the 1950's did not. Once you reached Tulsa driving from Pawhuska, you were still a long ways from downtown Tulsa where the stores and businesses were. With any traffic problems, it probably took another thirty minutes to get downtown, and then you had to figure out how to park. The roads between Pawhuska and Tulsa were narrow, only two lanes, had very few safe opportunities to pass another car, and you had to pass through a number of towns to get there. If you went one way, you passed through Wynona, Hominy, Skiatook, Sperry, and Turley before you reached Tulsa. Another way, it was Barnsdall, Avant, Skiatook, etc. Any trip south had to go through Lynn Addition and the businesses there so that took time. Each town had to be negotiated with all of its stop signs, traffic and reduced speeds within city limits, so it could take nearly two hours from our house in Pawhuska to reach downtown Tulsa.

My mother's 1941 Chevrolet made the journey more times than it should have, and we were regular visitors to an auto repair shop in Skiatook. When it had problems, it was invariably at Skiatook and the problem was usually an overheated engine. Thermostat entered my vocabulary.

When we got the 1956 Oldsmobile the journey became easier but still tedious at times.

The old Chevrolet had its headlight dimmer switch on the floor on the left side. When it went up a hill, the windshield wipers quit because they were vacuum powered; if the engine needed power, it stole it from the other systems. The 1956 Oldsmobile had electrically powered windshield wipers, and they were not affected by the power needs of the engine. The dimmer switch was still on the floor.

Perhaps those roads contributed to Pawhuska having the number of new car dealers that it did. It was easier to stay at home so you bought the family car at home. And then, there were some differences in consumer law. If you bought your car in Tulsa, some dealers advised you to have it serviced there as well.

Cars had character then. They weren't perfect and probably not as good as the cars of today. But just the names of cars, Thunderbird, Corvette, Rocket 88, Coronet, Lancer, Roadmaster, Monterey, Hawk, Clipper, Star Chief, Belvedere, sounded classic, powerful or beautiful. At my age of twelve, I had no idea where or what Monterey, was but it sounded good to the ear.

Many of the cars had the look of a wild and magnificent beast. Our Oldsmobile had an oval grill that looked like the mouth of a large fish. Mike Avery said it looked like a pregnant guppy but I thought it looked like it was eating up the other cars. The 1954 Buick seemed to have a mouth full of angry teeth. All cars seemed to be a reflection of their human creators. The grill mimicked a mouth, the head lights were set up like eyes and the brand identifier looked like a nose. We drove by a car that was stranded on Main Street with the hood up and a mechanic had boosted himself up over the radiator so that his feet were off the ground; it looked like the Ford was having him for dinner. The only thing that they ever ate was your pocket book.

The Buick brand had holes along the hood on each side and the Special, the entry model, had just three holes while the top of the line Roadmaster had four. We referred to the number of holes to indicate the level of luxury, a three hole Buick, etc. One of the boys that we looked up to told us that he had seen a five hole Buick, which impressed us; it just wasn't true. There were only three and four hole models.

Many cars in 2007 are named with little imagination. There are the Element, Scion, HHR, Rio, Passport, RDX, and Tribute. Few of them excite me like the old, proud and fiery names from my youth. Frankly, I'm holding out for a Klingon Battle Cruiser.

AND SERVICE TOO

I worked for an oil company for thirty-three years but never in a service station. A service station sold gasoline, but they gave service. When you drove in, a (usually) cheerful man appeared at your car and asked, "Fill 'er up?" Often we said, "Put a dollar's worth in her." And as he did, he washed the windshield, lifted the hood and checked the oil and gave the engine, rubber hoses and belts a good look and often checked the radiator. He walked around the car and checked the tires and measured pressure in any that looked suspicious. All of that was included in the prices of gasoline, which was somewhere around thirty cents per gallon at that time.

When it came time, annually then, to put on a new automobile tag, elderly women, single mothers and pretty young women drove in and asked, "Would you put my new tag on for me?" He dutifully took the new tag, a screwdriver and wrench, removed the old tag and installed the new one, often without any gasoline being purchased. In return we gave them loyalty to the station and to the brand. We drove in and without asking the price said, "Put a dollar's worth in her." Just after payday we said, "Fill 'er up."

If we couldn't find the time to wash our own automobile, we took it to the same station and a young man, often one without a high school diploma, washed the car, cleaned the inside, emptied the ash trays and sometimes put a squirt of air freshener in it. For a few dollars more, he waxed it and made it shine as though it was his own car; he took better care of it than we did. Sometimes, when we had a little more money, we gave him a small tip, never more than a dollar. Sometimes we talked to him and learned that he had a young wife and two children, and they were barely making it. He didn't volunteer that to us; we asked him because we wanted to find out why he worked so hard. Sometimes the guilt led us to give him a little more on the tip, perhaps some change; thirty or forty cents more that we had in a pocket. We could give up a coke or something and buy our way out of our guilt—a little.

I have noticed that no one uses the phrase service station any more.

MERCURY

As much as I loved the old 1941 Chevy, I wanted my mother to have a new car. I had collected every brochure in town and researched heavily in *Popular Mechanics Magazine*, and she and I had together decided, based upon the technical data that I had collected and the way the grill looked, that we would get a 1956 Mercury Monterey. Every week for her, every day for me, we had gone to the Mercury dealer and looked at the Mercury we wanted. Bobby Hughes had gone with me several times, and he and I had driven it quite a bit alternating turns at the steering wheel. Of course, in our test driving we never left the showroom floor, but that's what imagination is for.

One evening Bobby Hughes and I were returning from our dance class at Evelyn Whitsitt's when we saw a 1956 blue and white Oldsmobile Rocket 88 parked next to our house. It could have been my Aunt Ola Mae's as she favored Oldsmobiles. Bobby and I walked around it, looked it over, touched it and discussed it. We did not kick the tires because we did not know to whom it belonged. The only way to find out was to go inside and ask. Bobby came in with me as he was loath to pass a mystery by.

As we entered through the side door that was our back door, I heard the strong voice and laughter of my Uncle Bud Lessert. Bud always drove a Cadillac but, there he was and there was the new Oldsmobile. Before I even said hello to him I was asking, "Did you get a new car, Bud?"

"That's your car Stevie." I was feeling pretty good about that; twelve years old, never had driven a car, didn't have a license, and I had my own Oldsmobile. He saw the light in my eye. "Let me say that it's yours and your mom's car." My spirits sagged. "How..." I began. "Your grandma Louise and I bought it for her in Tulsa," he said. My mother had to pay for the Oldsmobile, with her weekly salary from the Southwestern Bell Telephone Company, and she had no decision in it. I knew she was going to be frustrated and she was. I suppose that she could have taken it back but, it was here, at our house, parked at the curb, and things like that had a tendency to grow on you. At least Louise had made the down payment and negotiated the deal.

It was late and Bud had left his Cadillac in Tulsa at Bradley Oldsmobile, and we had to take him to retrieve the Cadillac. He drove the Oldsmobile while my mother was just another passenger in her own car. Uncle Bud drove fast too. My grandmother was quirky for if my mother reached thirty-five miles per hour, my grandmother would hang on to the door frame and call for her to slow down. Bud drove eighty-five and she calmly smoked a Lucky and chatted with him as though they were in her own front room. Maybe it was because Bud was a man and my mother was a woman.

My mother and I drove home in the new Oldsmobile while Louise rode home with Bud. Bud was twenty minutes ahead of us. It was very late and I hoped I would be able to get out of school the next day but it didn't work out. I did get to stay up and watch Jack Paar though. My grandmother tried to kill Uncle Bud by fixing a major meal after eleven o'clock. My mother wanted to kill Uncle Bud.

In the end, it all worked out. I hoped that I would now get the 1941 Chevy, but she put a sale sign on it and sold it for $150.00, what she had paid for it three years before but she had invested more money than that in the car. I have heard that Roy Adkins cried when she sold the old Chevy.

While it sat on the lot waiting for a customer, it was a submarine, a B-29 bomber and a space craft. It was an old friend, and all of us boys missed it when it was gone.

WHEN EAGLES SOARED

I was a salesman for a number of years and as a salesman, I began to take courses in selling, which led me to taking courses in goal setting. I had a course in goal setting before I was fourteen; but I didn't know it.

Goal setting is about turning dreams into reality. First, you must have a dream, and some say a dream is a dream because it can't come true. Turning a dream into reality requires specific steps for the dream must be clear, the desire strong; and it must have a time table to be achieved. The United States had a dream about space travel although most of us didn't believe it would become a reality. President John Kennedy made the dream a reality when he said, "It is our goal to send a man to the moon and return him safely to earth by the end of this decade." There it was; a goal with a clear and common vision: To send a man to the moon and return him safely to earth; the time frame was before 1970. More than just the United States, humankind had long dreamed of space travel. Turning a dream into reality requires one more thing, perhaps the most important element: you must have passionate belief.

To demonstrate the power of passionate belief, the ability of a clearly conceived goal to bring itself into existence, we must return once again to those thrilling days of yore, when the Eagle was King.

Not the bird; the motor scooter.

The Cushman Corporation, located in Lincoln, Nebraska and a long time maker of golf carts, once manufactured a line of motor scooters, and the top of the line was the Eagle.

Motor scooters and motor cycles have always been an important part of my life. I had my first ride when I was six, behind Gordon Hughes and Bobby, and it scared the geewhillikers out of me because I was the third one back and always in danger of falling off. Still, I loved it, and I was so excited by it that I couldn't wait to try it again. Only I wanted to sit further up next time, really, in the driver's seat.

Sometime later, my cousin Jerry Payne took me to Spring Lake in Oklahoma City, and I saw the first real motorcycle I had ever seen, a Harley-Davidson, and my heart was set on having one. I was in the process of goal setting without even knowing it and if I had realized what was going on, I could have written a book on setting and reaching goals.

I bought a copy of Cycle magazine and I began to learn everything I could about motor cycles. I wrote to the Cushman Motor Company and got brochures on their motor scooters. I began to focus on and collect items about motor cycles and motor scooters, and, most of all; I began to dream about them. Most of my waking hours were fixed on motor cycles. And, an interesting phenomenon was going on; all of my friends were young boys who shared my dreams of motor cycles. I can look back now and see that from about age ten on all of my friends shared the same interests in motor cycles.

I just didn't hang around with people who weren't of a motorcycle mind. And we talked them, walked them, dreamed them and were absolutely captivated by them. Several of us spoke about becoming engineers so that we could build them. And we had to play the game of "Can you top this?" by out learning each other on technical terms that we would never use or have reason to use.

I once knew how many foot-lbs. of torque a 1957 650-cc Ariel Square Four produces at 3,500 rpm. I didn't know what torque was but I knew this amazing detail from reading Cycle magazine; not just reading but studying it intensely. Of course, growing up in Pawhuska, some of the great motorcycles were obscure and distant for us as dealers existed only in the big cities. The great motorcycles were Triumph, BSA, Ariel, Matchless, AJS, BMW, Indian (British) and, of course, Harley-Davidson. The legends that were already gone were Indian (USA) and Vincent motorcycles.

Each of us had written to the motorcycle companies and, to their credit, they had sent representatives to Pawhuska to see us, each, individually. And it was a bit of an embarrassment as the men traveled to Pawhuska, sought us out only to find that they were meeting with twelve year old boys, at least two years away from their first motor scooter, let alone a great cycle. We were forming and fixing these goals, and they could have been written out as "I will have a shiny red 8-horsepower Cushman Eagle with dual chrome exhausts, windshield with canvas, buddy seat and rider foot pegs by the date of February, 12, 1958, which is my 14th birthday." I don't know that any of us actually wrote out a goal that way, but we talked, lived and breathed it so much that it was effectively stated.

My friend, Duane Titus, did not have much interest in motor scooters, but he felt the same way about aircraft as we did about motor scooters; he followed the same patterns as we did only for him it was Piper Cubs, Beach and Cessna aircraft. One night his father shouted, "Duane, get down here!" Sheepishly Duane crawled into the living room to find that Cessna had sent a representative to meet with him about the purchase of an aircraft. Duane's letter writing days were over.

But not Ronnie's and mine. We continued to collect information and each had a nice portfolio of brochures and color photographs. We began to shift our expectations from Harley-Davidsons, Triumphs and the like and to think more realistically about smaller motor scooters.

There were a number of reasons why we shifted our focus from the great motorcycles to the Cushman Eagle and several of them were quite practical. First, we could only operate a motor scooter of less than 5-horsepower by law so that took away our options for a real motor cycle until we could reach the age of sixteen, which was several hundred years in the future. Then, there was cost.

In 1958, a Cushman Eagle cost about $400, and that was reachable, with a little parental help. A Triumph Tiger was about $1,100, much less reachable. Then there was availability. There were Cushman dealers in Ponca City, Tulsa and Bartlesville. But the most important thing that helped to fuel our vision was presence. Eagles, owned by boys we knew, not much older than we were, flocked to Pawhuska. The presence of the Eagles, owned by boys we could see sent us the message that, if he can have one, then so can I.

If we happened to be standing around together, talking, and we heard the slight thumping sound of the exhaust pipe of a Cushman Eagle headed towards us, we dropped everything, opened our mouths, bugged out our eyes and wowed ourselves to near exhaustion as we watched it speed by us. Speed is a relative word as the top speed was around fifty-five miles per hour; still, it was faster than our bicycles.

That is turning dreams into realities; setting a goal, believing in it and seeking a solution without yielding until the dream is reality. Bring something into vision and develop a passion about it and, you can bring it into reality. The more passion you can muster, the greater is the likelihood of success. For our group of boys, all of the things for reaching a goal were in place. A vision: Each of us saw himself riding his own Eagle, so much so that they literally dreamed about this; passion, each one burned with desire for an Eagle; environment; each boy completely surrounded himself with everything he could about motor scooters and created his own environment.

We had Eagle pin-ups instead of girl pin-ups. Our closets were filled with Cycle magazines, brochures from Cushman, Triumph distributor Johnson Motors, and every dealer we could identify and write to. Ronnie and I both wrote to Triumph in England and discovered what "insufficient postage" meant. Our hope was so strong that it could just not be denied. We believed, without a doubt, that our dream would come true. We would have our Cushman Eagles.

Oh, yes. Obstacles: There have to be obstacles to reaching a goal or it isn't a goal; they were primarily two: parents and money.

Most parents did not want their young boys to have a motor scooter and most of the boys did not have the money. And even if you had the money, you had to overcome parental objections; there were plenty of those. The power of setting goals, believing in them with passion, and living life as though the goal has already been achieved is such that every one of the boys--except one--got a Cushman Eagle.

And the boy that didn't get an Eagle got a Harley-Davidson 165. I had mixed emotions as he was my friend, Ronnie Havens, and I wanted the best for him but not better than I had. On the other hand, it gave us another option for something to ride, since we all rode each others motor scooter. The hard facts were that the 165 was more motor cycle than motor scooter.

The Eagle was classified as a motor scooter, by law, and certain things made a motor scooter a motor scooter. It had to be less than five horsepower, usually had a step through for the rider and small, balloon tires. The Eagle challenged that a bit, for it did not have a step through and instead had a center mounted gasoline tank that had to be straddled, so that it had a *faux* motorcycle appearance. The Eagle had a centrifugal clutch and a two speed transmission; the centrifugal clutch allowed it to idle in gear. The clutch lever was on the left hand side and foot operated with the gear shift lever also imitating early Harley-Davidson motorcycles. The Eagle was a *faux* Harley. And then, there was the name, Eagle; it was, like many of the cars, a name with character.

Harley-Davidson built its small motorcycle in two models, the 125cc model, called the Hummer, and the 165cc, also a Hummer but known by everyone as the 165. The 165 had a standard motorcycle clutch, operated by the left hand, a three speed transmission, operated by the left foot; and it was fast. The Eagles were a four stroke engine while the 165 was a two stroke engine, and the 165 would do something no Eagle would do; it would run— backwards!

It wasn't by design, it was an accident of being a two-stroke engine, that if you started it with the piston just wrong, it would start running in a reverse direction; and it had to be stopped and restarted. We started these monsters the old fashioned way; we kicked them. We would let the Eagle lie on the kick stand, which was on the left hand side, then walk over to the right-hand side, raise the kick starter up, then stand on it and drive it furiously to the floor of the Eagle.

Most of us added a little theatrical Harley bravado to the starting process, and especially so if there were a girl nearby and looking our way. It had to look more difficult to be better appreciated. When the gear had worn a little through usage and slipped a bit, we sometimes negatively impressed a girl by falling over the gasoline tank and onto the ground on the left side. Or, failing an actual fall, you just banged your knee against the metal gasoline tank and said words that she did not know you knew.

The 165 was started by kicking straight backwards, and it may have been easier to kick than an Eagle; but it also had a mean back kick. If you didn't follow all the way through with the kick, it ratcheted back and hit you in the leg. That also was embarrassing if a girl were watching and heard more of those words.

The problem with two-stroke engines was that they mixed oil with gasoline for lubricant, so they smoked and they smelled. So no one really wanted to ride behind them, but sometimes we had no choice. If Ronnie wanted to flex the muscles of the 165, we rode behind him.

Another popular motor scooter with a two-stroke engine was the Italian made Vespa, although most of them that we saw were sold by Sears & Roebuck as the Crusair. It was a motor scooter with a step through, small round tires, smaller even than the Eagle's tires, but it ran well and relatively fast. The pale green Crusair with its small tires was sometimes unstable, and a gutsy Eagle rider could get ahead of it on the streets. And if the Crusair rider hit the throttle hard in first gear, it had a tendency to rare like a horse and go over backwards.

I think I was still at Union when, once again, that marvelous, underground communication system worked so well, and we heard that Dale Savory, a boy who lived on east Eighth Street, was getting a Crusair. Earl Brunger, Butch Daniels, some others and I went to Dale's house, and watched him and his father work with the new machine. Until then, I had only seen photographs of it in the Sears & Roebuck catalog. It was a pretty machine, pale green with Italian sculpturing, and a bit smaller than I had thought it would be. Dale was very new at it, and they were having some trouble starting it. Each time he kicked it through, we would get a whiff of the two-cycle oil and gasoline mixture that it used. It seemed like there were a hundred boys there and Dale, it was obvious, felt a lot of pride at having the only Crusair in town. He was eager to show it off.

However, he had never ridden one before. His father and someone else were showing him the throttle, how to shift gears and operate the clutch. Dale followed their instructions, mounted the small black saddle, raced the engine, released the clutch, and the Crusair reared like a horse and dropped Dale off of the back. He kept his footing though, and the engine died, leaving him holding the motor scooter and looking frightened and, what I later learn to describe as, chagrined. We thought he had done it on purpose though, at first, until he said a few things about it, which are better neither remembered nor written.

Of course, we all wanted a ride on it and, some of his friends wanted to drive it. After a bit, he finally got it going, and headed west along Eighth Street, a light trail of blue smoke lingering in the air. Of course, it fueled our desires to have a motor scooter.

I still wanted an Eagle though.

However, the first motor scooter I had was not an Eagle. My mother had some reluctance about getting me an Eagle, and in desperation and fear of not having a motor scooter at all, I yielded to various pressures. My first motor scooter was made by Cushman as the Pacemaker, but sold by Sears as the Jetsweep. It was a 4.8 BHP machine with a centrifugal clutch and a single speed transmission. The operating mechanisms were a twist throttle and a foot brake, so it was much easier to operate than the Eagle, but did not have the power of an Eagle.

Ironically, the day that my mother took me to Tulsa to buy the Jetsweep, none of my motor scooter friends were with me. I was involved in my Baptist Church then, and we had just acquired a new preacher, Dean Rainwater. Among his children was a boy my age, Terry, and I invited him to go with us. Amazingly, his parents allowed him to go and spend the day with us in Tulsa. They had just moved from

Atoka, Oklahoma, and it took a lot of trust to turn their son over to my mother for a day. Of course, I was the one that was a bad influence on him, not my mother.

I picked the scooter out, showed Terry, talked about it for hours, and my mother made the arrangements for purchase and for it to be delivered on Wednesday, several years away. But, like all days that can not be hurried, for things come in their own time, Wednesday arrived, and I took my first rides with it, unlicensed of course, for we couldn't get a license without having a motor scooter to demonstrate our ability.

Terry didn't get a motor scooter, but he has remained one of my close friends since that day in 1958.

The Jetsweep wore out between carrying newspapers, and some wild riding and in December, 1958, I at last got my Eagle. I was very pleased with it as it was an 8-horse power engine, blue and had a passenger seat, which we called a buddy seat, dual exhaust pipes and black saddlebags.

January 30, 1959, shortly before my fifteenth birthday, I was struck broadside by a 1951 Chevrolet, and my legs were badly injured. Again, I had no broken bones, but I damaged soft tissue, and I spent some of the year learning how to walk with crutches. My mother allowed me to have the Cushman rebuilt, and by summer, I was running with the wild bunch again.

For a brief time, I had both of the motor scooters. A boy, who had lived in Pawhuska and then moved to Ponca City, had a newer, light blue Crusair. He was visiting Pawhuska and was about to return home when five or six of us decided to ride to Ponca with him. On a cold December day we started out to have some fun. Bobby Hughes asked me if he could take my older Jetsweep instead of riding behind me, and I agreed. The problem was that the throttle was broken, and we had been using a jerry rigged wire that the rider had to hold with one hand and pull to feed fuel and relax to idle down. It meant the rider had to ride with one hand only on the handlebars. He assured me that he could do that all the way to Ponca City, and we set off. Excitement of the moment causes fourteen year old boys to believe about anything.

We started out of the alley behind our house, and as we passed the telephone company building, Jim Hicks, the boy from Ponca, turned around to say something, and Bobby hit him from behind knocking the new Crusair into the brick building. Bobby struck him again, lost his balance, turned over and slid on the cold concrete some distance and was a bloody mess. We really didn't mean to laugh at him.

Jim Hicks called him a lot of things, and then we picked Bobby up and took him home. Fortunately his mother was not home, and he could sneak into the house. After he got his jeans off and cleaned up a little, getting most of the blood and some of the street tar off, one of us suggested an alcohol treatment to prevent infection. At this stage, an alcohol treatment meant pouring it on; later it would mean drinking it. Bobby called us a lot of things after we started pouring raw rubbing alcohol onto his cuts, especially the big one on his upper thigh. Jim Hicks went on home to Ponca, his Crusair and his pride wounded. The rest of us didn't make it that day.

Somehow, all of us survived that phase and became adults. I have had a motorcycle much of my adult life, while many of my friends gave them up. A few still ride one but as we move into our seventh decade, it is admittedly more difficult to ride, and we ride less than we once did. Still, the motor scooters and boys who rode them together formed a special group, much like George Armstrong Custer's Seventh Calvary as they rode off that day.

SERVICE WITH A PAWHUSKA TOUCH

Pawhuska did not have a grocery store that we might call a supermarket, not in the sense of the great supermarkets of today. The Packing House Market on the corner of Main and Leahy was probably the closest thing to a supermarket until about 1955, when a Safeway store was opened on Leahy and Sixth Street across from the post office; it was about the same size as the Packing House. The Servall market, on Main Street between Prudom and Leahy, was probably the next largest grocery store.

What Pawhuska did have was a grocery store in almost every neighborhood. These were small, what might be called mom and pop stores, usually about the size of an average house with a white store front and about one hundred feet in depth. There was a counter up front as you entered, usually on the right, and a clerk or the owner helped you check out or find things that were not obvious.

Most of them had a pop machine outside that was a chest type rather than a stand up and usually painted pale green. The color might have been due to the sponsoring beverage company.

You put coins in a slot and then drug your chosen bottle of soda through a set of metal tracks to a gate that lifted and let you remove the bottle; sometimes I accidentally got the wrong bottle and faced the choice of drinking a soda that I did not like, not drinking it, or trading it to someone else, if I could talk him into getting the bottle that I wanted.

If I was at a grocery close enough to home, such as the one on Lynn Avenue near Eighth Street. I just carried it home and stored it in the refrigerator hoping to trade it to my mother for something. I liked Coca Cola, Pepsi Cola, Root Beer, and Strawberry and Grape flavors. I would hardly touch a 7-UP, although if I were ill with a fever, 7-UP was the best thing in the world, especially very cold or with vanilla ice cream. That was the only time I liked vanilla.

All of the little grocery stores had a unique aroma that announced their own something special when you opened the door. It might be candy, or vegetables or sausage or maybe even the aroma of the wood floor mixed in with all of the other aromas. It tempted you as soon as you walked in.

There was a grocery on 15th Street, west of Grandview Avenue, and just down the street from the Kiwanis Park and swimming pool, which was really only a wading pool. That was convenient if you had been playing in the park or swimming in the pool and needed refreshment afterward. We always needed refreshment afterward.

There was a grocery store on Lynn Avenue between Seventh and Eighth Streets and another near the pool hall on Ki-He-Kah Street. Also, I believe that there was another neighborhood grocery in Lynn Addition.

Then there was a slightly larger type of grocery store, not quite as large as the Packing House but large enough to serve most needs. It was in these stores that my grandmother mostly shopped. For years she shopped at Soderstrom's Grocery, which was just across from the Journal-Capital building at the foot of the stairs to the hill. Sometime later, she switched to Dowdy's Grocery store on

Sixth Street, opposite of the post office and a little closer to us. I think that she switched because she owed Soderstrom's money and got behind in paying and causing a problem. It was resolved, but I don't think they let her have the ample credit terms again that had previously made her such a loyal customer.

My grandmother, Louisa Victoria Lessert, was an Osage woman and her payment came every three months. She had built her business relationships, as many Osages did, with the commitment to pay her bills every payment; but one year, she had tax problems and was not able to make her payments to local businesses until the Internal Revenue Service debt was resolved. This might have been when and why she switched to Dowdy's.

My grandmother seldom went out in public because she had suffered cancer and had surgery, a colostomy for it, which made her uncomfortable in public in some cases. And she had never learned how to drive, safely anyway, so she had abandoned driving years before: Pawhuska was grateful. So she shopped by telephone; both when she had been at Soderstrom's and then when she switched us to Dowdy's.

She would call the store, identify herself and say that she wanted to place an order. When the clerk was ready, she started down her list: a can of Folger's coffee, a gallon of milk, pork chops, a frying hen, a case of mixed pop flavors, a can of Crisco, and so on. Oh, and a carton of Lucky cigarettes; the cigarette brand was Lucky Strike, but it was always just Lucky to her. The grocer might tell her, "Louise, I've got some nice cantaloupes in, and I think you would like them." "OK," she would say, "Put two or three of them on." Whatever he suggested, she took.

Once the order was completed, someone at the store filled it, boxed it, and Walt delivered it to the house. Not everyone knew it, but our back door was seldom locked. My grandmother wanted friends and relatives to feel free to come by and stop in, and she didn't want to lock me out so, it was left unlocked except at the latest hour of night when we went to sleep and not always then. Our front door was not locked very often.

Often I came home from school to find Walt, not only delivering the groceries but in the kitchen and actually putting them on the shelves for my grandmother. If he got anything extra for that, I don't know. I was used to it, and if I walked in I merely said, "Hello Walt," and talked with him a bit. He would complete his stocking, check his ticket and put it in the place he always did and leave. He was always pleasant, kind and helpful. I didn't know his last name, only Walt, but he might have been Walt Goodson.

I related this to Mary McFadden, and she told me of similar experiences. Mary said that her mother would call the Charles Cleaners and tell them that Mr. McFadden had three suits for the cleaners and tell them where in the closet the suits were. Someone would come from the cleaners, go into the house, pick up the suits and have them cleaned and returned.

I've lived in several cities of different sizes, one in North Dakota of only two hundred residents, and the Pawhuska of that time is the only place where I have seen service with a Pawhuska touch.

TRUST

Pawhuskans had trust: trust in each other, trust in the town, and trust in just the way things were. As I said, we seldom locked our doors, and I think my mother had to learn that for she had been raised in Oklahoma City early on, and some bad experiences had left her with mistrust.

When she had the old Chevy, she usually left the keys in it when we were downtown. Somewhere, she had got the message that the police or fire department might have to move your car, and it would be easier if the keys were in it, and it was left unlocked. Maybe you just didn't lose your keys that way. By the time that I had started driving, we had a 1956 Oldsmobile, and she continued to leave the keys in it when she parked downtown; so I did the same. There were times I removed them but that was only when I parked behind Irby's Drug Store in the big lot and went to a movie. If I parked on the street in front of Henry's, the Manhattan Café, the barbershop or anything, I left the keys in the car; just in case the police or fire department had to move the car; also, someone else might need to move the car for another reason.

I kept the keys with me and locked the car at the high school, not for fear of theft, but some of my friends played practical jokes. Some of the kids who did not like me might just vandalize the car, but it wasn't an issue of trust; it was one of prudence.

Many other people left the doors to their house unlocked, except at night, for you never knew who might stop by. And few people called to see if you were home; they just stopped by. I always knocked, but if someone didn't hear me, I might gently push the door and call out, then gradually move into the house and find my friend in the kitchen at the back of the house. I would apologize and be excused with a, "Oh, that's all right, just come on in if no one answers." It was an easy time, and it was an easy town.

One night at the drive-in theater, I accidentally locked the keys in the car. I knew where my mother kept her set at home, but how to get to the house? I was only sixteen and had barely a year and a half of driving experience, but I asked the first person I saw, Johnny Main, if he could drive me into town and let me retrieve the keys. Johnny and his girl did not want to leave the movie so, he thought a minute, and let me have the keys to his car, a 1956 Ford convertible. I drove to town, retrieved the keys, and returned the car to him. That was trust.

And, I had a great time driving his convertible.

PAWHUSKAN

I, like several other people, do not really like the term Pawhuskan to identify someone from Pawhuska. It is easy to fall into using it for by adding an n, it is done. I have used Tulsan all my life and never thought twice about it. I could use Pawhuska as in, "He is a Pawhuska," but it doesn't make much sense either. It is as though we are saying he is town, and we would never say, "He is a Tulsa." I can not neither be more specific than that nor can I say what I don't like about using Pawhuskan and Pawhuskans. Still, I am not comfortable with it. I do not know what people from Hominy are called, and perhaps it is always a longer, "She is from Hominy." I know a lady from Barnsdall, but I never thought of her as a Barnsdallan and so on with Wynona.

Since it is easy and seems to fit, I will use Pawhuskan with apologies to those who do not like it, including myself.

1957 FACES

The cover is faded now, once ivory, now showing yellow on its edges; its vinyl has small pock marks where other books have rubbed against it, as it has been taken from and replaced many times on its shelf. It has even been moved from house to house over the years, as I have moved from place to place. The letters are raised on the cover where the name that the Osage call themselves, Wah-Sha-She, angles across from left to right, rising in the right hand corner. At the lower right is a shield, with a flame in the center and tomahawks opposing each other on the left and right, and the letters PHS tell me where it came from; the top left tells me when: 1957.

It was my first year at PHS, Pawhuska High School, and I was not truly in high school, although I shared the building with those that were. We were seventh graders, the lowliest of the low, not worthy to be on the same grounds as those hallowed seniors, who were in their last year at PHS, the year we all sought so desperately, so that we could be out of school and on with living life. It was a time between shooting wars and only the cold war lingered on, still pervasive in our lives through television and movies. There were few dirty commies in our school, although we looked for them everywhere, and we guarded our words so that our own loyalty was never questioned. We even had an organization called Youth against Communism (YAC). I was a boy and usually wore jeans, probably genuine Levi brand most of the time, with a simple shirt, often plaid.

When I open the cover I am greeted by a two page black and white photograph of the old building that was taken from an airplane. On the east side are two white buildings, much like houses that were then the choir and band buildings. North of the main building is the gymnasium. It is difficult to tell in which season the photograph was taken although the choir building has a clear 58 facing me. There are few cars parked near so it may have been in summer, but it has a bleak look about it, as though winter has arrived and the leafless trees seem to confirm either late fall or winter. There are no people in the photograph. The front of the old building is magnificent with double white doors above cement steps, steps where most of the class photographs would be taken, and there is character about the face of the building, although she bears a tired look at the same time. There is no anxiety in her face though, for she has been through this cycle of new arrivals and tearful departures many times before. She knows what to expect; it is we who do not.

Usually we took the real people we knew for granted and thought that beauty was only in the films and television of Hollywood and New York. Yet, I am struck by one photograph midway through the yearbook. On the right is a page which introduces Sports and on the left is one of the most beautiful photographs I have seen, a young woman name Lynda Jackson, who is billed as the T & I Queen. She is perfectly coiffed and her face has that teasing sense that we would later see in actress Bernadette Peters. She wears large earbobs, and the shadows are perfectly cast upon her face, which is smiling as are her eyes. Perhaps there is even a bit of Ann-Margaret in her impishness. It is the same photograph that appears in the senior section.

One page towards the front is another beautiful young

woman, Redema Tharp, Football Queen, also a senior. It strikes me that such beauty was present in our high school, so far from the worlds of glamour and glitter. I was in awe of the seniors and in fear of some of the senior boys, for they commanded the campus. Some of the senior boys are quite good looking too. There is Richard Harrison, well combed dark hair, a coat and tie and smile to charm the wits out of you; he defines charming.

Johnny McFadden has all American looks with his neat flat top hair cut and bow-tie. There is a senior boy named Jimmy Adkins, in coat and tie. His photograph suggests we will see him as a country western singer or comedian.

On a page in Sports is a photograph of the cheer leaders, who have leapt into the air with a rousing Rah! frozen in time as I still wait for them to come down. I could not tell you who they are from that photograph, but above it is another with them seated on those same steps of class photographs, their black skirts spread out in fans: Sharon Dowdy, Melinda Liebenheim, Nancy Grinstead, Marla Templeton, Marcia Shimonek, and Marilyn Moyer Culver.

Marilyn Moyer and Tom Culver were married and still in school, two seniors sharing the last year, he in football, she a cheerleader, and I thought that they were attractive together. Years later I saw her at a restaurant; I took a moment to tell her who I am. I told her that she had been a senior the year I was beginning and that she was a role model to me, and I thanked her. She did not remember me, which I did not expect. Seniors did not know seventh graders, unless they were their siblings, and then they were ashamed of them. She was embarrassed at not having known or remembered me, which added to her charm. At least she took the time to talk to someone younger who had looked up to her; not everyone does.

There are some autographs in my yearbook and some notes: "A good clarinet player shouldn't have a broken hand" by Johnny Lawless; "Lot's of luck" by Jimmie Ann;

"Steve, too bad I am a little late (writing in your annual)" by Sherry Johnston. There is a cryptic message from Ronnie Havens, "You must be a good secretary and treasurer." Most of them are just the signature, and Ronnie signed it in several places. But there is one that even today gives me pride and causes a chill to come over me, and it is this: "Steve, I will never forget your 'strong' voice in reading class. You should be an orator. It's been nice having you in 7-2's. Your homeroom teacher, Miss Updegraff, Seventh grammar."

Beauty belongs not only to the senior girls Tonya Noel was only in the eighth grade, but her photograph is beautiful, smiling, looking directly at you, reminding one of actress Gale Storm. Gayle McCain's photograph is next to her, also beautiful but more serious. They are in individual photographs because they were class officers. Our class officers were Henry Hollowell, president; Charlotte Cass, vice president; Jackie Carlile, secretary; and Bobby Green, treasurer.

When I look at the photographs of Henry, whom I knew as Hughie, and Bobby, I have difficulty thinking of President Hughie and the impish look of Bobby Green worries me that he was the treasurer. Jackie and Charlotte are beautiful but almost opposites of each other, one dark, and one fair. I find my own photograph in the seventh grade section and my face is too round, my ears too big, my head in what seems to be a permanent tilt to the left. Ronnie is standing to my left, and Johnny Lawless is just in front of me. The girls look so good and most of the boys seem to have ears that are too big for them. My photograph in the junior high band section is better, and I wish it were the only one in the book. If you should see me in person you must tell me that my ears are no longer too big. I would like that.

They are only faces and yet most of them were people that I knew and felt their influence, and for the most part, it was good. I remember that year a quiz contest on live radio, and Abe Stice was in it; but I don't remember who won it or what they won. It was probably a scholarship and probably not a large one. There is a photograph of a banner that reads KWGS with the entire quiz panel and the students assembled on the stage. There are no captions and no identifications of the people in the photograph.

Too bad, for I expect most of it is lost to us now. We were grateful that they had it, for it got us out of class and in the auditorium for an hour or two. For some of us, that meant postponing a speech or presentation for another day, maybe even another day to study for a test that we had sacrificed to a good night of television.

Being seventh graders, we would always be behind the class of 1961, the eighth graders in every thing we did except, for some curious reason, in the 1957 year book the seventh graders are listed ahead of the eighth graders. So, for just one time, in regard to that special circumstance, let me, as Stevie Joe Payne, seventh grader, say to the eighth graders:

Na na na na nah.

THE LAST OF MY FATHERS

Bill Cosby said of Sheldon Leonard, "Today, the last of my fathers has died." Sheldon Leonard had been an actor who was usually cast as a mobster, filling his role well. He moved behind the camera and was the producer and executive producer of a successful television series starring Bill Cosby and Robert Culp. The series was *I Spy*, and it was one of the first to partner a black actor and a white actor as equals.

Sheldon Leonard was more than the producer for he was a mentor to other actors and visionary in his approach, witness Cosby's remark. For the first time I realized that I had had more than one father, though I had no father in my life for I had never met my father. I would finally get to meet him just after Easter of 1997, when I was fifty-three years old; but I was unable to create a relationship with him and meeting him caused damage in some of the family relationships that I had made over the years. Yet I'm glad that I got to meet him and have him look into my eyes and see truths that he had tried to deny. Perhaps that's all I really wanted at that stage of my life. I had obviously made it past the difficult teen years without him.

The other fathers that I speak of were those that were

around me and mentored me, cared for me and watched over me. They had their own sons and daughters, and I was often friends with those offspring, but not always. Gordon Hughes, Bob and Kay's father, was one of the first that I remember; he stayed with me well into my adulthood, giving me advice, which I did not always take, and moral support, which I always needed. He was there to guide me with tools and helped me learn the difference between a Crescent and a box-end wrench, and how and when to use each one. Sometimes I took a short cut and had skinned knuckles to prove it. He gave all of us a role model and life advice, although he did it in a bit of Gordon short hand. And, personally, he helped me one time in such a way that it is a debt I can not yet repay.

Later there was Russell Havens, a sage man, who was the first to open the doors of philosophy to me. While Gordon Hughes used a short hand, Russell Havens went the long way to explain things, and he intrigued me into certain books that were too much of a challenge for me then. But I kept them in mind, and I have read many of them since then. Russell Havens always seemed to me to be a bit like Judge Hardy of the Andy Hardy movies, wise, thoughtful, considerate and decisive.

Felix Lawless had the Phillips 66 station down the street when I first met him, and he was somewhere in between Gordon Hughes and Russell Havens, having a bit of the rogue in him, and an easy laugh. He knew tools and cars, and something about kids as well. It was almost as though he kept a lot of the child about him, and it made it hard to put things over on him. Humor seemed to be the common thread between Gordon Hughes and Felix Lawless. Wise as I perceived Mr. Havens, I don't think I saw him with that same sense of humor, and I probably had more respect for him but also more fear.

When I was in Union Grade School (no public school (PS #) number for us) I had only female teachers, and the two that I think of the most were Mrs. Theiss and Mrs. Scheirmer, respectively my third grade and fifth grade teachers. They gave me the most opportunities and the most encouragement, so much so that I would think of them throughout every thing in later years. When I was inducted into two different scholastic honor societies at colleges, I thought of both of them and wished that they could have been in the audience with me, to show in some way, that the faith they had shown in me then had been justified if even in a small way. So, my fathers included some mothers as well.

When I started in Pawhuska High School as a seventh grader, I was in a group called 7-3, and I went out for football. Some of the things that I had learned from my fathers till then quickly taught me one thing; that I had no business playing football. The second thing came slowly and with pain. When you are in the wrong place at the wrong time, you had better change, and, this is the thing that came slowly. It's no shame or reason for shame to change when you don't fit. So, I changed to band, and that was an accident, as I had a close friend in band; and it was for him that I changed to band. I had no musical gift or ability, and I had no clue what instrument to play. When Mr. Arnold asked me, I just reached up into thin air and said "Clarinet" and I still have no idea why I did, but the clarinet was kind to me; and I fell in love with it. I became quite good at it, and I learned to work very hard at something. I practiced long hours, and I took extra lessons every summer.

I loved the clarinet and I still have my Leblanc B flat clarinet; I play it once in a while though not as often as I did. Mr. Arnold was the father who would have the most influence on me, leave me with the most tools to help me get into adulthood and even through my three years, eleven months and twenty-three days of the navy. My other fathers at school were Mr. Wilson and Mr. Powers. Mr. Powers was another of those that scared me more than anything, yet I felt that I knew the meaning of the word respect for him. I would never dared have crossed him. I learned from all three of them, both the lessons that they were supposed to teach and the lessons that they gave me, just by living, just by being themselves.

I had two navy fathers too: my company commander in basic training, V. D. DeSelms, a chief petty officer (radarman, and I became a radarman) and Gordon Hakenjos, also a radarman, my first class (a rating, such as a sergeant) who was my friend and mentor and helped me greatly. At Phillips, in my thirty-three and a half year career, I had a father in Richard L. Clampitt, who saw potential in me and others and helped us into better positions and furthered our careers. He wasn't easy, and he demanded a lot, but he made us better women and men for his challenges; he gave us opportunities. What we did with them was up to us; but he took the risks and gave us chances.

At sixty-three years of age, I am facing that same moment that Bill Cosby faced. My fathers that remain are few, and they are getting older and several are frail now. I worry about them as they perhaps they once worried about me. I worry for different reasons, of course. They wondered how to set us on a path and keep us out of trouble. I worry about their health and what will happen to them. They are three now. That is all that remain of all my fathers. They are in their seventies and eighties, and I know that their time is limited, and I grieve about it for it is not just their lives, but all of the knowledge that they had and shared and the wonderful role models and mentors that they have been to me and others.

I do not possess them to myself, but sometimes I feel like it, as though they were my fathers and no one else's. And, of course, there is my own father Jesse Butler Payne, J. B., Jay as he is called. I got little from him, and for years I referred to him only as "sperm donor." I stopped doing that after my son's death, for I learned to respect J. B. somehow, even for his failings as a father to me. He treated my two older brothers well.

He is still my father, but I will never get to know him, and that's his loss as much as mine. But it was his choice; I gave him the opportunity. Even as these men have been my fathers, most without even knowing it, I must realize that to the young women and men I have helped, mentored and guided, I am in the same way, their father. Many of them were as I was, with no father in their family. They looked to me in the same way, for love, for respect, for guidance as I did to the men I have named. I have given many of these young women and men a book, *The Magic of Thinking Big* to help them see their potential.

I was addicted to cigarettes; some of them were addicted to more, to cocaine, heroine and alcohol. Some of them were outcasts to their family yet felt at home with us. Also, I have given away one hundred and ninety-nine copies of *The Seven Habits of Highly Effective People*. I know that this book has helped some of them. I don't know how many copies of Joyce Hifler's *The Cherokee Feast of Days* I have given away, but it is close to one hundred, and that has to have helped some too. I have given away a number of the book, *Over The Top* by Zig Ziglar to motivate many young people. I hope it is not for selfish or vain reasons. (I am in the book on page 106). I could do that, freely give so many books, because of the values that were given me by the women and men I have named, not because it was my lot to do so.

I know that one day, probably quietly inside myself and with deep sadness I will say "Today, the last of my fathers has died." I don't know when or which one it will be, but I hope it is still some time away. I hope that they remain here with me for some good time to come, and I wish them all the best. They gave me their best, these wonderful women and men.

THEATERS FOUR

As you drive through the streets of Pawhuska in the year 2007, it may be difficult to believe that there were once *four* movie theaters in Pawhuska. Around 1952, there were the indoor theaters of the Ki-He-Kah, the State, and the Circle A Theater, and then there was the Corral Drive-in Theater. I think that the Circle A Theater might have been closed for a while before this time and then reopened. Most people probably don't remember it, but it was fascinating to me for its western theme.

Outside of the ticket both was a hitching post and the floors on both sides of the ticket booth as you entered were wooden and had ranch brands burned into them; almost everywhere that there was wood, brands had been burned into it and everything about the theater kept the western theme. The lights overhead in the concession area were western lanterns affixed to wagon wheels suspended by chains. The Circle A was located on the north side of the street somewhere near B. F. Goodrich tires, perhaps just across the street from the Pullman café. The only movies that I remember being shown there were cowboy movies. The prices were probably the same as at the State, and the concessions were about the same: popcorn, soft drinks and candy. I didn't understand why it closed when it did because the house was always packed.

Then there was the Corral drive-in theater south of Pawhuska along highway 99 and across from the Osage County Fairgrounds. In the mid-1950's, Wednesday was a special event called Cash Night, and when you bought a ticket, you were entered into the drawing. The award was $25.00 and if no one won it, the $25.00 was added to the next week's award for $50.00 and so on. Sometimes it was quite a bit of money, especially since it was less than $1.00 to get in. When the cash award got to be large, there were long lines of cars out to the drive-in and then at the end of the evening, the same cars all returned towards town, taking quite a while to get back home.

Going to the drive-in was fun, not because of the movie, which may or may not have been good, but because of the experience per se. Some families that had station wagons might back into the parking spot, lower the back gate and park the children on a blanket.

For each two parking spots there was a metal pole that came up to the car's window and held a speaker on each side; one for the car on the right, one for the car on the left. The speaker was a gray metal device that connected to the pole by a black cord. There was a black plastic dial that controlled the volume, and the quality of sound on these was never very good. The speaker itself always looked to me like the face of one of the aliens from outer space in some movie I had seen. The speaker had a curved fixture that let it rest over the window of the car or over the door where it connected to the window. Sometimes a driver became impatient and forgot and drove way with the speaker still attached to the car door and the cord was ripped loose.

Sometimes the driver just cut the cord and kept the speaker as a souvenir. I think there was a posted reward for information on people stealing speakers. No, I never took one: honest.

The projection booth was towards the front and this

doubled as a concession stand and a place for the restrooms, although a few people thought the restrooms were just beside their car, especially for the little kids and in some cases, teenagers. At the concession stand was a patio with metal lawn chairs, which could be cold if the night was cool. To get away from our parents we sometimes went up there; it was also a meeting place for kids.

LIGHTS IN THE SKY

After the Second World War, there was a lot of military surplus that was converted to civilian use. I suspect that searchlight truck trailers might have been one of these for now and then, the Corral would have a special that it wanted to advertise, and a search light truck would be brought in to light the night sky. It was effective advertising as you couldn't help but notice the lights playing back and forth across the sky. Also, when the movie, *Earth vs. The Flying Saucers* debuted in Pawhuska, not that it was its world premiere, I remember the search light trailer parked in front of the KI-He-Kah. I suspect that an individual or a small company owned the trailers and rented them to the theaters. It is rare to see a search light trailer today, and if you do, it's usually at a new car dealer.

THROUGH RED AND GREEN GLASSES

The movie industry was getting hurt by television, although we did not realize it, and it was coming up with clever and innovative ways to get people into its theaters. In Pawhuska and all the towns like it, movies were one of the few things we thought we could do for entertainment, so we went to the movies no matter what was showing. Still, what happened to the big cities followed to Pawhuska and around then came: 3-D movies. Some of them had a plot.

We saw the coming attractions for them and learned about the special glasses, and we were excited. The first 3-D movie that I remember seeing was *Bwana Devil*. I remember nothing about it but the title and the effect. The film had been made with two cameras, off set, and to see it as it was intended required special glasses. When we bought our ticket at the box office, we were handed special glasses with one red lens and one green lens. The frame was made from a stiff cardboard and hurt our ears after a bit so we would take off the glasses and watch the movie with our own vision: mistake.

Without the glasses, the movie was two separate images of red lines and green lines, and it could make you queasy. So, we put the glasses on. It was a fad, it was fun; I'm glad it faded away.

THROWING PAPERS

I was a paper boy, not that I was made of paper, but I delivered newspapers to earn spending money. As we say, I "threw" the paper, and that is usually what happened to it. I started with the Pawhuska Journal-Capital (J-C), which was an evening paper that we delivered five days weekly. We did not deliver on Monday or Saturday but did deliver for the rest of the week. On Sunday, we delivered it early in the morning.

I had a red English racer bicycle with wire baskets, one on each side of the rear fender. I stored my papers in there and also in a cloth paper bag that we were issued. I do not remember the route number of my first paper route, but it began at the Journal-Capital office on Ki-He-Kah and Seventh Street, Soderstroms's grocery, all that side of the street to Main Street and then across all of the streets west of there and north of Main Street. So I delivered on Tinker Street and out to the cemetery area. It was not a bad paper route, and there were some very nice people along the way that treated me kindly. I had a number of elderly clients and a number of handicapped clients.

I liked throwing papers and a big part of being a paper boy, like being a Boy Scout, was the camaraderie. We paperboys gathered at the J-C after school and waited for the paper to finish. While we waited, we talked, exchanged ideas, and had good natured banter and a few fights. I didn't really like to fight, and I tried hard to avoid them; but one boy had a quick temper and was easy to set off. I had a fight with him one day over nothing, and I dreaded having to face him the next day and more. I never really tried to talk to him anymore or be a friend, and we developed a truce that avoided further fights between us. But he had a fight with someone almost every week. He was one of the smallest of the boys, but he was quick to fight and didn't back down. He lost as many as he won.

The J-C printing press was not the best in the world and there were frequent break downs. There was an order of getting your papers, probably based on how far out you had to go, so the same boys always got their papers first. A press break-down meant that you got your papers late and got a late start on delivery, which left clients unhappy but that was the nature of being a paperboy then.

We were not given these papers. We were business men, and we had to buy them from the J-C organization. To pay our paper debts, we had to collect money from our clients. The fee was $.25 a week for the J-C then. We were issued a book with two metal, rectangular plates and a two binding rings to hold the receipts in place. The receipt was a small, white paper that we tore out and gave to our client.

Although I liked throwing papers, I hated making collections. As incentives to us to collect and pay our bills to the J-C on time, we were given coupons to Irby's Drug Store, the G & L Drug Store, and movie passes to the Ki-He-Kah Theater, if we paid on time. I think that my net pay after paying my paper bill was around $5.00 to $7.00 weekly and that was nice because it was ours, or we saw it that way.

Some of my clients were not well off, and it took me several trips to collect my quarter from them, sometimes going into the next week, and it then became $.50 to collect. Difficult collections went like this:

[Knock on the door]

"Journal-Capital. May I collect, please?"

"Yes? Oh, it's the paper boy. Do you have any money? No?"

"Say, listen, we don't have a quarter now. Could you come back tomorrow?"

"Tomorrow?" I voiced, as my mind raced into thinking, I have to ride my bicycle all the way from downtown to here for one lousy quarter when you know good and well that we collect on Saturdays and we have forever so, why don't you have one lousy quarter and save me all the trouble?

"Yes ma'am, I'll be back tomorrow or Monday," I would say, as pleasantly as I possibly could.

"Thank you. Monday would be even better," my client would say.

To pay my paper bill then, I had to short from my own profits and pay it until I could collect the delinquent accounts. When I was an adult and had the paper delivered, I remembered that and I always put out the money for the paper boy first thing.

I left the Journal-Capital at some point, and I began to throw the Tulsa World. It was a guaranteed $5.00 every week and no collection. Alas, it was early in the morning. I woke up at four AM to get ready for it, went to the dock behind the post office and waited for the papers to arrive.

At the Journal-Capital, we folded our newspapers into what we called the J-C fold. The paper was laid out, folded over to make it smaller, and then we did a pretzel twist on it to get it into a flat form with a wing on it. That way, it sailed when you threw it, and it could be steered a bit. It also made the paper stiffer and easier to break a window with it.

The Tulsa World was a much larger newspaper, and we usually had to roll it and then bind it with a rubber band. We had to buy the rubber bands ourselves. Thursday always had dreaded "inserts", which were the supplemental advertising that came from a central source. These were not put in at the Tulsa World offices in Tulsa, so we had to do it and it took time. Time was precious when you were getting up at four and had to go to school after throwing the paper. We always hoped to finish and get another thirty minutes of sleep at home before heading off to school. Sometimes I got the thirty minutes in school, not intentionally but sometimes I was too exhausted to stay awake. I was always difficult to wake too, so if I got up at four, my mother and grandmother got up at four to get me started.

I stayed with the Tulsa World for a while, then I quit and threw the Journal-Capital again, and once, I had a Journal-Capital and Tulsa World route at the same time. Since one was an afternoon delivery and the other a morning delivery, I could do both but on Sunday, they were both morning deliveries. But it took more time.

I made more money delivering both, but I was supporting a motor scooter which I used to deliver papers, and the maintenance was consuming most of my earnings.

THE MOVIE SCHEDULES

I don't know who delivered it, because it always just showed up, but the Ki-He-Kah Theater published a single sheet advertisement each month that listed the movie schedule for the coming month. Not to say that life was dull in a small town, but most of us looked forward with excitement to the new schedule. Each month was published in a different color to make it easy for us to tell the current month from the new month.

The former Ki-He-Kah theater building

As soon as we received it, I eagerly studied it and planned for the movies that I wanted to see. Usually I had seen multiple showings of the coming attractions at the theater, and I knew what I wanted to see; it was just a matter then, of seeing when the movie would be on, planning how to get money for it and lining up friends or a girl to go see the movie with.

This sheet of paper was probably eleven inches high and nineteen inches across, and it had some advertisement from other local businesses. The telephone number for the theater was listed and the dates, times and prices for the movies. It was posted in a prominent place in our house.

I had paid a child's price for a long time, and I was approaching twelve years of age. In the eternal conflict between child and parent, I wanted to be twelve, even though it meant paying an adult's price. My mother wanted me to stay eleven forever and continue to pay a child's fare. She spoke about it often and to anyone, so that everyone knew I was going to be twelve and when. I wasn't really happy about that, yet, in a way, it was nice that people knew when my birthday was coming up.

I was born February 12, 1944, so I shared my birthday with the great and famous American President, Abraham Lincoln, although he was older than I. Eventually, I won out over my mother's wishes, and I got to be twelve years old. I almost didn't make it to fifteen though when the Chevy and the Eagle collided.

NUMBER PLEASE?

My mother, Bettie Payne, worked at the telephone company in the offices on Main Street. The business office was down stairs and the switch board was up one floor. Pawhuska did not have dial telephones then. We simply picked up the receiver and heard the very pleasant voice of a woman—it was always a woman then—ask,

"Number please?"

"1757," I might say.

"Thank you," she would say in the same charming voice, and I would hear a ringing sound, and a few seconds later Bobby Hughes might answer the phone. Or I might hear the operator say,

"I'm sorry, but that number is busy."

"Thank you, I'll call back later," as though I believed she cared if I did or not, and I would hang up.

Our telephone number was 187. My friend Ernie Daughtrey's number was 699, and my friend Ronnie Havens's number was 484, and later, my girl friend's number was 485. I called Ronnie one day and the operator gave me 485 instead of 484 and the girl said, after realizing the error,

"Oh, I know you. You're what's-his-face." I didn't know that we would be girl friend, boy friend later on and, struck by my shyness again, I didn't ask who she was. In fairness, I called her one day only to have the phone answered by Ronnie who said,

"Oh, I know who you are calling," as he laughed at the error. I saw the irony that neither of them knew.

The operators made errors occasionally, but I was allowed to see the switch board several times, and it wasn't a dial. It was a small section that my mother had responsibility for that had thick wires going everywhere. The wires were almost like tubes with a thick, fiber insulation over them and a plug end that was inserted in the panel of holes in front of her. When a call came in, one of the lights above a hole would flash, and she would ask, "Number please?" Then she took a wire from one place and connected it to another, and the call was completed between the two phones. I looked, but I did not understand how she knew which cell to plug into. But that's why we must forgive them the few errors that they made, for it was an acquired skill that could be improved but never perfected.

The phone directory was a small book, thin and about the size and shape of a 5 by 8 inch photograph with a section at the back for frequently called numbers. We all knew the numbers of close friends, our own number, and a few especially important numbers: The Ki-He-Kah Theater's number was 75; the State Theater's number was 10. You could call and ask,

"What is the movie?"

"*The Greatest Show on Earth*"

"What time does it start?"

"The matinee begins at 1:30"

My mother told me stories about the work that the operators did as they were the regular operators, the information operator and the long distance operator all rolled into one. The operators would get calls like this.

"Honey, this is Julia Griffin, and I don't remember the number, but I want to call the little shop that is across the street from the Packing House. Can you do that for me?"

"Ma'am, do you know the name of the shop?"

"No honey, that's why I called you. But they have little baskets that a lady who lives in Wynona makes."

"I know where you mean. One moment and I'll connect you.'

"Thank you honey."

The call was completed with no more information than that. The operator was polite, courteous and helped my aunt and a business owner get together. I miss that.

The number of 565 was stuck in my head, just as though it were glued there. For months I looked in my notes and old letters, trying to recall it. After I verified telephone numbers for people that I knew, I struggled to figure out why this one number was so persistent in my mind. Finally, it struck me. When I first went to work for Phillips Petroleum Company in the research department in 1967, our unit's telephone number was 565, after you got through the main PBX switch board. Two years later, we changed to a seven digit number system but the old number stayed with me, and it was so close to a Pawhuska telephone number that I believed it was.

THE LAST FIGHT

The last fight that Bobby Hughes and I had was when we were sophomores.

I mentioned the rotating and elevating teeter-totter in the park across the street. One night a boy and I were playing on it when another boy came over. He was the neighborhood tough and a bully. Sometimes we played with him all right, but generally, I was scared hairless of him. I was ready to yield my place on the teeter-totter to him and just go home, but instead, he offered to push us and he did. Faster and faster he pushed, standing inside of the circle and the other boy and I were hanging on, having fun and getting dizzy. One of us would have to fall off and I was getting close to it when I got an idea. I pulled my legs up, threaded them through the vertical loop and underneath the teeter-totter. There was no way that I was going to fall off now.

He pushed us faster still and the laws of science that operated then, centrifugal force in particular, forced the other boy off, flying through the air and rolling in the grass. I had won. Uh-oh. And then the teeter-totter, still moving fast and with all of my weight on it dropped to the ground, crushing my legs beneath me. I did not break any bones, but I had a very serious injury, tendons and ligaments, and it left me crippled for several years. I walked with a limp, and I ran with a limp, not very good for a star right half back, when they let me play there.

Jay Lynn told me that we did the Pledge of Allegiance in all of our classes, but I only remember the fifth grade for it. But the reason I remember is, that one day when I led it, was the first day that I had been able to plant my right foot flat and stand on it for more than two years. That was what I remembered, my success. There was a price to pay for that though. It had left me stoop shouldered, and I was made fun of for that. Bobby Hughes had called me Hunchback on occasion, and it hurt. I reacted by hitting him, which usually started a fight.

He had his own flaw and his own sensitivity though, and I did not realize how great it was until that sophomore day. We had had a verbal dispute over something in our physical fitness class, and we had not resolved it. As we were walking from the gymnasium towards the main building, he barked out, "Hunch-back!" and I responded, "Freckle-faced brat!" We flew at each other, arms grappling, fists flailing as our friends called out, "Hit him in the face! Hit him in the face!" I was trying to, but we had hold of each other in such a way that neither of us could get a good swing in. We were rolling on the ground, getting damp and dirty, ruining good jackets when the kindly hand of Mr. Jack Richey stopped us from rolling any more. Bobby and I were the only ones taken to the office, and Mr. Bean beat us nearly to death, for Mr. Bean. He didn't really hit that hard, thank goodness.

Mr. Bean had us apologize, which we did, and shake hands, which we did, sincerely for we had too many years together for such nonsense, and we were both sorry. That was the last fight that Bobby Hughes and I ever had with each other.

As we were walking out of the office and heading to our next classes, he looked at me and asked, "Can I catch a ride home with you?" "Sure," I said, "You rode here with me, ought to ride back with me." "Sure." And that was it.

A WHUPPING

There was a boy that Jay Lynn, others and I played football with at Union. I mention that because he went on to play professional football with the San Diego Chargers and later, the Denver Broncos.

In 1967, he was the offensive rookie of the year, and he was the rushing leader several years. He played in the Pro Bowl during his last year in football. His name was Richard Post, and he and I were friends. Others were friends with him too, but he acquired all kinds of friends from Pawhuska once he began his professional career. But he and I were friends before any of that. His family moved from Pawhuska to Paul's Valley, Oklahoma, and it was there that he was discovered and recruited by the University of Houston so, technically Pawhuska can't make a claim on him, but we do anyway. If you were there long enough, and that can vary depending on the contribution you made to Pawhuska and to its legends, you became a Pawhuskan.

Before he was famous and rich though, he was a student at Pawhuska High School and had a Cushman Eagle, red, and he was one of our Wild Bunch. Most of the time, we called him Richard, which was unusual for that nick-naming age, when we made diminutives out of almost any name. The San Diego Chargers billed him as Dicky

Post, which I don't believe any of us ever called him.

Richard and I had a study hall hour and we sat close to each other and goofed off more than we studied. The study hall monitor—which we called a teacher, even though they taught nothing in study hall—was Jack Richey. Mr. Richey had a tendency to get up and wonder out of the room. Since Richard and I were bored, we started playing a game. When we saw Mr. Richey either not looking or out of the room, we would hit each other in the shoulder, hard. He could hear it, if he were there, and he would look up but not seeing anything, he resumed his reading or nap.

Richard hit me, and when I got the opportunity, I hit him. We had been doing that for a while when Mr. Richey left and stayed out for a long time. So we really started hitting each other and the other kids around us were laughing and enjoying it. We should have known that something was amiss when those in front of us suddenly turned serious and spun about in the seats to face forward. But neither of us picked up on it, and we were happily hammering away on each other when a hand caught my hand in mid-motion and stopped it.

"Having fun boys?" he asked. We had been but we were not about to tell him that. We exercised our right to remain silent, and we would have asked for a lawyer if we could have got one. "I think I'll take you both down to the office and let Mr. Bean handle you." There was probably a whipping in this, but we had both been paddled by the Bean before and lived to tell of it. We were embarrassed by being caught in front of the rest of the students, but not worried.

After getting his facts, interviewing witnesses, pronouncing us guilty and quelling any appeals, Mr. Bean opened the cabinet, removed one of many boards, which I'm sure the shop class made from failed projects, and stepped into place. He told Richard to lean over the desk and then, at the last moment said, "Mr. Richey, would you like to paddle these boys?" We were in luck. If Mr. Bean were harmless, Mr. Richey would surely be more so. Richard smiled at me, and I motioned to him with my eyes, "Don't blow it, Dick." Mr. Richey stepped back, raised his arm as far and wide as possible and, "Kapow!"

It was the loudest whack I had ever heard. Richard straightened up and yelled out. Mr. Richey aimed and hit him again and that time, Richard went up against the desk, turned and said, "Please don't hit me again." I thought, oh come on Dick. You're overdoing it. The final blow was a very painful one, obviously, and I was beginning to think that Richard wasn't acting.

It was my turn and I took the position, and he hit me just as hard, and I thought I would never stop stinging from it. Then came the second one, and I beat Richard's record for climbing the desk. I was looking forward to the third and last one to get it over with and hoping that we would finally have that air raid by the Russians that we had been expecting since first grade. I tried not to anticipate it, but I could hear the air beginning to move, feel his muscles straining as he aimed, and hit true to his mark. The only time I ever hurt more was when my shoulder went completely out from an arthritis attack; and maybe when the Chevrolet ran over me. But the hospital gave me morphine for that. "Go back to study hall and sit down boys," Mr. Bean said. Sitting was the furthest thing from my mind.

I went home and wrote out an excuse to be dismissed from any further study halls and forged my grandmother's signature. I never went back to study hall. I thought back to when Bobby Hughes and I had just escaped Mr. Richey paddling us and how lucky we were; we just didn't know it.

I was watching a televised game with Dick Post playing against a tough defense one day when the announcer said, "Well that was a whupping," as Dick was tackled viciously.

No, a whupping was what we got in 1960; after that, everything was easier.

BY ANY OTHER NAME

There was a long period when we had our diminutive names; Bobby, Johnny, Jimmy, Stevie. At around age twelve, and probably in the transition between sixth grade and junior high, we started trying to grow out of them and into something else. We were trying to shed our cocoons and become butterflies and picking a new name, our own name, was part of it. We shifted from being called Bobby to Bob but not quite Robert. Bobby Hughes never sat down with me and said, "From this day forth I shall be known as Bob." I'm not sure how we signaled the transition but I know that my girl cousins Candy and Cathy would not give it up. I was Stevie forever to them, and I still am.

Many from high school knew me as Steve, and they are just as stubborn about giving that up. In my twenties and later, I discovered the sound Steve had a harsh, guttural sound to it and I began to use my given name of Stephen. At one time, for business reasons, I just used S.J. but so many people asked what it stood for and then called me Stephen that we reprinted my next box of business cards with Stephen J. Payne. I have used that, officially, since.

Bobby and I allowed each other to grow up, as we wanted, and we called each other "Bob" and "Steve" as we went through high school, but when we were alone we still used "Bobby" and "Stevie." It didn't bother me. In 1991 there was a reunion of sorts at the Elks Club in Pawhuska, and he called me and encouraged me to come. I wasn't sure if I should. My wife and I were married twenty-three years and then had a difficult divorce. I was uncertain how I felt about facing old friends and gloaters with a divorce. Then on the other hand, I had a new ALFA-Romeo Spider convertible that I didn't mind people seeing, so I put the top down and went. Zoom-zoom!

When I arrived and signed in, Bobby showed me a long banner and asked me to put my name on it. I took the black felt tip marker and signed with my famous signature and new arrivals were asking, "Who is that?" as though I were a new arrival from another place and had never lived in Pawhuska. Bobby took the pen and beneath my signature wrote: Stevie Joe.

Suddenly people were coming over and asking me to pay back loans and things. No, just kidding. They were coming over, talking to me, and we were having pleasant memories, whether they really happened or not.

One time I was experimenting with concepts about success and failure and I asked Coach Hurt (Jay Lynn as an adult) how many touchdowns he had scored. He knew. How many by rushing? He knew. How many by passing? He knew. How many times he had fumbled? He didn't have a clue. He said no one had ever asked him before. Others not only forgive our youthful mistakes but they also forget; we should too.

As we talked then, no one brought up unpleasant memories. No matter who it was, we had been the best of friends in high school and a couple of girls had even dated me, though I didn't realize it. Catch-me-red sports cars can have an interesting effect on people.

In our forties, we were still Bobby and Stevie to each other.

LATTER DAY STEVIE JOE

My cousin Candy Cooper and her mother Ola Mae always called me Stevie Joe, whether they were talking to me or about me. Candy said that they had told Candy's step-son, Jackie, many stories about Stevie Joe. They just never told him how old Stevie Joe was. They told him that Stevie Joe had built a lot of ships out of old lumber, and that they were all over the old house; in the rooms, on the porch, in the yard, under the house.

Art Brave found one of my ships many years later, when he was working on the house. It was in reasonably good shape, and one of my better pieces of work. I had carved the bow well, with a saw, and the turrets were still mounted, though some of the guns had rusted. The guns were always large nails driven into the turrets. This particular ship that Art had found was probably one of my battleships, as it was quite large.

They also told Jackie about the bicycles that Stevie Joe had taken apart and modified, and the motor scooters that had often been spread about the yard as they were being worked on. So, Jackie had a lot of Stevie Joe stories. One year in the mid-1970's, I was around Candy a lot, when she was living in Pawhuska again with Jackie and her two children, Richard and Libby. Candy had ridden on my motorcycle, a Kawasaki 750CC model, and Jackie seemed to eye us suspiciously.

"Candy," I began. "I think you ought to talk to Jackie, and explain our relationship."

"He knows you're my cousin," she said.

I was not sure.

"Candy," I tried again, with more desperation, "I think he thinks we are having an affair."

"Jackie," she asked, "Do you know who this is?"

He did not reply, and appeared to be puzzled. She then realized that, perhaps he did think we were lovers.

"Jackie," she took up, "*this* is Stevie Joe."

A broad grin swept his face. He had thought that Stevie Joe was still a teenager, much like himself, and not the adult he knew in me.

THE SWIMMING HOLE

Pawhuska did not have a swimming pool in the early 1950's. If you wanted to swim you swam in a pond or in one or two of the select swimming holes on Bird Creek. There was a small wading pool at the Kiwanis Park on Grandview Avenue at 15th Street, and there were water holes in places like Cedar Canyon, but no swimming pool. Some families went to Sunset Lake about midway between Pawhuska and Bartlesville, but we did not have a car. I couldn't swim anyway, so I wasn't worried.

My mother often talked about swimming in the Arkansas River amongst the sand bars when she was growing up in Web City. Anytime we crossed the mighty Arkansas River at Ponca City she would boast of her swimming ability. Naturally, I felt bad because I couldn't swim. Also, I was frightened of the water, especially dark water.

About 1953, Pawhuska finally built and opened the swimming pool on Lynn Avenue and 15th Street. I had never been to a pool before. To understand why most parents felt some relief at the pool's being built, that time must be placed into the context of a disease that struck mostly children and left them paralyzed: poliomyelitis.

I was scared to death of it, and didn't know how to avoid it. Every summer brought fun and excitement and the fear of polio. Donna Poulton had a cousin named Richard Wong, who lived in Wichita, Kansas. Every summer, Richard visited in Pawhuska at Grandma Jessie's. Richard was half Chinese, but I thought he was all Chinese. He did not speak the language, but he acted very Chinese—to me. We were great friends and I looked forward to his summer visits. He told me once, that the reason his parents sent him to Pawhuska, away from the bustle of kids in Wichita, was for him to avoid getting polio.

The pool was wonderful and I got to take swimming lessons, from which I learned nothing. I went through the motions with my instructor, but I just couldn't learn to swim. Still, I spent hours at the pool, in the shallow water, going from side to side and getting the worst sunburn of my life. I didn't know I was burning until I got home and had large, white blisters on my shoulders and down my back.

I always had a solution to things though, and I thought it was a frogman's web flippers, a diving mask and snorkel tube, which my mother bought for me at Greer's. I could swim underwater with that so I was making progress. Actually, with my imagination and the movies, I was playing frogman from one of the movies I had seen; everyone else was just swimming.

Accidentally, between the flippers, failing swimming lessons, and some friends helping me, I learned how to swim. Then I had goals which were first, to swim from one side of the pool to the other, then lengthwise, from the shallow end to the deep end. Then I bounced myself off of the low diving board a few times and swam the pool. I was getting pretty good. Then I went up on the high diving board. From the ground looking up, it is only about ten feet high; from the board looking down, it is some seventy-five feet. Of course, it was water so, what could happen? It's not like hitting solid earth; right. I dived, misjudged and hit the blue concrete below me that looked suspiciously like water but could not have been. Water is soft, and you can't get hurt falling into it.

When I finally got out of the water, a life guard, or rather a life guardette, a very pretty girl with a smile, asked, "Are you all right?" Why do they keep asking this question? I opened my mouth to speak and...no words came out; just a mysterious "aaaauuuuugghhhh" sound that I could make no sense of either. It did not get any better and she encouraged me to dress and go home. I nodded and walked, crab-like, to the dressing room and changed. Boys were trying to talk to me, and all I could say was, "aaaauuuuugghhhh." I had had the same feeling once before, when the chain on my bicycle broke in a hard race, and I hit the cross bar with force.

Several days later though, I was normal and I vowed to never try that again. I didn't either, until the navy forced me to in order to qualify and pass boot camp.

My friend Richard Wong from Wichita visited that summer. He, Donna and I went to the pool almost every day, when I wasn't too sunburned to go. Richard was one of the few friends I had in a distant town, and we wrote to each other, my first pen pal. I received his letter with shock. "Stevie, I got polio while I was in Pawhuska." I was devastated for he was a wonderful guy. At that age, Wichita was somewhere out there, nowhere specific to me, and I didn't know that I might be able to visit him. But the old 1941 Chevy kept us from that and, I suspect that my grandmother and mother did not want me to visit him; too much risk of getting it myself.

The next time I saw Richard—and every time—he was in braces and using crutches to walk. But it never took his smile away; it never stole one laugh from him.

Ironically, he was the only person I knew who contracted polio. As an adult, when I could think about it, I doubt that he actually contracted polio in Pawhuska. He was a wonderful guy and everyone loved Richard Wong.

AROUND THEY GO

Like most kids my age, I had a pair of roller skates. They were not fancy or special. They were two metal frames with four metal wheels. The middle part had an adjustment system with which they could be loosened and moved closer together or further apart. The metal frames fit over my regular leather street shoes but never very well, and I always experienced frustration with that. I would tighten them as much as I possibly could, and then they would loosen and cause me to fall off of my skates. A few years ago, I figured out that the leather sole was gradually giving in to the dual pressures of the metal and the physical force of my skating; this meant that the fitting could never be made completely secure.

I knew only one girl who had real skates, that is a built in skate and shoe so that they could not come off.

The sidewalk around my own block was smoother, but it was frequented with adults so I usually went off to Bobby Hughes's block and skated around it. On the north side, there was a section of sidewalk that was badly broken up, and it was a challenge; one I often failed to negotiate. Skating was fun, but it was a lot of work, and we all had our share of trips and falls.

Then Pawhuska got a skating rink. It was on the south part of Leahy Avenue close to the old rail road station. It was the first time that many of us had been on real skates. The rink rented skates in various sizes for both boys and girls. It must have been around 1958 for I remember the girl I was in love with and the songs that she liked. There was music at the rink, which we could barely hear over the noise of a thousand skate wheels. Surprisingly, there were a few excellent skaters, and we would see them gliding by, turning and skating backwards and doing a few tricks. Most of us skated as fast as we could, in a long oval pattern around the rink, over and over. I was carried away and I over did it my first time, so I paid dearly on Monday for my Saturday fun. Still, it was one more place that we could ask a girl for a date. It was one more place where we could meet girls.

It was very busy for some time, and then the business began to wane and it closed.

Later, a bowling alley opened, and I think it was in the same building. I bowled there with friends one time while I was living in Bartlesville and before I was transferred to North Dakota.

SON

In Pawhuska, he was just called "Son." I liked him in the movies before I knew that he was from Pawhuska, and the truth is that he wasn't. He was from Foraker but that is close enough to be called a Pawhuskan, and he called himself one. To me, he was Trooper Travis Tyree and Sergeant Tyree in *She Wore a Yellow Ribbon* and *Fort Apache,* the John Wayne movies. I liked him best as Greg in *Mighty Joe Young* though, and I best liked the way he looked in *Hang 'Em High* and *The Wild Bunch* with his dark, devilish beard.

The first time I saw the man, Bobby Hughes and I were standing on Ninth Street, just east of Pamela Ray's house when a 1957 Buick rolled by, a man low in the seat with a gray cowboy hat shading his eyes. As he passed us, he turned and raised his hand in a wave, a smile breaking over his face. "He waved at us!" Bobby shrieked. We had waved back, as we had been taught to do. "Who was he?" I asked. "That was Son, Stevie. Don't you know anything?"

I did not know that he was a living, breathing, human being; I did not know that he visited Pawhuska regularly. I was deeply impressed. The next time was years later at the Osage County Fair when I saw people passing him, stopping, shaking his hand. Red Davis asked me, "Stevie, did you see Son?" I only saw him as he passed by, the same wave and smile I had seen years before with Bobby. I never got to meet Ben Johnson, Jr.

But my mother knew him; my stepfather, Art Brave knew him, and my younger brother, Charles Brave knew him. My mother was in the Cowboy Hall of Fame one day when a crew was filming a documentary. She and the children had moved to one side to not interfere with their work when she heard, "Just a minute, fellas, I know that lady and need to say 'hi' to her." Then she heard, "Bettie?" and turned to face him as he said, "Hi, Bettie. Ben Johnson," as though she would not know who he was. By all accounts, he was a genuine person, not a drop of Hollywood or movie star in him.

Charles Brave

Anyone and everyone from Pawhuska was proud to the ears when he received, first a nomination, and then, the Academy Award for his Sam the Lion in *The Last Picture Show*. He did Pawhuska proud.

And I am probably the only Pawhuskan from my generation who will admit never having met him; I wish I had.

LOSING A SON

My wife and I had a son in 1967, and named him Stephen William Payne. The William came from the long line of Williams in the Hardy family and my wife's father, William S. Walling. Stephen developed type I or juvenile diabetes at age thirteen while we lived in North Dakota. He fought a brave fight with his disease, eventually losing his eyesight to it, and then his kidneys failed him. He was on kidney dialysis three times weekly for the last seven years of his life. Stephen lost his fight, September 6, 2003. I later wrote the essay that follows.

My son, Stephen William Payne, 1967-2003

A SON'S FAREWELL

"Dad, I'm scared!" Stephen said into the phone. I could hear the fear in his voice, sense the anguish that gripped him. My entire intellectual life flashed before me, all the things I had learned from books, movies, the Bible, management seminars, counseling, my college career, the Navy, all the things I *should* say as a father: "Chin up!" "Keep a stiff upper lip." "There is nothing to fear but fear itself." "A good soldier does his duty, "Never give up!" I opened my mouth for one of those gems and heard my voice saying "Son, I'm scared too." It was the right thing to say.

Stephen, at thirty-six, prided himself on not breaking any bones--so far--unlike me; I had broken seven before I was twenty-one. Diabetes had blinded him six years earlier and trips and falls were just part of his life, but so far he had suffered only skins and bruises. He always counted the thirty steps of the stairs between his apartment and the taxi waiting to take him to his thrice weekly dialysis sessions. That morning, he miscounted.

In spite of the broken bones in his left ankle, he managed the three hour treatment and was even planning to return home and rest before going out to perform that evening. That was his anti-psychotic medicine talking, medicine that helped him get through dialysis. A nurse made him go to the hospital where surgery reconnected the bones.

His mother called me that Friday evening, letting me know that I did not have to rush the three hundred fifty miles to Tyler, Texas. She would keep me informed, and I was grateful. I talked to him over the weekend and then again on Monday, when the doctors conceded that the device joining the bones was failing.

Years of diabetes and dialysis had left the bones too soft. He was so upset that he had his mother place the call for him, the one when he told me he was scared—about the amputation. It wasn't certain but it was likely and he would not know until he regained consciousness. He would go to sleep with two legs, one badly broken, and he would awaken with either two legs or just one.

Or he would not awaken at all; it was a possibility. I hurt for him then as I had never hurt before, wanting to trade places with him as any father does. I prayed hard. He kept his leg, for which we were all grateful, but it never really healed. He seemed to settle into the hospital routine, and we called each other often; and I traveled to see him as soon as I could. I stayed in a motel and spent what time I could at his side in the hospital. He was drowsy from the medications so our talks were short and intermittent but just being with him was enough, for both of us.

I couldn't stay for all of his long hospital time so I drove home and returned later. My younger brother Charles Brave, who was close to Stephen (as only five years separated uncle and nephew), drove from Pawhuska to Tyler to be with him. And Stephen had his mother and many friends. He was not alone yet he was all alone; alone with the things he had to go through. No one could do it for him. No one could do for me what I was going through either.

His fear was not of the pain, not even of the dreaded amputation; it was of losing his independence. He had seen my mother lose both of her legs and her independence to diabetes, and it had left hopeless images for him. That was not how he wanted to end up.

He was considering an option that he had touched upon but not discussed much. He might go off of dialysis. He had talked with his doctor about it, and she told him that he would take about two weeks to die, that a hospice would take care of him with analgesics. (We don't use the word painkiller in a family of Paynes).

The selfish father in me did not want him to do that, yet I understood both his reasoning and his wishes. He had suffered more than he should have. He had suffered more than I could have born to suffer. He had been diabetic since he was thirteen, and I could not argue with the logic he had for letting his life end. An earlier heart attack had removed him from transplant candidacy so living longer just meant more organ and tissue failures. There was no hope of getting better, only worse, only sicker, and then dying. This decision gave him some feeling of control in his life, and there was little left that he could still control.

Diabetes wasn't Stephen's only fight. There were also those with drugs and his need to feel loved. He *was* loved, but I know that there were times when he didn't feel like it, and sometimes it was my fault. Sometimes I had been too stern, too much a disciplinarian; sometimes I had yelled when I should have spoken softly; sometimes I had said no when I should have said yes, and sometimes I had said yes when I should have said no.

Still, I always felt loved by him, even when I was more a father than a friend, even when he was angry with me. When you have a child who has problems, some people consider him less worthy to live, that his life has less value, and sometimes, he saw himself that way; and sometimes that was my fault.

Sometimes it was his mother's fault. I tried to counter that as much as I could by telling him that I loved him every time we talked, by giving him the things that he needed and wanted that I could give and, surprisingly, these were often simple. He needed batteries for this guitars and tape recorders. He needed lots of blank recording tapes, and I had learned to skip the Christmas and birthday wrappings as he needed them already opened, one less thing for his blind eyes to struggle with.

When we were together I took him to the movies he loved and listened to the remarks of people who did not understand. "Is that kid blind?" "He's using a cane so he must be." "Why would you take a blind person to a movie?" Because he was worth it, because it's what he wanted to do and movies were still one of the special bonds that we shared; movies and music. And he could still hear and follow the movie. He still had other senses, perhaps more acute than those of the people wondering why a blind kid would go to a movie.

On a September Saturday in 2003, Stephen lost the final round in his long fight. "I'm tired" he had said to his Tyler friends Eric and Mike. Between Thursday and Friday Stephen saw his uncle, his childhood friend Pete Inda and me. He asked me to talk, to say anything, just to hear the sound of my voice. He loved my voice, he said. I talked for a while, and he slipped into a gentle sleep. I was stepping out to let him rest when he stirred for a minute, rose up on his pillow a little and his voice became strong, surprisingly so since he had been speaking so softly. "Dad," he said, "I'm *so* proud to have had you for a father." I stood at the door for what seemed a very long time, feeling his words more than thinking about them. It was the most magnificent thing anyone had ever said to me, and it made it difficult for me to speak; I didn't know what to say.

Against my will, tears forced themselves from my eyes. I looked at him, saw him on the verge of tears himself, and I struggled to find words equal to his. My voice was weak from talking, weak from the illness in my vocal cords, and I felt the shakiness in my overtired voice as the simple words, "Thank you son" croaked out of my throat. A son's farewell: *"I'm so proud to have had you for a father."*

Stephen died about 5:30 Saturday morning.

RONNIE'S SONG

My friend Ronnie Havens lost a son before I did, in 1988, and I hurt for him as though I had lost a son. In many ways, he prepared me to deal with losing Stephen. Ronnie is more eloquent with words that I and with his permission, I am using his 2002 poem, *I Don't Recall* from his *A Book of My Dreams*.

I Don't Recall
(Upon remembrance of the day he left)
I don't recall the day that I realized he wasn't there.
Oh, I knew he was gone alright, and I had seen him and touched him that last time,
But I really didn't think him gone, vanished into that twilight mystery.
But there surely was a time when the wind blew and rumbled against the house,
And night bore down its deep, black blanket, engulfing me in its dark, silent tears,
But even then I didn't really know he was gone.
I would wake and feel him sleeping in his room, his quiet breathing echoing in the halls of night,
And in the darkness I would find myself dreaming the dream that had awakened me was real,
But half a dozen steps toward his room and I knew he wouldn't be there,

And so I struggled back to the bed that still held my warmth while-his lay cold,
To stare at the ceiling in the darkness until the tears ran even colder into my ears,
There to slip back into the vanquished dream.
I don't recall the day that I realized he wasn't there, the day I *really knew*.
Dreams and years rolled by and I would hear a car turn into the drive then stop,
Its slamming door would get hope up to greet his return and then he would vanish again,
Becoming someone else and he would drift back to the edge of sorrow's twilight reality,
The one I fought and fought and fought, over and over and over,
Wearing myself down drop by salty drop as tears carved the sadness deep into my face,
And still I didn't know, at least for sure, that it was *not a* dream
And I would fight the fight more than once again.
I think it may have come in spring, after my hair had turned mostly gray,
And my bones no longer jumped and ran with the fireflies that filled the cool night.
Or perhaps it was on that autumn day when the chilly north wind snatched me up,
One with the swirling leaves, blowing me into the land where the fence rows dance
With dead reds and crackling yellows,
Caught for the moment until they, and I, were crumbled to dust and gone.
Or, if memory serves, that day the summer heat of the hottest August noon ever bore down,
Drenching me in its white-hot, sun-sweat furnace called self-pity.
No, maybe that winter morning I awoke to find only the

still, silent whiteness dressing the yard,

Having fallen like the cat's step in the night to lie a surprise through the frosty pane,

And looking out at it in its peaceful stillness, seeing it wrinkled by the garden's stones,

Perhaps then I knew and then I fell to my knees, opened my heart,

And let it break at last into its thousand waiting tear-shards.

I really don't recall the day that I realized he wasn't there, isn't here,

Perhaps I never will.

TO HAVE AND TO HAVE NOT

Like Ronnie and thousands of fathers and mothers who have lost a child, I don't sense the reality of it. I turn the corner, hear a sound, hear a song, see someone, and hear a boy's laughter, and I am reminded of Stephen. Every few months, I see a boy that looks like him, a motorcycle jacket, unkempt hair, a dreamy look and I stare and take him in to remind me once again that Stephen lived. And it's not the same boy, but different ones in different places, who have much in common with him. We have two words that are like the binary switches of a computer, 1's and 0's, on and off: Life and death. But they are not that simple, for life begins with the union of a man and a woman. Before it began, what was it? Do we call it death? We have no name for it. It is pre-life, but does it really exist? It exists for those who believe we exist, and then enter a human body. Death does not apply to those who have not been born. It is the word we use only to say that a life has ended and some form of the word exists in every language for death is a universal experience.

I had Stephen for thirty-six years, almost thirty-seven, and I am grateful for that. I have been blessed, for I have had many wonderful experiences in my lifetime. Many were in the form of something I wanted: a car, a motorcycle, a college degree, a job, a book to write. But there is nothing in the life we are given to live, nothing in the human experience that can compare with the feelings of having a child. *All* of the feelings, the joy, the frustration, the anger, the tears and the laughter for they are all standard issue with a child. I miss him but I count the days and years of his life as my blessings, and I am thankful to God for those gifts. How can I ever complain about him being taken away for having been given those gifts? And I have more. As long as I live and can remember, the gift of his life continues to fuel my life. I would rather have had, loved and lost my son than to never have had him at all.

TODAY I AM A MAN

I don't think anyone ever says the words, "Today I am a man." We are children and teens, and we want to grow up, eventually, for it is the debt that we owe. We can not stay children forever though Heaven help us if we completely lose our child's way of seeing the world.

I was an insurance salesman in California and making a call in Whitaker when the little girl on the other side of the door said, "Mommy, there's a man at the door." I promptly turned around and looked to see who he was. Self definition: I did not see myself as man—yet. That would come later, when I was thirty years old, or forty, or fifty. It still seems elusive. One statesman said that you become a man the day the last of your fathers dies. One said it is when you lose your father. I think it is asymptotic. We can approach it, and get ever closer, but it eludes us. We become adults but still hesitate to call ourselves "a man." It is easier to answer the forms question: Sex: Male.

When we had a change of command aboard ship, we had a ceremony and the incoming and outgoing captains read their orders, saluted each other and said, "I now relieve you of command of the U.S.S. Point Defiance." "I stand relieved, Captain." And that is it; he becomes the captain when the old man says that he is. Perhaps we should formalize a ceremony and someone we have called a man and he knew what it meant, names us one. There was no mistake about why we called him a man. We looked up to him, admired him, respected him and learned from him.

Gordon Hughes, Russell Havens, Louis Bean, C. G. Arnold, Father Joe, Dean Rainwater, Coach Doug Dugger; those were men, and I knew it the first time I saw them. Perhaps that is when I will feel that I am finally a man, in the sense of the word that those men were and are; men of honor. Perhaps someday, one of them will tell me, "Today, you are a man." Then I will believe it.

FATHERHOOD IS FOREVER

Stephen Joe Payne at age 62

But I knew when I was a father, no question about that. And once you become a father, you are always a father.

This section is dedicated to two friends. One is from Pawhuska, and I have known him a lifetime. The other I have known more than twenty years from my career connection; that is time to establish friendship. What they have in common, besides their connection to me, is that they both have lost a child. We three fathers have that in common, that is the club we belong to. Both of them lost a child suddenly and unexpectedly, to an automobile accident, Ronnie Havens, a son, Dennis Goldwood, a daughter.

I lost my son to a slow and progressive disease, juvenile diabetes. I had many years to prepare for his death and each year, for many years, Christmas was a gift. I accepted those gifts hungrily, and spent as much time with him as I could. I had the opportunity of having a good goodbye with him for we spent his last day together, and we exchanged good thoughts and love. I could still be his father, but I no longer had to stand tall and be made of steel as I offered him advice on how to get through life.

I could forgive all of my failings as a father and not spend his last day agonizing about where I had gone wrong or even where I had succeeded. We were just two friends together talking about songs we knew, movies we had shared and loved together and all of the funny things that we had seen and done; just as Ronnie and I had done in another lifetime, another place. We laughed a lot and not at jokes for we told none but at everything else. I had to have one very serious moment with him and that is when I had to ask him about his last wishes. "Dad," he said, "I want to be buried in Pawhuska." And so he is. This was the most difficult conversation I have ever had to have, but I was glad that I did for I did not have to guess at his wishes nor argue with other people about what Stephen wanted.

Even with the knowledge that one is going to be a father it comes upon you swiftly, in a single moment and it changes your life. Many of us look at a small, helpless form and see the future as one burdened with debt and preparation for college. But then we get past that stage and find something else to worry about for there is always something. One moment you are not a father, the next moment you are and it never goes away. It is a question that I have had to ask myself: Am I still a father, after my only child has died? I would be in church on Father's Day, and the preacher would ask for all of the fathers present to stand, just as he did on Mother's Day. Should I stand? The answer was and is—of course. I will always be a father. My two friends had other children, so they had to turn to the additional task of helping the surviving siblings deal with the loss of a brother or a sister. I will always be a father for once ordained a father, the office is perpetual.

So, to these two friends, Ronnie Havens of Pawhuska, Dennis Goldwood, now of Houston, Texas, fellow members of a club that we want to keep very small, my dedication to you: Fatherhood is forever.

MY HEROES HAVE ALWAYS BEEN...

Cowboys?
Well, yes and no. My early heroes were certainly cowboys; they were Roy Rogers, Lash Larue, the Lone Ranger, Red Ryder, Tim Holt, Johnny Mack Brown, Gene Autry, all certified cowboys. Ben Johnson, jr. was one even before I knew he was from Pawhuska, or thereabouts.

I found new heroes in Crash Corrigan, Commando Cody and others. Then I saw Fess Parker as Davy Crockett and got to meet Mr. Parker in person and he was my all time hero—for a while. Audie Murphy was my hero for life, and I missed him after his death, even though he had not made a movie in awhile. Later, as I reached adulthood, technically, I found heroes in Steve McQueen, James Coburn, James Dean, Sean Connery and others.

Elvis Presley was my hero for he came from nowhere and went to the top. Buddy Holly was my hero because he succeeded with average looks, and he made me think that maybe I could too.

One day I looked at the world with a very intense glass and found that I had been looking in the wrong places for heroes. Most of those that I had chosen were not real; they were on the screen, in books and distant. I should have been looking closer to home, and in fact I was. I just wasn't putting the right perspective to it. In many ways I have remained at some unchanged age from my youth, perhaps seventeen and that causes me to have a childlike fascination with much of the world. That is what keeps me so interested in movies and how they are made, and why I enjoy talking to actors and directors so much. Physically and chronologically I am older and I show that, as I should. But remove the aches and pains and stiffness of arthritis, and I don't feel much different than I did at seventeen.

Here are some of the heroes, the real ones, that I found when I looked closer:

Wimpsey Gilkey is my hero for he was a good man. He helped other people, and he became a role model for us when we were trying to learn a new society. He was a good friend and he was hilariously funny as well.

Jay Lynn Hurt is my hero. He was athletic, gifted, a star and just a good boy to model on, and I did. I could not reach his example, even when I stretched but looking up to him and trying to be like him made me a better boy then; perhaps it has made me a better man today than I might have been without his positive examples. He strongly influenced me; got me into the Boy Scouts and I tried harder because of him. Ultimately, I had to learn to be my own person, and that is one that is very different from Jay and anyone else. Yet I could not have become better without him.

Jay Lynn Hurt coached high school football for thirty years and was inducted into the Oklahoma High School Coaches Hall of Fame in 1999.

Bobby Green is my hero for he was delightful to be around, usually smiling, very funny and always telling funny stories and jokes. He too was athletic, and he had tremendous courage on the baseball field. Bobby became a highway patrol trooper and continued showing his courage there.

Pamela Ray is my hero; she was beautiful and she had more talent on the dance floor than anyone I have ever seen. She was flexible and could do amazing splits and back bends. She was so far ahead of most of us, that we would quit and just watch her and wonder how she could bend so far back. She could tap dance, glide with ease in any boy's arms and make us think that we knew how to dance. She was patient and would show us steps she had learned; I never heard her criticize a boy for his clumsiness. Of all the kids then, she was the one that I thought I would see on Ed Sullivan someday. She was my date at several proms, and I felt I was the luckiest boy in the world to be with her then; and I wondered how I had got her to go with me.

Frank Ikenberry is my hero because Frank was quiet and seemed older by many years. He was a good role model and never got into any trouble. He was difficult for me to make friends with because we were so different from each other, but still he was a loyal friend, not only to me but to everyone he knew.

Donald "Butch" Daniels is my hero because he understood my lack of confidence as a boy. He never held that against me and just became a good friend. Don taught me how to use wrenches and other tools, and he let me try things so that I could learn. He was a solid friend and he risked himself to protect me from bullies, but if I started it, then he left me on my own to learn. I needed that lesson, to learn that even a friend has to admit when you're working without a net and let you fall on your own. He taught me about bicycles, so that I could fix my own and change tires. When I was teaching my son to fix his bicycle, it was Don Daniels being channeled, because all of the things that I had forgotten came back to me as though it had only been yesterday.

Roy Mitchell is my hero because he accomplished so much in his life. Roy was heroic in his fight against cancer too but long before then, when we were just kids, he was the boy that most of us looked up to and learned from. If Roy could help you, he did. Roy taught me one of my most valuable lessons long ago, and it was painfully learned. It was this: You can't run from trouble.

Ronnie Haven is my hero for his great intelligence, his humor and his friendship. He was the best cornet player I was ever around. More than that, he taught me many things, and he helped me begin to gain some social graces. The courage he showed when he lost Michael helped me deal with losing Stephen. He prepared the way for me.

Robert Gary Malone is my hero for being a United States Marine. He didn't have to make the ultimate sacrifice to be my hero, but he did. His brother Jerry is my hero for being a Marine.

Earl "Chunker" Brunger is my hero for the many things he taught us; some that he probably should not have. Earl was never in band with us, and it was hard to think of him as a musician; but he loved music. Earl bought a Silvertone electric guitar and amplifier from Sears and learned to play the guitar. He mostly taught himself and he had courage as anyone who has ever mounted a stage and played and sang will know. It's harder when it's in front of people you know. He has always been an inspiration to me and, he's been a good friend to all of us.

My cousin Cathy Smith Alburty is my hero. She quit school but didn't give up, raised her family, finished high school and went on to college. It takes special courage to do all of that, and I admire her for it. I am proud of my little cousin for her successes.

Bobby Smith is my hero. For years, I have greeted and introduced Bobby Smith as The Great Bobby Smith. Bobby Smith is my hero, not for his accomplishments on the football field, when he was the quarterback, but for the way he conducted himself in defeat. Bobby never gave up, but when the team lost a game, Bobby lost the game. He took his responsibility seriously, and he felt a loss deeply. I never got to see Bobby in those private moments when the team was in the locker room, but other boys told me about it, and I was impressed with his character. I always wanted to say that to him, but I never did. Perhaps it's too corny, even if it is true, and I get too emotional when I try to tell people things. Every time I see him, I think back to then, and how much respect other boys expressed for Bobby Smith. Not everyone can move a team like that, and I don't mean just down the field. That's why he is The Great Bobby Smith.

My son, Stephen William Payne, is my hero; he courageously dealt with facing death. He did so with quiet dignity and made sure that everyone knew he loved them; he brought the grace of God into the lives of those around him in his last few days.

And yes, the Red Avenger is still my hero. He had more courage, bluff though it was, than he had toughness. He never shirked his higher calling, in spite of formidable opposition, and it got him beat up regularly; that's courage.

Heroes are all around us, not just in movies, books and fables. We just need to look to find them. And if a stranger told us a story about someone we didn't know, who had done just some of the things that the people we know, touch and talk with had done, we would stand in awe and say, "Why that person's a genuine hero. Why don't you do something for them? Give them a medal, have a parade, hold a banquet for them—you have to do something for them."

Indeed we do. Why don't we just tell them? *You*—are my hero.

A TRIBUTE

About two years ago, I saw Billy Mitchell, in Tulsa, at the Cracker Barrel restaurant, and we talked a little. His brother, Roy, was very ill and later in the week, I called Roy. We talked about fifteen minutes, and he said, "Let's get together and have dinner some time."

We didn't have the opportunity to do that, and Roy died not too long after that. I did say, "I love you, Roy," during our phone conversation. I might have embarrassed him, but I wanted him to know that. There had been too little time over the years to see Roy and to talk to him, although many of us, Jay Lynn, Ernie, Hughie, and others had wanted to see him.

The next time I saw Billy was at the funeral service of my cousin, Candy. I asked Billy if he knew how I could reach Ray Mitchell, Roy and Billy's brother. It had been a number of years since I had seen Ray.

At one time, we had been close friends and then, we had just drifted apart, as boys do when they age and change.

I was in Sambo's Restaurant, in Bartlesville in 1978, when I saw a man that reminded me so much of Ray that I could not stop looking at him. We were standing at the door, waiting for a hostess to seat us, and the man was at the far side of the restaurant, seated at the counter, drinking coffee by himself.

The man and I looked at each other, and then he rose,

walked over to me and asked me if I were Stevie Joe. Frankly, I was frightened, for it had been so long since we had seen each other, and I was unsure of our relationship. But Ray gave me a warm handshake, gripping my hand firmly, and continuing to hold on to my hand with his strong grip. He asked about my mother, and we talked a bit, until my wife and I were called to a table.

I saw Ray often after that, for he was working in security for the same company I worked for. We always spoke, smiled at each other, had a few friendly words and sometimes we would talk a bit.

And then, one day, he was gone again. Someone told me that he had moved back to Arizona.

I asked Billy for a telephone number for Ray, in Arizona, and I called him. Ray drives a truck and his schedule is a difficult one, so it took me several attempts to reach him. I had left a message with his wife, giving my telephone number and my name, Stephen Payne.

When I finally contacted Ray, we talked a bit, and then he asked me, "Sir, what is your call about?" I told him that I only wanted to convey my condolences about Roy, and tell him how sorry I was. He thanked me, and then asked, "How did you know Roy?"

"Ray," I said, "I knew all of you when we were at Union and in high school." I sensed that he was still very puzzled. "Ray," I said. "I'm Stevie Joe."

Then the tone of the conversation changed, and he asked me all about things; about Pawhuska, my mother, and so on. I told him that my mother had died in 1993, and he expressed condolences to me. Then he paid the great tribute to my mother.

"Stevie," he said, "when we were growing up, your mom would take us somewhere; to a movie, to some game, something. And when she did, if she bought you a coke, or a hamburger or anything, she always bought Roy and me the same thing; whatever we wanted. We never felt left out when we were around your mom."

I was so grateful for his saying all of that, and more. There are so many times, as the man I am, that I have wanted to back up in time, to the boy I was, and say something like that to someone. I've wanted to say thank you, I've wanted to express how deeply I felt about something that someone did for me. I've wanted to say, "I love you," to all of those for whom I have felt love, and for whom I have failed to let them know.

And there he was, Ray Mitchell, an adult, American male of some sixty years, remembering kindnesses from long ago, and expressing such deep felt thanks and remembrances. And, Ray made me feel good, because my mother did a lot of simple, but nice things for many other people. I'm glad I called him.

We miss so many opportunities to say things to people. It can be because of our shyness, our awkwardness, our lack of courage. There are so many times that we want to tell someone how much he or she means to us. We never know the effect we might have on someone by telling them. Some say life is short and then…. We can fill in the omitted words with anything. Life is short and we shouldn't waste opportunities, not opportunities to tell people important to us how we feel.

THE OLD RESERVOIR ON THE RIDGE

December 26, 2005, Ronnie Havens and I toured Pawhuska. We met at the Memorial just off of Lynn and Main streets where the great flag flies and monoliths bear silent record to the wars. Lists of names, there remind us to think of them, to remember them, and to honor them; in some cases all are now gone; in other cases, some are yet with us.

For our trip around Pawhuska and back in time we used Ronnie's car, a black Mazda Protégé with a compact disc player, so when we had lunch, I paid the $19.62 (the same number as our class year of 1962) as he had been out for gasoline at about $1.91 a gallon or so. Our previous trip had been at $.34 a gallon or so but the Mazda was kind and used little fuel. Our 1956 models used a lot.

Ronnie asked me if I remembered an old reservoir located on the ridge between the old brick plant on the west side and Pawhuska Cemetery on the east side. "Yes, I remember it."

The first time that I had been there was in about 1955 and Earl Brunger, whom we called "Chunker," had told some of us about it. We were a group of boys with rifles and shotguns, and one of us had suggested that we go to the brick plant to target shoot. We gathered Earl Brunger, Don Daniels, a few other boys and walked through the center of town, past the police station and out to the brick plant carrying a .22 caliber, single-shot Stevens rifle (mine), an over-and-under .410 gauge shot gun with .22, a 12-gauge double barrel shotgun, several air pistols and rifles and ammunition. People waved at us and greeted us and good naturedly shouted things like "Going hunting boys?" No one stopped us, the police didn't pick us up; we weren't a gang, and we didn't intimidate anyone.

That's the way it was in Pawhuska in 1955. Boys could walk through town with rifles and were not a threat. I'm not sure about adult men but at least we were considered to just be having fun. I don't remember everyone in the group that day, but Tommy Daniels might have been with us; I think we were about seven in number.

Don Daniels, mentioned earlier as my 4-H gun safety partner, was usually called "Butch," except that we had "Little Butch" (Bob Hughes) and "Big Butch" (Don Daniels) and later another Butch.

We had killed about all of the tin cans, glass bottles and other targets that we could—and run out of ammunition—when Earl told us about the reservoir on the hill; only he said it was a swimming pool.

Because other people were still shooting down below we couldn't go straight up the bluff in front of them so Earl led us in a long trek around the side of the hill. It was still quite a climb with the rifles we were carrying, and although we ranged in age from about ten to thirteen years of age, it was exhausting. When we finally reached the top of the hill, Earl found the swimming pool and he convinced me that it was a swimming pool. Even then I had the good sense to ask, why in the world would anyone build a pool up here? The hill was covered with small trees and bushes and there were no discernible roads. We could not figure out how anyone got to it yet it was there.

It was odd for a pool, even to my mind then. It had the same depth on each end and it was deep and I think it was square in shape. We examined, experienced, played and theorized as much as we could and then the reality struck us that we had to climb down the hill, around again to avoid shooters, and trudge the long way back home. And being the geniuses that we were, we had brought neither water nor food with us and the day was getting long. One of the boys said that he thought that the cemetery was on the other side of the hill, and if we could find the path, it would save us a lot of walking as it was a *short cut* back to town.

At that age, I was usually game for a new adventure, and tired as I was, I was excited at the idea of finding a *new* passage, perhaps a *secret* passage that only we would know. We followed him and soon, we were at the cemetery but on the wrong side of a high fence. We climbed the fence, handing our rifles over according to the way that Big Butch and I had taught our class mates and walked through the cemetery, to 15th street and then home, down the hill and across town; there was no short cut to it. When we were back at school on Monday, we asked other boys if they knew about the swimming pool. Some did and some didn't, so it was a secret only to those who didn't. We were now in the group that knew. It was special information and set us apart. For some reason, I went there one more time, later, perhaps when I was seventeen or so.

Ronnie said that he had wondered if it had been only a dream, and so he had gone traipsing up the hill, from the cemetery side and found the old reservoir and proved to himself that it had been real. He told me that there is a road that goes almost to it, and it is easier to get to now, so I asked him if we would mind going there again.

He parked the Mazda at the top of the cemetery, and we walked a short distance where the fence opened and admitted us to the trees and bushes. Ronnie began to walk in the direction of the reservoir. I was grateful that he knew because my sense of direction was off, and I would have walked a diagonal away from it. I might have found it— eventually, but his knowledge saved us time and energy. We are getting shorter on both.

I thought back to us climbing the fence in 1955, and I wondered if the passage around the fence had always been there. I decided I would not tell any of the boys if I saw them again, and it came up. It had to have been a reservoir for it makes no sense as anything else. We could speculate that it might have been Pawhuska's first reservoir since it is high on a hill. Still, it is difficult to get to and probably always was. There are remnants of roads, two tracks in the dirt with rocks strewn about.

All of the ways to get there seem challenging, and it is difficult for me to imagine trucks of about 1912 or so carrying men and materials to such a an isolated place to build a reservoir. It is disintegrating now and beneath the smooth cement veneer, blocks of sandstone are visible and one corner is now completely down. It was through there that Ronnie and I walked into the reservoir. In 1955 we jumped down; it did not seem prudent in 2005.

The reservoir floor is broken in places but still visible. It seemed to be a smooth cement cover, again, probably over sand stone blocks. It seems to be a place that begs to be written as a Hardy Boys like story; *The Mystery of the Old Reservoir,* and maybe that was what was always so intriguing about it to me. And then Ronnie told me something that broke my heart. He said that there had been parties up there with beer and liquor and girls. I wasn't upset that there were parties just that I had not known about them, and I had missed all of them. Ronnie told me that he had only learned about them later, and he had missed them too. Ronnie, most of my friends and I were wall weeds (girls are wall flowers), shy and always came late or not at all to the fun, questionable though it might be.

When I first saw the old reservoir, Pawhuska was bigger then, further across and the hills were higher. Even so I, like Ronnie, am glad that it existed, that it was real for it was part of our adventures as boys, and I wondered if any girls ventured up there. I know one who might have, but she never said anything about it. Maybe it was one of those things, like tree houses, caves, swimming in Bird Creek and exploring Cedar Canyon that *seemed* to be reserved for adventurous, even reckless boys.

THE LAST STOP

There was one last stop we had to make, and we were near. That was the cemetery itself where Ronnie and I both have sons resting, gone too early, missed too much. He eased the Mazda down the hill, where we stopped at my son's grave, and Ronnie walked with me. There were still guitar picks on the stone from a visitor who had left them. When I first saw them, there were twenty-two of them of different sizes, colors and shapes, and I knew that they had come from Tyler, Texas from his friends who always said that he never had enough picks. His mother may have delivered the picks for them, but the pickers in Tyler were behind it. My grandmother and my mother rest beside Stephen.

We took the short yet long walk northward to Michael Scott Havens's grave, and as we passed I pointed out where Florien McKee, Blackie Ricketts, and my cousin Candy Cooper are. Ronnie said, "You know, I'm starting to worry because I know more dead people now than I do live ones." Buried very close to Michael is Frank Ikenberry, a quiet, sturdy man from the class of 1962 and Henry Roberts, the man that we boys called "The Old Man," lies close by.

Michael's stone is a beautiful work. It is gray marble with his name and the dates of 15 Feb. 1970 - 6 March 1988 and at the bottom are engraved two roses meeting each other as in a kiss with the word "Tulsa" over the rose branch on the left. The other side is magnificent, and one day when I was there I called Ronnie to ask him if he had taken it from the book *The Little Prince* because it reminded me of the spirit of the book. He told me that he had written it, and if you have read his poetry you can see the similarity to that. These are the words:

He laughed
He cried
He loved
He was loved
He made music

I could think of my own son, Stephen, of whom the same could be said. Stephen was a musician and played cornet, guitars, piano and keyboards. Ronnie and I were musicians, so it is not surprising that something of both of us has been passed on to another generation. Stephen has acoustic guitars carved on his stone and the words "God's Picker," which are not nearly as eloquent or as beautiful as Ronnie's words and I feel that I should put a small sign by Stephen's stone, which directs people to Michael's and says "See this for my sentiments also."

The day was decent for December 26, and we bided our time there for a while. As we walked back I asked Ronnie to make one last stop in the cemetery, and I directed him around and back up to the top of the hill. We walked to Sergeant Robert Gordon Hughes's small stone. We stood there a while and talked about some of the things we remembered together about Bob. It didn't seem a good time to recall all or even some of the tricks that I had played on Bob, yet we found something to laugh about as there was always something to laugh at about Bob.

I had a birthday party at the Legion Hut when I became twelve, and Bobby pantomimed hilariously to the song,

"All American Boy." There is a line where the singer said, "my Uncle Sam says...knock, knock: Here I am," and Bobby made a knocking motion on the back of his head with his mouth open. Some of the girls thought he had really made the noise himself, and he was so successful that he was asked to do it again. He was a ham so asking him to repeat a performance was a given. He did.

We left the cemetery and drove one more time down Grandview Avenue and over by the Indian Agency, down the road behind it and by old Castle Hill, where a house that was shaped like a castle once stood. Then it was down the hill and by the old ice plant where we were in front of the old Chevrolet Garage. It was time to eat, and we drove west to the bar-b-que only to find it closed and one of us said "pig sandwich" so we drove to the Pig Stand, which I did not know still existed. We sat in front of it for a few minutes remembering how good a pig sandwich was, yet fearing heart burn if we went in.

In a moment of prudence we decided the Pizza Hut would be better for us yet there was something foreign about the idea of a Pizza Hut in Pawhuska. Pizza Huts should only be in the bigger towns like Bartlesville and Ponca City, places where you went to get away from where you were.

The Pizza Hut won out, and we ordered personal size pizzas and an order of wings and iced tea and we spent a long time talking about things and listening to some music, music that was tolerable for us. We had been listening to some CD's in Ronnie's car and, to be on the safe side, I had brought my own collection of the Everly Brothers, the Fleetwoods, Elvis Presley, and, of course, Buddy Holly. Ronnie had an excellent collection with him, and we had listened to it for a long time.

I asked him if we could play the Buddy Holly, and that's what we were listening to as we pulled into the driveway of the Pizza Hut. A lot of our talk was about writing and about things that I will write later. There are things to be said about binoculars and old buildings and elevators and pea shooters, about bicycles and dogs and bad movies, about snow ball fights and football games and most of all, about friends.

AN ESSAY

Bobby Hughes died March 19, 1993. I was at a car show in Tulsa and returned late to find a message on my answering machine. It was the third death in a short time that year, and in spite of any maturity and strength that I had, I was grieving. I wrote an essay that I shared with a few of my friends and classmates. I have modified it several times, and I hope I have made it a better piece of writing with each modification. The essay, *Three Stars*, follows:

Three Stars, Shining at Pawhuska High School

There was old Wink Martindale recording called "The Three Stars." It was written after a small plane crashed in a snowy field near Clear Lake, Iowa on February 3, 1959. There were four people in the plane; the pilot and the three stars: Charles Hardin (Buddy) Holly, "The Music," Ricardo Valenzuela—known as Richey Valens—and J. P. Richardson, "The Big Bopper." I remember it well because I was flat on my back listening to a lot of radio after a Chevrolet had broadsided my Cushman Eagle (with me on it)

Do not try this stunt at home.

I thought Three Stars would be appropriate about this

memorial note for there were three stars shining at Pawhuska High School: the Big Man, the Funny Man, and the Running Man.

Carl Jech (pronounced with a Y for the J), was the Big Man. The first thing that struck anyone meeting Carl was his size. I met him for the first time in that all hectic seventh grade, our first year with the big people, and I looked high above me to see his face. I still thought I was going to grow another five or more inches before I left high school (which I didn't thanks to smoking enough cigarettes) but he would have still been bigger than I was.

One of my first thoughts was that he was a teacher, but after talking to him for just a few minutes, I realized that he was as confused as I was so he had to be another student. I never had a face-to-face conversation with Carl in school because I was always looking at just about his navel, but I had come to know him better since the reunions at twenty-five years and the 1991 gathering at the Elks Club in Pawhuska. He said that he wished he had not been such a "jerk" (his word) in high school and had met more of his fellow students and come to know them then instead of waiting until twenty-five years later. He said he was having a lot of fun getting to know more of us, and he was making up lost time for those years in school.

A lot of us attended Carl's funeral, and I will take just a moment to list some of them who did; forgive me if I leave someone out as it is not by design: Bob Hughes, Susan and Jay Hurt, Juanita Hurt, Jimmie Ann and Joe Maxwell, Carlos Gripado, Dwaine Orr (late of the eighth grade, PHS), Terry Rainwater, Nelson and Pam Carter, Buddy Ricketts and Georgette Pratt (Ricketts), George Hazlett, Charlie and Shirley Wadsworth, Florien McKee (Griggs), Tommy Maddox, Bob Moore, Sherry Kendrick (Ramey), Mrs. Ruby Duke, Mrs. Mavis Bacon, Gary Carson, Dr. & Mrs. Walker, Billie Whitcraft, Mr. & Mrs. Speck Horn, and others.

Oh, and one more thing; it's all right to cry at funerals for friends, even if you are a guy.

Carl was a Star on the basketball court and Pawhuska reached its glory in state annals while he and his teammates wore the Orange and Black.

The team had Jay Hurt, Carlos Gripado, Wimpsey Gilkey, the twin brothers Cleo & Leo Brown, Charlie Bighorse, Tommy Maddox and Carl Jech.

There was more to Carl than what happened thirty years ago. Carl was a giver and chose to give most to the kids in Skiatook and other places he could, coaching young people in basketball and teaching younger people where he worked.

His wife Joyce often had to make sacrifices, so that Carl could take care of his many charges. The preacher, Don Branscum, told us that Carl and Joyce took a kid with them on their honeymoon. He also said that Carl had a quick temper and expressed himself, sometimes scaring gray hair onto young heads, but he was over it just as quickly.

Carl had a silly rule that he wouldn't come to any of the reunions if he weighed more than 300 pounds, so he was on a crazy diet pattern every time one was due so he could look good, like the old Carl at playing weight. That was Carl in the present. Carl absolutely hated for anyone to pronounce his Jech with a J so that it came out "Jek." Jimmie Ann said that there was a radio announcer in Tulsa who should be on the lookout for a big, angry basketball player dressed in Orange & Black.

The second Star was Robert Gordon (Bobby) Hughes, the Funny Man. If I write more personally on this one, it is because I knew him better than I did Carl and I knew him a long time; forty-four years.

Most of us knew Bob by his nickname, Butch, that his dad Gordon gave him, and his sister Kay called him that most of the time. I called him Bobby and this has been the hardest death for me and the hardest to accept, even though I was preparing for it after Carl's funeral when we learned that Bobby was having serious health problems. He joked about them.

Jimmie Ann, Bobby and I rode to Skiatook with Florien for Carl's funeral. Bobby was on a high dosage of blood thinners, and he told several people there that the doctor had warned him about cutting himself while shaving and bleeding to death. I said that at least he wouldn't cut himself combing his hair (I'll wait for it). He spent quite a bit of the time talking about his experience with doctors and about his narrow escape from the surgeon's knife just days before Carl's death; all of it with humor and exaggeration. He was scheduled to have open heart surgery ninety days later, but he fell short of that.

Bobby died on March 19, two months before his forty-ninth birthday, which he shared with Nelson Carter.

I met Bobby when we moved to 643 Prudom Street from Girard and that was before we started school. Bobby and I had our first fight shortly after that, then made friends and then we had a fight and, on and on over the years. Sometimes he was a close friend and sometimes I couldn't stand him, and I know that he felt the same way about me. I was too young to understand how much alike we were, and that we competed for friends, attention, and position. I would never have admitted then to being jealous and coming now to know that this emotion was at the root of any problems we had has been growth for me.

I think Bobby had the same experiences with me. One of my comforting thoughts is that when I was at the Hughes family home in Pawhuska, when Gordon died, Bobby called his daughter Robyn over and told her, "When I was your age, my best friend and I were never more that this far apart (motioning with his thumb and first finger together)." He meant me. It was good to know that any angers and regrets had been forgotten, and we were friends again and forever.

When I say that Bobby was the Funny Man I mean it in the best sense as Bobby was a comedian, and if you never got to see that side of him you missed the essence of him. He never meant anyone any harm, but he got so caught up in funny stories about people that he got wild tales started that weren't true or that were true, but the people he told them about weren't the people about whom they happened.

Everybody has been the victim of one of Bobby's funny tales too, from Jay Lynn to Jimmie Ann, from Nelson to Earl Brunger, from Miss Hill to Lewis Bean and, of course—Stevie Joe.

When Kay and I were standing over Bobby's casket, we were both scanning his face. Kay asked me what I was looking for and I told her that I was looking for the two scars I had given him. She showed me the two she had given him, and I showed her my two. Her major scar to him was when he wouldn't leave her alone so she hit him in the head with the swing on the back stroke. My major scar to him, that his bald head showed well now, was when I hit him over the head with a wooden rifle for calling me a name that years later wouldn't have mattered. He cried because I almost killed him, and I cried because he broke my rifle.

Bobby had two small scars on both lips that I can't resist telling how he got. He came to our house early one summer Saturday, and I was just opening a stick of Black Jack chewing gum. He asked me what I was going to do with it and in a moment of pure, flippant inspiration, I told him I was going to smoke it. The thought had never occurred to me before, and I didn't know if it was possible but we were going to find out.

We conversed briefly about the joys of smoking Black Jack gum with all of it being made up, as I went and then I rolled it up just as though it were a roll-your-own cigarette. As I was about to light it, he asked if I would let him smoke that one; so I handed it to him and offered him a light from a kitchen match.

The Black Jack flamed instantly burning all the way to the end and sticking to both of his lips. I helped him get it off which wasn't good for his lips because it pulled his skin off. And I couldn't help it; I laughed. He didn't forget it, because he always brought it up telling how I tried to kill him with a stick of Black Jack gum, but it was always with humor (I think).

Nelson Carter wrote a poem for Bob's funeral and I was asked to read it publicly at the funeral. My voice broke, for only a minute, and then I gathered my strength and read the entire poem without further problems. I miss Bobby today, and I probably always will. I have dreams about him sometimes and don't understand why.

So long Bobby Hughes.

The third Star was the Running Man. He wasn't a member of our class of 1962, but sometimes someone will remind me that I am not technically a member of the class of 1962 (because I didn't graduate until 1967 and then from College High School, Bartlesville). It's not important in the scheme of things. When you're six years old you seem so much older than a four-year old that you don't have anything in common. When you get fifty or sixty, that four-year old is forty-eight or fifty-eight and two years don't seem to make much difference; ten years doesn't seem to matter much

Wimpsey Gilkey was in the class of 1961 and I could have called him the Black Man instead of the Running Man. That was certainly one of his features and the one you would see quickest if you just happened to meet him on the street and didn't know anything about him. If you knew Wimpsey, you knew he was kind, gentle at heart and worked hard at almost everything he did. I remember in 1957, when we started high school that, in addition to just being scared to death because we were now back at the bottom of the pecking order, some of our parents were scared for us, and they were scaring us because we were going to be going to school with black children.

When I look back over all of these years, and when I have been in Los Angeles when people were burning cars, attacking people just because they were different, I try to get a perspective on the whole thing. I think we were very successful at our integration. I think it was partly because we were a small town and partly because it happened slower in our town. But I also think that it was because of Wimpsey Gilkey and all of the people like him.

I wasn't an athlete, so I wasn't in the trenches with Ed White, Kenny Templeton, Jay Hurt, Jimmy Rector, Raymond Stice and the others so I don't know what happened there. But I was around Wimpsey, and I never heard him say a derogatory remark about anyone and certainly never a racial remark. I never heard Wimpsey find an excuse for not doing something when he easily could have. I had some years in Bartlesville around Wimpsey and his wife, Pat then, and he was a lot of fun; good sense of humor, a joker, and he was always a role model.

From my own experience, he did a lot to help young kids, most of them black and struggling, but I never saw him exclude any another kids from his helpful and helping spirit either. One day I was looking in the Wa-Sha-She, Pawhuska High School's annual publication and I saw that Wimpsey Gilkey had been awarded the Ormand Beach trophy. Today, I'm not sure what the award is given for, but I admired Wimpsey. I have the feeling that it is a spirit or accomplishment award and not just for yards gained, touchdowns scored and on-the-field accomplishments. I like to think that.

I don't remember the details of any plays at a football game but I remember Wimpsey was a Star, along with others. I remember Wimps carried the ball and our hopes for the state championship football title.

Wimps was on the 1961 state basketball championship team though; and we did make that.

We didn't make it, but as Robin Hood said, "The fool who jumps for the moon and misses surely jumps higher than the wise man who only stoops to pick up a penny."

I listed some of the people at Carl's funeral. Most of them were at Wimpsey's funeral the next day in Bartlesville plus a few more: Merl Powers, Mr. Terrill, Travis Finley, Ray Finley, Peggy Gilkey, Dora Gilkey. The same thing for Bob's funeral in Pawhuska. The same people plus a few more, minus a few. Hugh(ie) Hollowell and Judy, Pam Singmaster (Ray), Bob Roberts, Jim Javellas, Brenda Brunger (Bleuer), Charlie Wadsworth, Mike Avery. Some of you wanted to be there and couldn't. That's OK. Those of us who were there were just lucky that we could be, and we may not be able to go to the next one; you may have to be there in our place; and we'll feel like we should have been there. Don't worry about it. Go if you can, forgive everyone who can't and don't gossip about those who could not attend; It's not important.

What is important is that we spent some time together; that we learned some things from each other, and that we love one another now and we don't forget to tell each other that we do. The words aren't so hard, they aren't so bad, and no one ever died from just saying, "I love you," to a friend. If you can't say, "I love you," try, "I care about you." They'll understand; we'll understand.

I began with a choice, to write it as a third person narrator and keep my feelings out or to be an involved first person. I chose to leave some of me in it. If I have done so to the point that you are offended by it, I hope you will get over it. One choice I could have made was to not write it at all. I have spent too much of my life not doing something, fearing how someone would see me, and I have missed a lot of things for that reason. I won't do that anymore, and I don't think you should either. It's OK if you don't like my personal words in it. I do apologize for any real errors in spelling or facts.

I want to close with two things. The first is to share a moment with you. I learned from Jimmie Ann, via my answering machine that Bob, had died. I called her back, and we talked long into the morning. The next day, I went to Pawhuska and there was a little informal gathering at Chunker and Brenda's house. When I went to the door, I knocked, and Brenda came out. We put our arms around each other and wordlessly held each other for a long time—a long, long time. There was no need to talk because holding each other was all the communication we needed; it was the way of saying something about our feelings we could not have said in words. That is the moment I want to share with you. That feeling that something was special, that words could not have been spoken that would have added to it in any way, and that everything we shared about Bob and the others that are gone was known between us. As Nelson Carter said, a special feeling exists for our class mates, because each of us has been formed by the experiences of each other.

We would not be the persons we are today, whatever that is, if it had not been for the experience of knowing each other and growing up together, bouncing off of each other through love and war and the times that changed us and the times that we helped to change. Remember that we are just as much a part of our history as were the people who lived with George Washington.

The second thing is this: it's all right to cry at funerals for friends, even if you are a guy.

THE MESSENGER ON THE BRIDGE

Ronnie and I were heading west on Main Street until we came to Rogers, and then we turned north and went by Eddie Allen's house. We passed by the place where Union Grade School once stood, proud and mighty, and then we turned onto streets that led us to Flanagan Hill on Prudom Street and up to 11th Street and by Ronnie's old house. It looks different now, older, less cared for, and yet it once seemed to me to be a grand house, much larger, much richer.

I thought of the meals that I had shared there with Ronnie and his mother and of the model airplanes, ships and cars that we had put together and painted, trying to make them as real as possible, trying to make them come alive for us. Ronnie had had a great dog named Spot that was black and white. I remembered that we would throw a brick, not a stick nor a rock, but a whole red brick and Spot would run to it and bring it back so that we might throw it again. He slobbered on it, of course, that's what dogs do.

Behind the house had once stood an old garage where things were stored and the upstairs, a loft, had been turned into a kingdom for twelve year old boys with makeshift chairs and magazines, a club house for a club that didn't exist; a club that had no name, no charter, no offices or officers yet was somehow a club. The garage has been gone for a long time. The club still exists in a kind of phantom brotherhood, though it has been more than forty years since we last met; brotherhood yes, for there were no girls allowed in a Calvin and Hobbes way.

We went downtown where stores we had known were once part of our childhood and in some cases, the building remains but the soul is gone. They remind you of what they were: the Dairy Queen, Pitts Furniture Store, the General Electric Store, Longstreet's, the Army-Navy Surplus Store, Oklahoma Tire and Supply Company (OTASCO) "ka-ching. Thank you, here's your change." The old library which had once been a bank, the Packing House Market, old gas stations where we spent a dollar, Irby's Drug, Crawford's Bakery, T.G. & Y. the bus station, and, of course, the bones of the once great and proud Triangle Building, rotting, standing, perhaps, in the way of something we might call progress. I want it left there though, to remind us of what Pawhuska was. It is a Holy place.

We went by Patsy and Dean Lozier's old house and down on Girard, where I had once lived before we moved to Prudom. I showed Ronnie where the house, now gone, used to be.

We came to the Swinging Bridge and the discussion was brief. "Should we…?" "Ronnie," I said, "This is Holy and we can't be here without going out on to the Swinging Bridge." It was warm for a winter day and the sun reflected off the water and off of the chain links of the bridge. We walked out to the center of the bridge, and we looked back towards the low water bridge up the stream, Bird Creek. The water was like it had always been, dark green, dirty looking, and it was difficult to believe that I and others had swum in parts of Bird Creek, although never under the Swinging Bridge. I was always too afraid of it there. It's not the same bridge for the boards are newer, and there were no holes in the bridge, but it has a precarious lean to the south.

I told Ronnie about the time Johnny Lawless dared me to ride my Cushman Eagle motor scooter out on the bridge. The motor scooter weighed 450 pounds, and I weighed about one hundred and fifteen and was scared. I maneuvered it slowly out onto the bridge and about half way, there was no turning back, I began to feel funny vibrations and movement of the bridge. I heard a strange laugh behind me, a laugh that sounded too close to me and I turned expecting to see Johnny standing on the bridge close to me but what I saw was his Cushman Eagle, on the bridge, right behind me, with him on it, double the weight now. Any fears that I had had were gone then, because I was sure that we were going through the bridge, down into the green water and the only comfort I could ask for was that we were drowned and quickly. A parent's wrath was much more severe than death then, and I knew that we were going to face a parent's wrath, my mother, his dad. We made it across and I vowed never to try that again. I've kept my word.

The Swinging Bridge

Before I am judged too harshly, Frank Hulse later told me that he did the same thing, on the same bridge on a dare from someone, and he experienced, hair follicle by hair follicle, almost the same fear as I did.

As Ronnie and I looked upstream we saw a car's wheel rising just above the water line at the bank of Bird Creek, and we looked a little further and there was another wheel and—a third wheel and then, Ronnie said it first, a whole car! It lay upside down at the water's edge, next to the bank and we pointed and questioned how it could have got there. Had someone dumped it from the banks above? Was it trash or was it the result of an accident. I had a small camera with me, and I took a few photographs of it, just to prove that I had seen it. Ronnie then told me that he had been reading Thornton Wilder's story of *The Bridge of San Luis Rey*, and it's been years since I had read it but we both knew the theme, of how strangers come together and happen to be on the bridge at the same time when it collapses and they plunge to their death in the ravine below. We both shared the same feeling about the questions posed in *The Bridge of San Luis Rey*, questions that are not answered but left for us to answer. And then he appeared; the messenger on the bridge.

He came on a bicycle, a new and modern bicycle, a mountain bike with shiny wheels and color in its frame, gears to spare and authority. He dismounted at the bridge's edge and walked his bicycle up the ramp and on to the bridge, and we stepped aside to let him pass. But he didn't pass. He stopped just before us, and I could see that he was not the young man I had thought him to be. He was an old man, with leathery black skin and a beard of gray stubble. Fatigue was in his eyes and yet he smiled, slightly, as though he were entrusting himself to us somehow. He was old, but then I realized that he was younger than the two boys who stood with him on the bridge. Ronnie asked him about the car.

"Oh yeah," he said. "He was goin' hundred eighty five miles an hour when he run off the bridge."

"Off the bridge?" Ronnie asked.

"Yeah, off the bridge. The woman driving, she be killed and all. Yeah, he was going hundred ten miles an hour. Come right off over there."

"Over there?" Ronnie asked.

"Yep. Did you know that I made up to $400 cutting wood?" the man asked.

Were we still in the same conversation I wondered?

"$400?" Ronnie queried.

"Yep, I made up to $400 cuttin' wood."

"Tell us about the wreck" Ronnie said.

"Yeah, they was a woman in it, three years ago. I made up to $400 cuttin' wood" he said

"Really?" Ronnie asked.

"Yeah and my brother, he live in Bartlesville, and he had thirty guns and I tol' him not to have them 'cause someone break in and steal his guns, and they did and shot his leg clean off. Now he don't have those guns."

"Really?" Ronnie said.

"Yes and you know, I made up to $400 cuttin' wood out there in the country side." He swept his hand broadly to indicate where the country side was.

He told us more about the wreck. All of it in excited conflict with what he had already said.

"I live over there, you know. Been born and raised there, right there. Right here in Pawhuska." He said.

"Yes," Ronnie said. "He and I are both from here, both Pawhuska boys, but it's been a long time ago, when we were kids."

And, for some reason, at the moment it occurred to me that I had not jumped on the bridge, and I grabbed the iron strand that tops the chicken wire, put my hands over it and I began to jump, high, coming down heavily on the boards, Red Boots flailing wildly in the air, I was having a moment of pure fun. Ronnie did not like my doing that. The bridge leaned far to the south and shook. It was fun, and I was safe. The old, black man who was younger than we were did not seem to notice my jumping. Perhaps he was used to it somehow. When the noise had subsided and the bridge quit swaying he took up again.

"Did you know I made up to $400 out cuttin' wood in the countryside?"

By then we had pretty well gathered this basic fact about the man, that he had made up to $400 cutting wood out there in the country side. He wasn't dull, or stupid. I'm not even sure if he was slow. It wasn't what he said, but the look in his eyes and the almost smile. Then he seemed to run out of things to say. Ronnie and I made our excuses, bid him farewell and walked off of the bridge. We went over to the side of the bank, to see how the car got there. There is no way it could have come from the top of the bank, and my own conclusion is that it was washed from the low water bridge down to the place where it rests. We could not tell the year or model of the car, and it could have been in the water for three or ten years. We left then and I asked Ronnie.

"Ronnie, was that a messenger from God?"

"I think so" Ronnie said.

"What was his message then?" I asked.

"I think it was this; that somehow we come together as friends, to exist at the same time in a small town, that I can't explain why we were there when we were there. Somehow we are connected and there is meaning in just that, knowing each other, sharing things, times and events and friends and people we knew. Sharing the town itself and the movies and music and things we shared and now, sharing this moment together with each other and the messenger on the bridge."

We had shared much that day, and I was home.

Charlotte and I had dinner that evening in Copan,

Oklahoma, and I told her about the messenger on the bridge and she was in hysterical laughter. As we were at the counter to pay out, I said to the cashier, "Nancy, did I tell you that I met a man who had earned up to $400 cutting wood?"

"No," she said, "but I'll bet he did. A guy comes in here that cuts up to seven ricks, and I know he makes that much."

"Really?" I asked.

"Yes," she said, "so, he could make $400 cutting wood. I believe that."

"Yes," I said. "He had made up to $400 cutting wood."

I smiled and watched Charlotte stifle the laughter, as she wondered where I was going with this. I didn't know. I know this. That I felt a moment of connection with an old friend, one with years of friendship and shared moments, of deep connection that goes beyond the words we say, and the new people who came into our lives later after we had left school and even Pawhuska behind.

And I felt an odd connection with the man I had just met, that he was more than a man for he had simplified many things, much like a Forrest Gump, and boiled them down to what I am. The bridge didn't collapse, we didn't fall into an abyss, we weren't lost to society yet some change has come over me for my moment on the bridge with the messenger. Ronnie is better than I am at these things, and he spent more time in conversation with the messenger, listened better to what he said and responded to him better. I was more the observer, and I observed, both Ronnie and the messenger. I also observed myself. I took him seriously, I was not disrespectful, and I wasn't sarcastic as I might have been.

My only sin was jumping on the bridge, and maybe he made me do that and it wasn't my fault. Perhaps I caught a glimpse of the messenger's spirituality which was greater than my own, and I envied him for that simple spirit. His bicycle was new and might have been a Christmas gift, and I am seriously doubtful that he has pulled the wood he cut with that. I don't think he could drive so, that he has made $400 cutting wood is in itself a miracle. But his presence and what Ronnie said reminded me of something: back there, although it has been more than forty years since the last meeting, somewhere in time, in an old garage behind a house, a club of brothers met.

WE'RE LOYAL TO YOU PAWHUSKA HIGH

That is what we sing; our school spirit song, and generally, those of us who have passed through Pawhuska High School remain loyal to her. I had many years in Pawhuska, and then there is my strong connection to Union Grade School, so it is expected of me. Interestingly, I find many people who passed through Pawhuska, spending only a year or two at PHS, that have deep loyalty to her, even though they might have graduated from another school. Patsy Lozier was there a few years, moved away and graduated from another high school yet, she rarely misses a school reunion. Kay Hughes from Pawhuska remains her closest friend more than, ahem, shall we say enough years after high school. Patsy is a lady and I would not divulge a lady's age, as I am a gentleman, sort of. But if you look in the 1958 Wah-Sha-She....

Jimmy Thompson of my 1962 class still attends our reunions and keeps in touch with the class. Jimmy told me, "You were the first person I met, when we moved to Pawhuska. We went to the fair, we ate a whole bunch of stuff, rode on a wild ride, you got sick and threw up, and we got in a fight. It was a lot of fun."

Through attending the University of Tulsa, Tulsa

Community College and working in Tulsa, I have met many people from Tulsa. Often they tell me that they did not know everyone in their class, let alone everyone in high school. They can have loyalty to their high school, Memorial, Hale, Ethan Alan, but there is not a school that captures their total loyalty in both town and school as does Pawhuska High School ours. Loyalty to PHS is also loyalty to Pawhuska, the town.

Pawhuska High School, the old building

Some who graduated from there but have lived elsewhere all of their adult lives remain financial contributors to Pawhuska scholarship funds and openly say that they are the success they are because of going to Pawhuska High School.

In 2006, Pawhuska held a ceremony to induct several classes into its Basketball Hall of Fame. This was not Canton, home of the National Football League hall of fame; there was no all star game; there were no television cameras from national networks and no former President of the United States spoke. Yet former players came from Tennessee, Pennsylvania, Texas and other states and all parts of Oklahoma to both participate and witness. Men, now elderly and a bit frail, who coached there, returned and accepted well deserved praise and they were openly humbled and honored. Coach Jim Killingsworth, who went on to coach college basketball at the University of Tulsa, Idaho State Unversity, Oklahoma State University and finally, Texas Christian University, returned to accept the accolade.

Unfortunately, the Pawhuska basketball team lost the game.

I can not say with certainty what creates such deep and lasting loyalty to a small Oklahoma town and its lone high school. I can speculate and I may be right; I may also be wrong. I think it is because of friendships. We formed them at some point, and we have kept them. As we have moved further away in time and distance, we have formed new friendships and new loyalties. Our new loyalties are to new towns, colleges, the army, the navy, a ship, our company, fraternities, sororities and a host of other things. But the distance and time away seem to create a veil through which we look backwards, and the veil lets us see things the way we want to more than the way they were.

Someone with whom we competed bitterly in first grade has become a friend as we have matured and gained deeper values. We have forgotten that he or she made fun of us or maybe even hit us. Going back to Pawhuska gives us a physical place to reconnect and while we are there, seeing the same things together, an old building that was once the fabled Dairy Queen, looking up to see Whiting Hall and recall a bus filled with black musicians with a national hit *In the Mood* in a still *de facto* segregated south, remembering a white sports coat, pink carnation, and a girl in our arms, all these let us reflect on that friendship and deepen it. Our loyalty is really to each other but the physical and enduring metaphor for our loyalties and our loves is Pawhuska, and the lasting symbol of Pawhuska is not the Triangle Building; it is not the magnificent court house high up Grandview Hill. The lasting metaphor for our loyalties and loves is Pawhuska High School no matter what form it may take.

That is why, "We're loyal to you Pawhuska High..."

PAWHUSKA KIDS

That is what we were, Pawhuska kids: Ronnie, the others and I. And Pawhuska kids we remain, for it is the spirit that counts and our spirits are of Pawhuska, with deep loyalties and lasting friendships. Our sons—who were not raised there but now rest there—have become Pawhuska kids. It's a good place, and if you live there, or are from there, be proud, be thankful for there is much to be proud of, much to be thankful for.

NOT FADE AWAY

Memories are reflections of something that has *already* happened, usually in the distant past. In my three years aboard ship I saw many shorelines disappear behind us as we sailed away. The shoreline seemed to grow smaller and fade as it became distant. Memories are like that too. They recede into the distance until we are no longer sure that we can see them. Perhaps the light flickers and filters the colors, giving them a golden hue that the events themselves lacked. We can trust them but not completely. But like the receding shore, we must know where they are, for us to ever find our way back again. The shore is where we began our voyage. Memories are not things, solid and tangible; perhaps they are not even real. Still, they help us to understand our journeys to faraway lands and give us a point to look back and see how far we might have traveled. And if we remember, perhaps we can find our way home.

    Stevie Joe Payne, February 8, 2007
    Pawhuska High School class of 1962,
    B-flat Clarinet, Pawhuska High School Marching Band

AFTERWORD

I had many assumptions growing up that turned out to false. For example, I thought that I lived on Prudom Street; it was really Prudom Avenue. The only avenue that I knew was an avenue was Lynn Avenue. When I began this I would write Prudom Street from fifty years of habit. When I learned that many of my streets were avenues, I grudgingly made my changes throughout these pages. That is minor, but I wanted to be as accurate as possible where I could be.

Flanagan Hill, though known as such, is not marked. We've climbed it, sledded down it, had snow ball fights on it, and knew its name. But I had never seen it written so my assumption was the traditional Irish spelling that I knew of Flannigan, which I originally used. After many conversations with other people and Dean Campbell's advice that the only Flanagan he knew said, "all a's and no doubles," I accepted and settled on using Flanagan. I also found records of an agency employee in Pawhuska with that spelling.

This was not meant to be a comparison of between then and now, but some of that is inevitable in writing a personal narrative. It has been a bit of a time machine for me as I have been able to go back in time some fifty years, visit a while and see some of the things that made us what we are. Then I could come back to the present and see how much things have changed, yet how much remains constant of what I knew.

I remembered the movies I mention, in genre if not by title. I did not trust my memory on the dates of release so I have used the International Movie Database (www.imdb.com) to confirm the year of release on the movies that I cite. That has been my only use of IMDB for this document.

I enjoy the technology of today and wouldn't want to be without it. As a photographer I use a digital camera to take photographs, and I use a powerful computer program called Photoshop Professional to process my photographs. I use a cellular telephone, a digital voice recorder for making notes; we have satellite television and digital recording devices, so that we never miss a television show we want to watch. I used a cassette tape player and then a CD player to have my own class room and teach myself other languages. I took my class with me in my car, when I walked, ran or rode a bicycle. I learned Spanish, French, German, Russian, Italian, Portuguese, Japanese and some Chinese. I have goals to learn some Arabic, Swahili, Greek and Cherokee, and I can do that because of modern technology. That is what we have gained since I first lived on Prudom.

What we have lost since then is a simpler life. I knew men then who retired from a job as a milkman after thirty long years. Staying more than ten years with any company today is a challenge as the companies experience unprecedented and rapid change and jobs themselves disappear. We have lost a sense of loyalty that existed, and I miss that. The values that I learned at Union, in Boy Scouts, Pawhuska High School and band and church are still important to me; they have kept me from wandering too far from the good path. It is a case of wanting to have our cake and eat it too, I suppose, and we can't do that, can we?

We can use the tools of technology to help us remember values from a simpler time and a simpler life. We could be using technology to make records of our aging citizens and capture their memories; we could make both video and audio records of them. It is important to support the museums of Pawhuska and preserve as much as we can through photographs, letters and written records and any recordings that we can capture.

The things we are doing do not seem important, and our children won't listen when we tell them. But when we begin to disappear, one by one, and they notice, then they will ask, "What was life like then?" We must tell them as best we can. It won't be perfect, but it will be recorded and the palest ink outlasts the strongest memory.

If I were asked to describe the most important thing in making life better, without a second's hesitation I would say, "Reading." It was the teachers who taught me to read and taught me what to read that have been most important to me. I hope that reading never goes out of style.

Stevie Joe

In Memoriam: Pawhuska High School Class of 1962

Beverly Adkins
Mike Avery
Tonya Brunt
Roger Dixon
Robert Gordon "Bobby" Hughes
Frank Ikenberry
Carl Jech
Henry Jones
Dean Lozier
Robert Gary Malone
Eddy Mansholt
Florien McKee
Robert McQuay
Roy Mitchell
Jerry Todd
Goldie Glasgow Todd
Carolyn Smith
Pat Warrior Beasley
Mickey Wharton

CPSIA information can be obtained
at www.ICGtesting.com
Printed in the USA
FSHW022334230820
73202FS